Perspectives on Development in the Middle East and North Africa (MENA) Region

Series Editor

Almas Heshmati, Jönköping University, Jönköping, Sweden

This book series publishes monographs and edited volumes devoted to studies on the political, economic and social developments of the Middle East and North Africa (MENA). Volumes cover in-depth analyses of individual countries, regions, cases and comparative studies, and they include both a specific and a general focus on the latest advances of the various aspects of development. It provides a platform for researchers globally to carry out rigorous economic, social and political analyses, to promote, share, and discuss current quantitative and analytical work on issues, findings and perspectives in various areas of economics and development of the MENA region. Perspectives on Development in the Middle East and North Africa (MENA) Region allows for a deeper appreciation of the various past, present, and future issues around MENA's development with high quality, peer reviewed contributions. The topics may include, but not limited to: economics and business, natural resources, governance, politics, security and international relations, gender, culture, religion and society, economics and social development, reconstruction, and Jewish, Islamic, Arab, Iranian, Israeli, Kurdish and Turkish studies. Volumes published in the series will be important reading offering an original approach along theoretical lines supported empirically for researchers and students, as well as consultants and policy makers, interested in the development of the MENA region.

More information about this series at https://link.springer.com/bookseries/13870

Warda Samara · Malaka Samara

The Power of Perceptions in the Middle East

A Study of Contradictory Political and Economic Interests

Springer

Warda Samara
Berlin, Germany

Malaka Samara
Dortmund, Germany

ISSN 2520-1239 ISSN 2520-1247 (electronic)
Perspectives on Development in the Middle East and North Africa (MENA) Region
ISBN 978-3-030-99149-4 ISBN 978-3-030-99150-0 (eBook)
https://doi.org/10.1007/978-3-030-99150-0

Proofreading: Rachel Hardy

This Springer imprint is published by the registered company Springer Nature Switzerland AG
The registered company address is: Gewerbestrasse 11, 6330 Cham, Switzerland

Preface

Exploring the different perceptions of the eco-political and social dynamics in the Middle East (henceforth, ME) is not an easy task. There are too many contrasting views in the sight of the mass load of information that lead to conflicting indicators. The region has layers of complex intersections that increase political, economic and social complexity, that is for the benefit of some forces. While others consider this complexity deepening the destruction dilemma in the region. Some even consider this as underneath eco-political global agendas. However, these conflicting perceptions are not new to the ME, but rather historically based.

This is not a historiographical text. Rather this book is an exploration and questioning of the main narrative and the historical sequence of events. This reviewing and understanding the ideologies that drive common behaviours and activities is essential if we wish to enable future prosperity for all. I discuss varying ideas and how certain perceptions could be incorrect while others could provide solutions. Considering a world that is rapidly transforming more than ever; global floundering, regional chaos and local ignorance thrives while a certain narrative is absent. I am here, like many people keen to seek what is going exactly behind the scenes. Namely, where is the ME going, and what kind of future are we leaving to the future generations?

The sequence of the topics in this book are representing the research and the professional experience of both authors in more than 25 countries; in the MENA region, the US, the UK, Europe and Asia through designing, supervising and implementing several economic, social and educational development projects. This is further supplemented by the authors' own academic experience in Europe and South East Asia by raising the local public's understanding through evaluation of their way of life to develop answers that might help the region emerge from this dark age. Believe this as process-based learning on the common understanding of contemporary history where information, data and knowledge are crucial.

This book intends to stimulate the reader by switching back and forth between two topics of focus. The historical focus and its relevance to contemporary events, as well as the development focus, going through the chaos and the Arab revolutions and the attempts to reshape the capitalist system. This was followed by the regional response to Artificial Intelligence (henceforth, AI) and the Fourth Industrial Revolution (henceforth, 4IR) as remarkable events in shaping all aspects of future life. Throughout history, major forces have always acted in accordance with their own vision of a global order. Some are almost adamant about altering societies reality or framework to fit their ideology. Thus, investigating the eco-political and social issues in the MENA is a somewhat harsh enlightenment process. It contains a combination of intersecting factors of ancient history and the emergence of civilisations in the region and the interaction with the current global political and economic dynamics.

WWI and Geopolitical Divisions

This book presents the different perceptions of the ME after WWI and the subsequent diplomacy that led to the division of the ME as we know it today. Consequently, unending conflicts have emerged in different parts of the whole region that caused the destruction of the bases of economic and commercial life. Denying the rights of the indigenous people and resulting in multi-dimensional disastrous consequences caused by the Western colonising forces accompanied by the internal players' roles. However, all the subsequent events lie somewhere between the perspectives shaped by reality and propaganda and those who can control perceptions with it and use them to their advantage in the future.

Wars are studied and recounted based on decisions taken and then designing the "macro history" of their pivotal military and geopolitical outcomes. This macro history as a common narrative focuses on wars and the illusion of control while the suffering of the indigenous environment and the subsequent radical change is ignored. The real suffering of marginalised groups and indigenous people hardly feature in these perspectives. The details of societal experiences, peoples dynamics, and interaction with the variable factors all contributing towards collective knowledge—that I will refer to in this book as the '*machine experience mind*'—are underestimated and neglected especially in the West narrative concerning the MENA region. It is commonly known that history, particularly on a macro scale, is written by winners and therefore only considers their perspective. These narratives later become realities that influence possibilities and decisions. Where the narrative of '*the machine experience mind*' becomes a thorn in the side rather than considered part of the huge economic and political structure. Consequently, the region turned from an open Arab World to several divided small countries claiming the protection of the security of their borders from one another. From rejecting the divisions of the map to fighting to protect the map.

To provide some context, an analytical and critical discussion of the "Sykes-Picot Treaty" is necessary, especially to avoid similar iterations with possibly worse consequences. Due to the consequences that allow a century of suffering under the narrative one single treaty that undermines the peoples of the region. Whereas, what has been happening in the region is a result of a series of multidimensional events interspersed with a series of ongoing threats and multiple agreements between the global forces. The internal failures of administrations in the ME are also a major part contributing to the disastrous consequences. This cannot be excluded from the discussion and one cannot continue to blame others. In particular, the ME journey is marked by a series of divisions, first appearing in the geographical form, the economic and now evolving into the digital. While the regional leadership has proved its limited capability to strategically respond.

Regional Chaos and the New Middle East

In addition, the global floundering in the era of COVID 19 has indicated that the strategic balance is shifting in many aspects. Particularly in the political, as the power of perceptions espoused by the current ruling parties and grassroots organisations became even clearer as well as their impact on all pillars of development including the interactions with the new economic world order. Simply put, the global economic actors cannot survive the rules of the current capitalist system in times of economic crisis. Especially that capitalism remains under threat by 4IR, as it has always been defined by its material nature—in other words, possessions, property and capital. With digitalisation replacing materialism, it poses a direct conflict with its more driven aspects. Therefore, if any economic system wants to survive now, new sets of institutional procedures and policies on all levels have to be fundamentally reshaped. This includes the shape of the government and citizenship as we are now familiar with. A response to the crisis is therefore described by the World Economic Forum (henceforth, WEF) as "the great re-set" which was recently introduced through Davos Agenda in 2021. This initiative already carries a lot of fundamentally conflicting viewpoints with it. However, with this dramatic shift, the persecuted ethnic minorities in the ME perceive the *status quo* as a historic opportunity to establish their independent states and self-administration. Here, it is important to realise that the concept of borders has changed as well and the dynamics shifted from geopolitics and geoeconomics to something else. The future has all the potential to adapt to what I will describe as '*geo-tech*'.

There is currently a great sense of ambiguity in many of the new treaties between the states in the ME, especially including those with Israel. This thereby maintains "the constant chronic headache" of the Palestinian-Israeli issue in the background and emphasises the necessity of establishing relations with Israel. A serious discussion about con-federalism among the different political actors including on the grassroots level has also come to the forefront, where divisions are, suddenly viewed as the only solution as a political compromise that ensures stability and as a social-economic solution that boosts the region's development. Counting on the possibility of regional economic success would allow new divisions to develop. This promotes other unannounced interests for the external and some regional forces. Others believe that this discussion is promoted only to misdirect the local leaders' attention away from the fundamental issues. It is wrong to confine solutions to one traditional path, without taking into account the new global changes and its advanced tools.

Others argue that Israel's influence in the region is minimal to Palestine by underestimating the importance of its primary intelligence and security role at the regional and international levels. As a result of this underestimation, Israel also plays an important role in affecting the true independence of most Middle Eastern countries, both stable and emerging. Especially in light of technology advancement in Israel. Moreover, the internal stability of these states can remain dependent on outside interference. Subsequent channels of forced partnerships and cooperation may follow which, again, may not be in the interest of the people. This is neither pro-preference nor a rejection of independent and federal administration as an idea. The remaining question is who will be the general umbrella government of any future federal and con-federal association in the region.

The way people act, interact or respond to the manifestation of reshaping systems remains the fingerprint that will shape the future and perhaps even reproduce new terms like the '*digital ME*' where people can interact and operate their businesses beyond the geopolitical borders. A vision intended for the ME is inspired by the EU experience that suggest an economic field different from the current one. But this vision is based fundamentally on AI programs.

Reshape Capitalism and the Fourth Industrial Revolution (4IR)

While the knowledge-based economy dominates and became the driving indicator of the competitiveness between global forces, the countries in the ME and North Africa (henceforth, MENA) continue to suffer ongoing wars, conflicts and more destruction rendering them the last to respond to the new technological advancement. This continuous horror in the region begs the question of who is allowing this to happen, who are the decision-makers in the region. One could argue the ME as it currently appears to be no longer prioritised, in the traditional way, by any dominant forces. Yet the features of a new ME are already underway on the ground as part of the new world order. It is remarkable to note that these changes are taking place due to the pressure of global powers to restructure the regional forces in line with their global interests and aspirations, which does not necessarily coincide with the interests of states and peoples in the region.

The current competition to dominate the region and access its rich resources is not only a struggle between two parties, but it remains an ongoing struggle in which global forces participate in various facades of various sizes. It is a multilateral collision, and the weakest parties from a material perspective are the residents of these areas, some call it a "resource curse". The complete deception of the domestic systems and ill-equipped, foreign-backed leadership caused the "Arab Spring", calling into question—who are the systems really serving, their own people or the external forces that support them to be in office? However, the structure of global forces and their historical formation is not clear. Hence, the book is exploring ancient myths and their current expansions in contemporary societies promoted by some forces. So the way we are going on will potentially lead to a conflict resulting in change. Unless there is a well-organised alteration coming from inside, of course.

Russia, China and their allies have already made many steps in the MENA to replace the US decline, a foregone conclusion or a new methodology of foreign policy? China maintains their balanced relationships with different ME countries which became clear through the Belt Road Initiative (henceforth, BRI), where Saudi Arabia, Turkey and Iran joined the Asian Infrastructure Investment Bank. Moreover, the interest in Chinese defence strategy indicates a notable shift in the ME away from the US as a strategic alliance.

Con-federalism and '*Digital Classifications*'

The continuous domestic powers supported by major regional allies, benefiting superpowers with their uncertain strategy strengthen the roots of chaos in the region, leaving their own people in a passive position under conflicting information and data overload. This, once again, makes the region vulnerable to a new form of divisions like the digital divide which can be seen on the ground in the form of con-federalism. This allows certain outcomes are imposed from outside.

Those closely observing the political and economic scene of the ME soon realise that the struggle between the Global forces has never truly ended. It was, over time, simply transforming from one form to another and from one player to another. For instance, beginning with the military colonisation of the MENA, evolving to military bases and economic control, to political interventions and ending with the current ideological and intellectual conflict that might end up with what I refer to in this book as '*digital classifications*'. The lifestyle becomes a matter of which '*digital classification*' are you or your business is operating in. After 2003, this became more visible on a large scale.

The Power of Awareness and Perceptions

Amidst the roar of capitalism, the experience of the indigenous people, (henceforth, '*indigenous perception*' is in a struggle to find the balance between the capitalist system and the communal system as a way of life. As of now, technology is advancing in a direction that increases technological dependency rather than emancipation for the people through technology. The focus is really to maintain the current global order. The '*machine experience mind*' was in a way therefore 'hacked' in order to manipulate popular perception, using all the possible tools like production of ignorance, creative destruction, mind wars, the geographical division and '*digital classifications*' yet to come. All with the purpose to shift people's attention to the fictional part of life experience while reality is unequipped with the right tools to lead societies to their rightful purpose with less suffering. This might be the end of indigenous people like the Palestinians and the Kurds.

Even though societies and people are the bedrock allowing for even the existence of politics and economic transactions. These struggling societies are still seeking intelligence in order to organise themselves and under the right circumstances could be capable of devising their own solutions that could stun even the most powerful forces. Maybe even opens the doors for renegotiation. Nevertheless, the dominant narrative and the truth are both present in the same field, but each of them operates on different frequencies. Illusions form part of reality for many people, for so many even that it can become accepted truth, thereby making the search for truth difficult or even impossible. However, there is no doubt that there is already a significant shift in the population understanding of events and the moving dynamics.

Development Opportunities

The other focus of the book considers the possibilities of prosperity, the pros and cons of the 4IR, the knowledge-based economy, and the need of developing appropriate tools which support a world transition. It also discusses perspectives on educational systems and learning processes, and sustainable development in the region. The competent workforce is one of the fundamental requirements for reconstruction and growth in the destroyed areas with a focus on digitalising cities and employing technological advancement. This requires a response of the Educational system and policies to adapt to 4IR requirements.

Focusing the entrepreneurship and the role of women are discussed as a key element that could lead to potential higher solutions. Emphasising the way of perceiving each element's details as the main discussion where politicians and economic institutes should be no longer the only decision-makers. Comprehensive cooperation is needed, where The Public Private & Society Partnership (Henceforth, PPSP) is appealed.

Future Perspectives and Suggested Strategies

The MENA region could remain subject to chaos and instability for a longer period but in the end, large-scale reconstruction and development will take place. The question is whether the domestic players then invest in these changes for the benefit of their own people or will they stick their heads in the sand and let the region be subject to the new dominating powers. Already in a remarkably short period, the MENA region is going under several events; ongoing conflicts and wars, militias dividing states, COVID-19, AI and the potential of great re-set. One needs extraordinary capabilities to reimagine how the MENA will come out of this afterwards.

This book is also focused on the power of collective perceptions and understanding on the eco-political and social cultures. As well as the understanding of historical events and the influence of global forces in the ME. Furthermore, there will be a discussion on the importance of developing new channels of regional relations to negotiate alternative deals.

The last chapter draws new perspectives and outlooks of the future that urge the exploration of new methods on how to respond to the current situation. Only through critical thinking, exploring new models, methodologies, solutions and possibilities can one really identify visions and goals for the post-transition era. Above all, emphasising that people in the MENA no longer accept the *status quo*. Where inner issues like leadership corruption and underdevelopment are no longer accepted as fact and now require radical solutions. The era of scapegoating is now over. As part of this, new models for development will be suggested, for instance, alongside analysis of the current model: *Public Private Society Partnership model (PPSP)*, countries *'centring' strategy* and *reform policies framework*. Furthermore, while implementing any strategies, there must be a high consciousness, focus and awareness of the role of '*digital classifications*' in the future which is already taking a hold on the ground.

This book is intended for everyone. But it is intended to be of significance to researchers, academics and students who study the political and economic science of the ME. It is recommended for investors who are new to the region. Nevertheless, it is for everyone who wishes to understand the current popular image of the region as well as its intersections and contradictions with the reality of political and economic developments at all levels.

This is a vital call to people to open their conscience and shift to a new status of awareness through an alternative perception of human history, the economic dynamics and everything else along with it. It is clear, societies are not satisfied; a re-set is required. The decision as to which direction to go, at which frequency to operate and what to connect on, remains the decision of the people.

Berlin, Germany

Warda Samara
info111.samara@gmail.com

Acknowledgments

To my dearest friend Rachel hardy from England for her generous support, time and effort to proofread this work.

Contents

About the Authors

Warda Samara acts as a development expert specialised in improving cooperation and negotiation of West/East projects. She is a businesswoman and managing director of a consulting and coaching firm based in Berlin (Germany) and Palestine, working in the Middle East and Europe. She teaches courses in microeconomics, development, transition management and entrepreneurship.

Malaka Samara acts as an education expert specialised in improving Technical and Vocational Education and Training (TVET) practices. She is a researcher in Palestine, Germany and South East Asia, she teaches courses in Human Resources Development, curriculum development, sufficiency economy and work-based learning

Acronyms and Abbreviations

4IR	The Fourth Industrial Revolution
AI	Artificial Intelligence
GCC	Gulf Corporation Council
GDP	Gross Domestic Product
IMF	International Monetary Fund
IoT	The Internet of Things
ME	Middle East
MENA	Middle East and North Africa
SDG	Sustainable Development Goals
SME	Small and Medium-Sized Enterprises
TVET	Technical and Vocational Education and Training
UN	United Nations
US	United States of America
WEF	World Economic Forum
WWI	World War I
WWII	World War II

List of Figures

List of Tables

Chapter 1
The Future of Ancient Interests in the Middle East

Warda Samara

1.1 Sykes Picot and the Formation of the Middle East

In general, wars result in political and economic treaties that lead to a "new world" order. This order which then becomes the newly defined status of the dynamics during peace. Naturally, the winner is the one who decides the new geopolitical structure based on ideological expansion, all forming the main narrative. In the long term, this dominates the perceptions of future possibilities of the other and forces them to submit to the new laws accordingly.

As to be expected, there were lots of overlapping fronts taking place in the ME. Although most of the ME was under Ottoman rule, the Western forces maintained colonies which allowed trade privileges, military presence and consuls throughout the Empire. For instance, Algeria which was subject to French colonisation (Jansen 2010) recruited its youth into the French army and spread the French language and culture (Roccu 2020). Meanwhile, Egypt and Iraq were under direct British control. The European countries exploited the privileges to serve their interests by interfering in the affairs of the Ottoman states at one time and dodging taxes at another. This allowed them to maintain colonies in the region.

WWI eventually became a time to declare war against the Ottoman Empire. To further emphasise that the complexities in the ME were not borne arbitrarily, but formed part of Western ideology is characterised by their ability to realise the importance of long-term strategic plans and how to deal with the people of this region.

In 1919, the Ottoman armies were forced to withdraw from the Arab region and relinquish their control there, see Fig. 1.1 which represents the Arab areas that were still under the Ottoman's rule until 1912 (Esemono 2008). They evacuated their military barracks and subsequently abandoned them after being defeated on several fronts while the Arabs groups advanced to the villages and suburbs. The Arabs demonstrated great valour, especially considering the significantly larger size of the Ottoman army and its increased execution operations against Arabs in that period. All Arabs, both women and men, Muslims and Christians, came together to defend

W. Samara and M. Samara, *The Power of Perceptions in the Middle East*,
Perspectives on Development in the Middle East and North Africa (MENA) Region,
https://doi.org/10.1007/978-3-030-99150-0_1

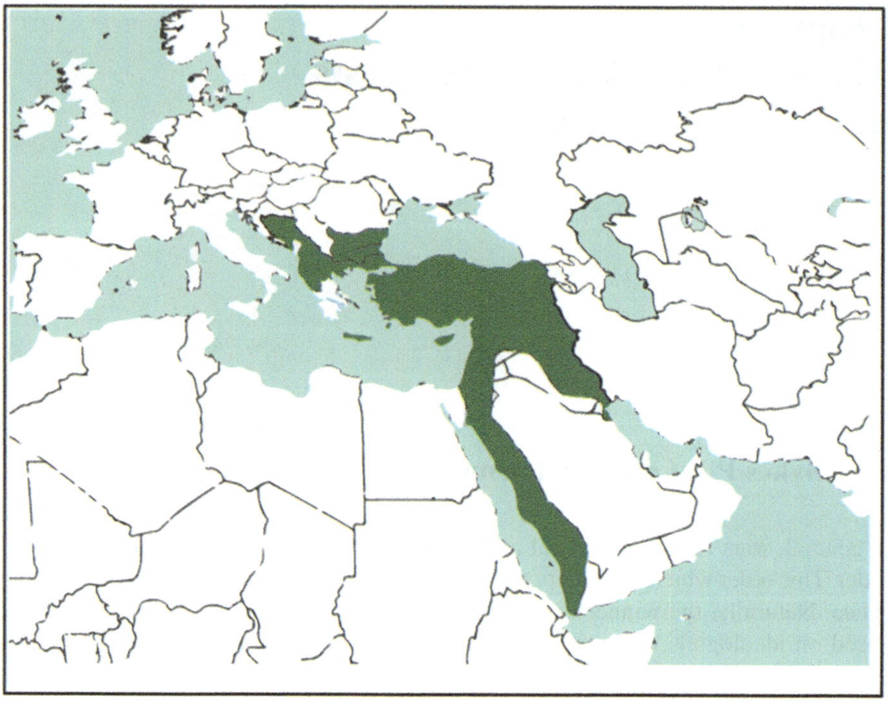

Fig. 1.1 Ottoman Empire concord area 1912–1919 (*Source* Author's own design)

their villages, for their "lives and livelihoods" (Awwad 1993). However, any final decisions concerning their lives and livelihoods remained out of their control.

War treaties are not absurd, otherwise, there would be no need to start wars in the first place. So is the Sykes-Picot deal. It was agreed upon by the three main forces; England, France, and Russia to protect their political and economic interests in the region (Britannica 2020a). Consequently, the treaty contributed to a specific roadmap within the framework of what the future of the ME should and would look like—at least according to Western powers' point of view.

The Sykes-Picot deal from 1916 was quickly followed by the Balfour Declaration in 1917. Where British foreign secretary, Arthur Balfour issued the letter to lord Rothschild (Library 2016). In the First Zionist Congress in Basel in 1897, Theodor Herzl had failed to get such a formal declaration. In April 1920, we saw the signing of the San Remo treaty, which laid the foundations for the border structure that we know in the region today. The treaty was to form the basis of a later treaty with Turkey, the treaty of *Sèvres* in August of the same year. This finally confirmed the deposition on the Ottoman Empire. The San Remo treaty gave final approval to the basis of a treaty with Turkey, which was eventually signed in *Sèvres in* August 1920, where the Ottoman Empire was deposed. These events were openly endorsed on an international level by the Council of the League of Nations in 1922 (Karsh 2020).

In 1923 the Treaty of *Sèvres* was originally promised land of minority groups like Kurds was replaced with the Treaty of Lausanne which, in other words, declined the rights of the minorities; the Kurdish self-administration and Armenian independence ("Treaty of Sèvres and Lausanne" 1920). The Treaty of *Sèvres* was also notable in its recognition of indigenous groups such as the Kurds and their right to sovereignty. However, in 1923 this treaty was replaced by the Treaty of Lausanne which outright rejected this. This naturally sparked the beginning of declining rights for minorities in the region on one hand and confirmed the geographical division on the other hand.

After intense negotiations between England and France as well as other global players, all agreed to divide and share the ME. Russia, of course, was too preoccupied at this time with the Bolshevik Revolution, thereby leaving France and Britain to divide the Arab world between themselves. Area 'A' was declared to be under French influence and control, while Area B was under British influence and control, as shown in Fig. 1.2 (Wood 2015). Thus, the period between 1916 and 1923 is marked by a series of landmark treaties all carefully implemented to ensure a certain outcome for the region. A contempt for hundreds of millions of people, the indigenous inhabitants of the region, was reduced to a single war agreement, 'Sykes - Picot'. Though this

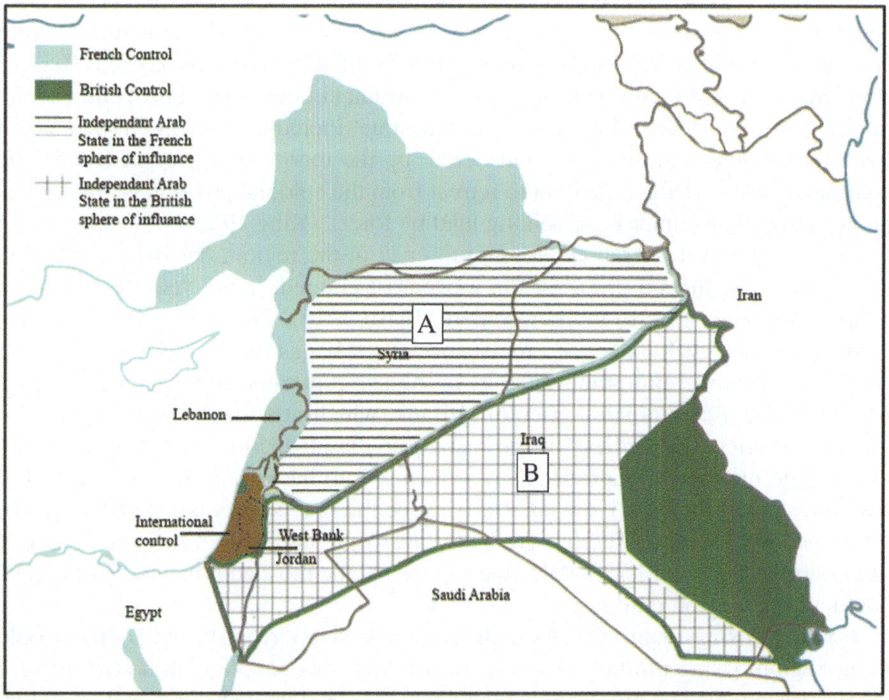

Fig. 1.2 Division of area A (French) and area B (England) (*Source* Wood); Division of area A (French) and area B (England) 1916 (*Source* Author's own resource)

was the start of a supposed "Anglo-French Peace", it was simply the beginning of a disastrous era began for the Arab-Muslim nation.

When the Arabs realised that the European forces were simply replacing the Ottoman empire under a different guise, they convened the first Syrian conference in 1919 and declared: *the independence of the Levant.* This consisted of rejection and abolition of the Sykes-Picot deal, rejection of the Balfour promise and any other project that aims to divide Great Syria—referring to the ancient geographical Syrian landmass which included (Syria, Jordan, Lebanon and historical Palestine). Moreover, all international guardianship or other mandates were rejected (Alaraby 2020).

Regaining control of the region was not just an option for France and Britain but was part and parcel of their colonial ideology. Although a commission of inquiry, the King-Crane Commission, was established during the *Paris Peace Conference* in the summer of 1919, where the victorious allies created the *League of Nations.* Both countries avoided the King-Crane commission because they were certain of the results that were against their will (King 1922). As a result, the King-Crane committee report was completely rejected by France, Britain and the Zionist movement where the desire of the population for self-determination was intentionally ignored, although the report acknowledged the ability of the Arabs in Greater Syria to form a state and run its administration (Reimer 2006). The expectations of the three forces were correct, according to the Commission report, 72% of all petitions throughout *Greater Arab Syria* were directly against partition, an unanimous rejection of the Zionist programme altogether. Where historical Palestine (including present day Israel and trans-Jordan) that time was all considered, by the report, as a part of Syria. The committee acknowledged that not to retreat from the colonial position is "insistence on displacing Palestinians and seizing land by force" (King 1922).

In order to cut the Arab economic presence in the region, the British mandate issued many facilities to the Zionism movement granted, in the year 1930, tens of *dunams* for cultivation to the newcomers (Bsiso 2016). The British mandate also allowed for the development of Zionist specialised banks for example by providing support for Jewish immigrants such as in the agricultural sector. Meanwhile, they had abolished the Ottoman Agricultural Bank, which provided similar support for the Arab farmers. Regardless of the incredible dissatisfaction from the Arab side to the large numbers of European Jews flowing into the region, the task started to be implemented forcibly. Now one starts to see the first confrontations between the Arabs and the Zionists. Though gradually over time the conflict has been reduced to the simple binary of Israel-Palestine. Arguably, the most complicated ideological conflict in the region until now.

Both colonising countries ignored the commission report and the will of the people in the region. Using military power against indigenous people with no defence for themselves allowed an uninterrupted and continued colonial presence in the region. As Plato says: "A tyrant seizes power by force and exercises it by violence, after which he first seeks to get rid of his most dangerous opponent" (Al-Azabi 2020). Both France and England acted accordingly in the year 1919, the British army had annihilated the resistance in Iraq through a fierce military campaign. Meanwhile,

France assassinated most of the members of the first Syrian National Congress. The death of the first demarcate institute in the region was declared (Alaraby 2020).

Historian, Elizabeth Thompson, argues in her book *how the West stole democracy from the Arabs* that European colonisers feared that Arab democracy would threaten their rule in North Africa, thus they would lose easy access to Iraq and the Gulf. The leaders of the Paris Peace Conference therefore decided, in cooperation with the new League of Nations, to destroy the regime the "democratic nascent in Damascus", which could have united the Arab nations and established a sovereign and impenetrable democratic state (Theompson 2020).

The French historian Henri Lawrence asserted that if independence was achieved in Syria, "France would have opened a door on itself in the other colonised countries in Africa" (Alaraby 2020). This emphasises that the French position was deliberate and determined to eliminate this movement to protect its interests not only in the region but in all its colonies.

In an age of flourishing philosophical thought, we find some philosophers have justified colonialism in the context of powerful countries rightfully spreading their values and rules (Kleingeld 2014). Invasion of other lands could be considered as a logical expansion of the powerful force to access resources and protect interests. On a more sinister note, this expansion in the eyes of these forces, is essential no matter the human sacrifice and communities lose.

Some historians view the Sykes-Picot treaty as the last real act of Western colonialism in the region. As this treaty was concluded during war time, these treaties had to be concluded as soon as possible in order to consolidate strategic allies. As a result, all destruction resulting from this can be seen as unintentional from the global forces and were not part of any political strategy directly concerning the ME.

> "colonialism is silently embedded in the genes of the West integration since its inception".

The other perception views colonialism as an extension of external forces enlightenment, which served to perpetuate this idea of "Western superiority" over the world (Saeed 1993). This is a systematic formation of political outcomes that guarantees illusion borders and gives its inhabitants new identities. This is the transformation of the form of economic intervention into a direct political and military presence (Roccu 2020) that becomes ingrained in the '*machine experience mind*' in the region. Especially that the proposed borders were not absurd, they were based on the western historical interests in the region, which even pre-dated the Sykes-Picot deal (Alaraby

2020). At the same time, the convention had already sketched out the Zionists on the territory of historical Palestine (Pappe 2006).

The '*machine experience mind*' in this book represents the collective experience of society. All aspects, including its people, nature and wider surroundings form this experience, akin to cogs in a machine all working together to create this collective experience. Experience can then become awareness, allowing individuals and groups to make decisions and solve problems. It represents opportunities on how people see themselves and how to observe and interact with others, including their physical surroundings. This connection with the self and the environment in the '*machine experience mind*' poses a great threat to any external power that has its own agenda outside of this collective experience. This is why it is imperative to degrade the machine experience mind to make it vulnerable to external influences. In short, it is the cumulative natural intelligence of societies.

To implement external ideologies, a tremendous change had to happen and hit the '*machine experience mind*' within. Global forces ideology goes beyond colonialism, rendering it not an easy force to counter. Western ideology possesses a monopoly on science and knowledge—plus its access. It also demonstrates malleability as it opts for different colonial models and philosophies (Greek, Egypt, Iraq, India, China, etc.).

Shaher Shaher, a professor at the Universities of Damascus and Euphrates, argues in his study "*post – Sykes-Picot maps, from partition to deconstruction*", that Sykes-Picot deal was designed carefully to not allow the space of forming any regional ideologies. Ideologies and non-materialised means are considered as the greater threat to the West force ideology (Shaher 2017). This is an emphasis on "armies do not fight by material means alone, but at the same time by moral means" (Al-Hussari 1951). The elimination of any national beliefs was necessary for the colonial forces. It hinders any attempt to develop the Arab national consciousness. Ideas and movements were politically appropriated from supporting Arab counter-groups that also aspired to govern in order to import nationalism beliefs from the West. Thus, there was a division among the people as a part of an ideological clash indicating a radical change in the local societies. Some scholars believe that Arab nationalism as an ideology has failed in the face of West military power, especially since Arab nationalist movements were promoted by the secular elite and used the tools of the West to defend Arab civilisation without the ability to employ it for the Arab benefits (Ashmawi 1996).

The historical association of France in the region has a traditional view. That resulted in close relations and interests that should remain under European control from France's point of view. The European vision in the region would not be possible and rather incomplete without deep studies on Islamic history, Arab history and the history of minorities throughout various Orientalist campaigns. Planning for domination does not simply operate only on a military level but also requires political research and diplomatic efforts. This research was not only crucial for understanding the people in the region, it was essential for producing a certain image of the region in the mind of the European armies and people to induce them about the necessity of these colonial missions. Moreover, England and France have been promoting to their people that the Arab groups who are demanding independence are nothing more than uneducated and troublesome Bedouin groups and have no capacity and ability to run their own country (Alaraby 2020). One should not underestimate the common narratives in the Western collective consciousness where manipulating popular perception was an effective tool implemented by the colonial forces. More importantly to gain support and justification for their interventions, often involving destruction and loss of life. These perceptions of societies and peoples, begin to be transmitted to the new generations as facts, leading to intergenerational stereotypes which only serve to hinder solutions and cooperation (Register 2017).

1.2 Liberation and Independency

There are states such as Egypt and Iran, which have existed since ancient times and have consequently always played an important role in economy, politics and history. There are other countries such as Turkey and Saudi Arabia, which are the modern forms of the Ottoman Empire and the Kingdoms of Hejaz respectively with new political borders (Al-Hussari 1951).

Lebanon, Syria, Jordan, Iraq, and Palestine, on the other hand, are all modern political entities as a result of the West colonialism in the region. Even Israel was created by external forces on some parts of the historical, already existing Palestine. Says American historian: These six countries pose a problem because they were mainly formed out of Anglo-French deal in the region (Oakes 2009). Therefore, the differences between Arab Islamic nation, in terms of independence, is huge. Some of them are completely independent, some are somewhat independent, and some do not own the decisions of their countries.

The Second World War in 1939 broke out and the balance of power and the laws of the global political dynamics began to change again, in transition to a different global political and economic system, shifting the economic and political power. Thus, all the Western countries returned to their old borders, except for Poland, which expanded at the expense of Germany. Europe was divided into two spheres the Soviet influence in the East and the US in the West. Germany was fragmented into occupation zones between the US, UK, France and the Soviet Union, which controlled political capabilities. To the world, a new international body was established based on geopolitical divisions.

Despite this, colonialism in the US is also considered an example of an extension of European ideology—itself a result of the European Enlightenment. Especially that the European intellectuals were influenced by classical Athens, Sparta, and the Romans when forming the United States Constitution (Berman 1992). This the emergence of the US and the Soviet Union as superpowers led the ME to believe that they would support their own liberation movements. However, the revolutions in the whole region did not subside, and then these countries began to become independent one after the other.

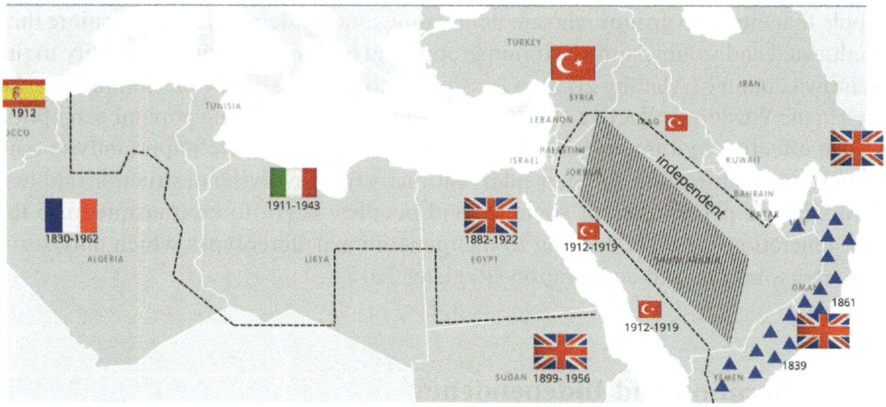

Fig. 1.3 The colonial power in the MENA (*Resource* Author's own resource)

Liberation movements and revolutions increased against the European forces; Algeria, Mauritania, Morocco, Tunisia and Syria were against France; Libya against Italy; Yemen, Iraq, Somalia and Jordan against Britain, as presented in Fig. 1.3 that shows the West colonialism in the region until the independence of the MENA countries (Rekacewicz 1992). The demand for independence continued for several years on a very large scale which exhausted colonial forces, both militarily and economically. While there were increased military withdrawals from the region, colonial forces remained eager to ensure that their economic interests, especially oil, were preserved. In sum, they would grant states independence, provided it would not pose a direct threat to their interests. Thus any newly independent states were entrusted to army generals or certain families interests were loyal to the colonial systems (Karatas 2019). Although the liberation movements and resistance were not excluded in Palestine, no liberation was ever declared.

The political system was either a republic ruled by a military regime or a monarchy that was hereditary within one family. The will of the indigenous people was out of the question for these so-called democratic regional forces. Thus remains the persistent power struggle between the ruling elites and the people (Karatas 2019). Therefore, the independence of states did not guarantee freedoms for its citizens in any way. Except for the pleasure of the early announcement of victories, the domestication of celebrations, and the transformation of revolutionary energy into colonialism of another form. This form remains unchallenged and strong in the region.

The people's patience was exhausted against the tyranny, oppression and corruption of the system of government established by the Ottoman centre and later by the Western mandates and control. On the one hand, local leaders were fascinated by Western industrial development. Hasten as to attempt to imitate their models of development in their own societies, regardless of its incompatibility with the region's environment. Simply due to their desire for advancement and personal stability provided Western colonialism. This form of colonialism is an ideological form seeking to divide the region and its people according to the ideological expansion of the West (Malhees 2020).

Therefore, some analysts view the so-called "state independence" as a strategic political manoeuvre and illusion as most of the major decisions that affect domestic politics, economy and society in the ME are still subject to external political power. In other words, the so-called "former" colonial class! This was stipulated even before their military departure, that certain political and economic arrangements were made to guarantee continued dependency. For example, the higher category of major merchants during the last decades of the Ottoman rule, turned into owners of local agencies for import and export. However, these major merchants simply works as proxy influences for European companies that had abandoned their branches. Thereby, all the main decisions remained in the hands of the Western forces (Al-Saleh 2020) in short, colonialism by other means. Hence, the departure of the coloniser was, in fact, just a redistribution of the balance of power between the coloniser and the loyal elites (colonial class) in their favour (Studies 2021), and not comprehensive independence. A further post-colonial strategy was the introduction of conditions for independence. For instance, the independence of Iraq's e in 1932 was dependent on maintaining British military bases inside Iraqi territory. This situation applicable to most of the countries in the ME where the military presences is still strong till nowadays. Figure 1.4 shows the foreign military presence in the MENA between 2015 and 2020 where Fig. 1.5 represent France military presence in 2018.

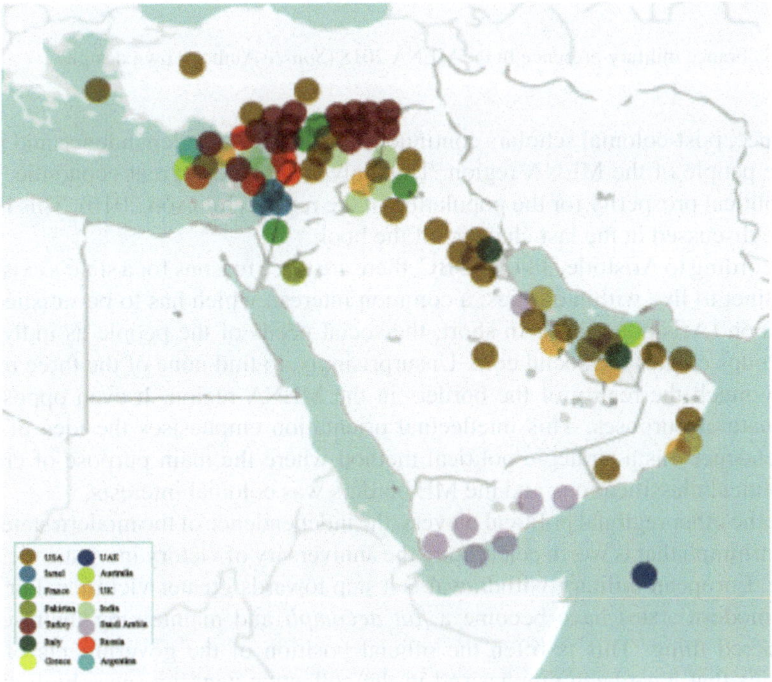

Fig. 1.4 Foreign military base in the ME (*Source* Author's own design)

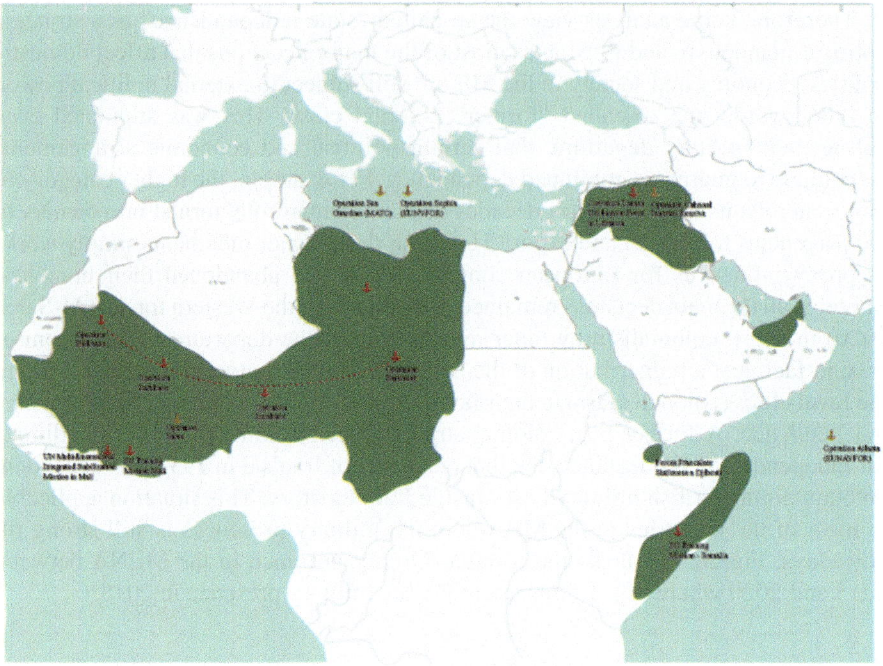

Fig. 1.5 France military presence in the MENA 2018 (*Source* Author's own design)

Hence, post-colonial scholars continuously call for real independence and justice for the people of the MENA region. This only will achieve great economic, social and political prosperity for the population of the region (Johnson 2016). This is what will be discussed in the last chapters of the book.

According to Aristotle, 384–322 BC, there are three reasons for a state's existence: an instinct to live within entities; a common interest, which has to be satisfied; and protection (Aristotle 1959). In short, the social needs of the people as individuals and groups creates the social core. Unsurprisingly, to find none of the three reasons is very much the reality of the borders in the MENA region. It even opposes the three natural purposes. This intellectual orientation emphasises the idea of "state independence" as a strategic political method where the main purpose of creating geopolitical classifications and the ME borders was colonial interests.

For the other regional political players, the independence of the modern states is an actual triumph that is worth celebrating the anniversary of victory in a patriotic event. Hence, European military withdrawal is a step towards greater victories. For them, these modern states have become a *fait accompli* and maintaining their security is a sacred thing. This is often the official position of the governments of these countries that have been emphasised in the collective consciousness by trampling these boundaries in schools while simultaneously bragging about Arab victories and revolutions.

For the authorities, the many aspects of failures are attributed to external interventions and pressures and the lack of capabilities. This allows for the gradual degradation of the "*machine history mind*". Neglecting the natural desire of the indigenous communities and manipulating the reality with the political phantom under the name of 'democracy' and 'freedom'.

1.3 Geopolitical Division and Dispute Over Borders

The complex human mind can easily surprise us with its own limitations, such as fixation of socially constructed concepts like political borders that even shape one's own identity. Consequently, this identity becomes more important than anything else as it represents a practical meaning for someone and their rights where justification becomes valid for any attitude. This was very vital for the colonial forces in the region and so they smartly and forcibly planted it.

The redistribution in the ME has consisted of uneasy and overlapping processes of state-building, where the interventions were not only within the borders, but also the introduction of electoral systems for political representation in the ME (Meshrek 2019). This subsequently contributed to the consolidation of modern concepts of citizenship, identity and ethnicity as new forms of political competition to control collective perceptions, including political parties, unions, and professional associations, and these processes have transformed national struggles from an elite-dominated activity into mass political integration movements.

The acceleration of state recognition of the modern Arab states was to assert the consolidation of these divisions, which strengthened separation between the Arab world as much as possible. This has produced the borders of these contemporary states (Studies 2021). What has worsened the situation is recognising the Zionist entity as a state in the core of 'the great Syria' without even identifying its geopolitical borders. This created a historical complicated conflict, perhaps for forever if no discussion is even considered.

These were not limited to these implications, but the withdrawn colonial forces began to wrap-around education, media, and institutions in the whole region even in schools teaching the liberation of the ME. However, emphasising the boundaries that were drawn by the Allies (Meshrek 2019). Many Arab school teachers ensure (often unintentionally) continued confusion among their students with misinformation. A female teacher even informed me: we celebrate illusionary events of state independence and teach this to the young. This continues with lessons concerning victories throughout the Arab World, yet when they grow up they find themselves still under occupation or devastated control leaves them frustrated with very limited choices and no future.

Each country protects its borders from the neighbouring Arab countries and some countries have become a security threat to others. In many cases, this situation has triggered many wars between the countries of the ME, most notably the Kuwait and Iraq wars, the repression against the Kurds, the ethnic cleansing and the displacement of the Palestinians. Many border problems that began to escalate one after the other to this day. The acceptance of the colonial borders fearing the alternative would be endless wars and conflicts even though these borders might not make sense from the ideological belief of many people in the region especially the ethnic groups those who struggle a lot for their rights "reality was forced to surrender" (Harrari 2020).

This is how the implementation in the ME benefitted the external forces, bringing the region and its inhabitants into a dark age with several repercussions. Nonetheless, still including achieving great economic gains for the former colonies, especially from controlling oil. However, all the subsequent events lie somewhere between the perspectives shaped by reality and propaganda and those who can control perceptions with it and use them to their advantage in the future.

1.4 Aftermath

Capitalism since the industrial revolution has formed by much part and parcel of Western identity and structure. Naturally leading to greater consumption and therefore greater need for more resources dependent on the labour force in the colonial countries. Since capitalism is based on free market economy, it was necessary to introduce this system in the markets of their colonies as well as to ensure the region participation (even if limited to a specific role). Materialism and consumerism started gradually to move to the MENA where the industrial communities were introduced and expanded through controlling the channels of commercial channels in the region.

After the Middle Eastern Arab and Turkish merchants became insignificant for their control over some commodities and the land and sea trade routes, the region became subject to the new European rule and were replaced by European merchants. For example, in 1925, a monopoly on exploration and production was granted to the Turkish Petroleum Company. In 1919, the ports at Alexandria and Haifa became open to both countries' trade with fewer rules (Britannica 2020b). Neither country paid tax and Britain became the sole owner of the railway connecting Haifa to Area B and had the right to move products and army troops along this line at any time. Where the top-ranking British in the region were concentrated mainly in Haifa (Mansour 2006). On the other hand, the indigenous people's activities were eliminated through reinforcement and the creation of customs barriers along with the concord areas, which impeded the movement of individuals and goods. The Iraq Petroleum Company (IPC) was founded in 1929 after significant oil deposits were discovered in 1927. It was owned by a consortium of British, French, Dutch and American oil companies, and operated by the British (Wali 2013). This constituted one of the biggest obstacles to economic progress in the ME which affected the ability of productive markets and thus the rise in unemployment rates until now.

In 1922 the terms of the Mandate Deed issued by the League of Nations referred to the economic policy that the Mandate Power was entrusted to implement in the colonised areas in the region. First, concluding international agreements with the local authorities to bring the Mandate countries into the economic space of the other

Mediterranean countries. Second, satisfy the needs of the Mandatory country by the development of the exploitation of its natural resources that satisfy the needs of the local authorities. Both deeds are to be implemented along with the economic development in the region that the locals pay for its administration (Al-Saleh 2020).

Two main historical political issues have appeared immediately: The Kurdish issue, a population of more than 36 million who were distributed over four countries. Some of them were displaced between the borders, which ensures a permanent conflict between the most significant countries in the region (Iraq, Turkey, Iran, Syria). The second issue is the issue of Palestinians, when Zionists began to affirm their ideologies on the ground. This later became the state of Israel which was announced in 1948 on Palestinian land, denying the rejection of the Palestinians themselves and intentionally ignoring the King-Crane report. More details about both cases in Chap. 2.

The historical problem in the region began with the obligation of purely material identity, stripping the people of their indigenous knowledge, and strengthening the physical connection as a determinant of the identity of individuals. Deepening materialism by creating artificial borders that divide the whole region into smaller countries under the French and the British mandates. By differentiating the people among new identities, their new security rested on protecting their new identities. These geopolitical divisions were claimed to be a major line of defence against the project of the Zionist project in Palestine. When the clashes between Arab countries and Israel started, it was a confirmation of the significance of these borders.

Referring to the colonial project in Palestine, Ilan Pappe, an Israeli historian argues that the Zionist project in Palestine is like hunting two birds with one stone, one of which is dissolution the issue of Jews in Europe, and the second is the invention of a small Western system in the core of the spirit of Arab-Muslim world. Thus ensuring that they are not united forever and ensuring a secure ally in the heart of the region for political, economic and military access. Where Israel is surrounded by "enemies" on all sides and is therefore in a state of eternal need for Western forces to ensure its survival.

The region has gone through several events in a very short historical period. One example is The Great Arab Revolt during WWI which resulted in affirming the contemporary political states including Israel as a symbolic representation of the most powerful forces in the world. This was followed by the emergence of charitable societies, trade unions, and the formation of political parties in the region (Al-Saleh 2020). Whereas WWII has emphasised the position of borders and has enhanced the government's systems in each state especially with the discovery of oil in the Arab region. This was the beginning of the era of economic classifications.

The League of Arab States (LAS) was founded in 1945 where the sovereignty and independence of the member states that joined the League were recognised and affirmed, with their already existing borders. One of the founding principles of the LAS was cooperation with international bodies supposedly to ensure security and peace. Commitment to the principles of the United Nations became a basic requirement. Thus, the form of modern states was approved by the governments of the region, and then the processes of building and developing infrastructure and promoting investments in various sectors started. This new environment became a fertile ground for a new order. On the more optimistic side, it could be an opportunity to divide and organise society according to. Or, could be a chance for global powers to divide and take advantage of its resulting weaknesses. All parties were, in different ways, forced to respond to the new data when the Western colonial powers retreated in the region and the American rise began.

The new situation has shifted the ME economy to a war economy instead of focusing on economic and social development. In 1990, the Arab military defence budget of eighteen Arab countries together amounted to more than 50 billion US dollars. Within a few decades, this spending saw further stark increases, see Fig. 1.6 that represents the military expenditure of some countries in the MENA in 2017.

Not simply in relation to their own increase in spending over time, but also in comparison to the rest of the world. In 2017, seven of the top ten countries with the biggest military budget were in the ME. As a result of this focus, numerous regional actors have engaged in violent conflicts that have caused enormous devastation and have stifled economic development (Wezeman 2018).

Moreover, during WWI the communication and transportation networks were both developed and determined primarily in line with the strategic, political or commercial aims of colonial forces. This, obviously, serves their needs rather than domestic or regional needs. The Suez Canal which plays a major part in the international trade serves only a minor role in the ME economy (UN 1951). Most of the railway routes

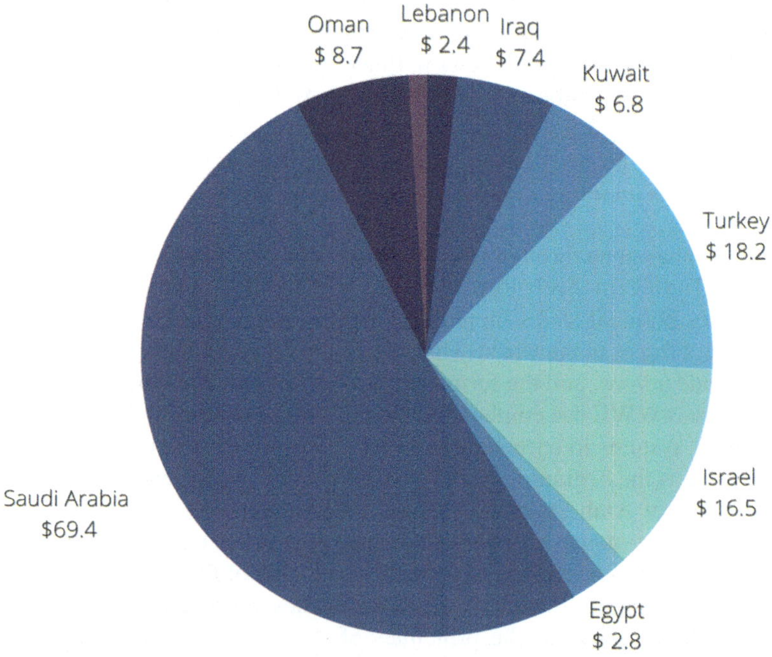

Fig. 1.6 Military expenditure in 2017, US$ billion (*Source* Author's own design)

and services only fulfilling the necessary function for locals interests in the region to a level that also suffices to serve international stability.

Since the discovery of oil in the ME, the West has sought to stifle any attempt for the producing countries to control their own resources. For example, the decision to nationalise the Suez Canal and move its assets away from the British to the Egyptian Government ("Nationalization of the Suez Canal Company" 1957) in 1956 was bloody and led to the declaration of a tripartite war against Egypt by the French, British and Israeli forces (Lahav 2015). Even though the military presence could leave a negative impact on Britain as well, it was still a choice they had committed to. The British treasury bore a severe burden as a result of their defeat in the Suez war, with the total cost of the war reaching 328 million pounds sterling at that time. Meanwhile, France also experienced a major loss as Egypt cut their trading ties, not only straining economic relations but also leading to a total loss of 400 billion francs. This loss demonstrated that direct military intervention is no longer practical with most countries. Until now, the Suez canal has handled approximately 12% of world trade, accounting for 30% of all global container traffic and over USD $1 trillion in annual commodities (Cairo 2021).

Of course, the great forces did not give up so quickly. They started looking for new tools to interact with newly acquired information after the first and second wars, first leading to the emergence of international relations and foreign policies. These tools were used then followed by the emergence of many new economic and political concepts, including those who carry the human social cover. For example, the development concept seemed to rise after WWI and has soon become a prominent role in the ideological struggle between the East and the West. In response to globalisation, the local governments in the region started to put more effort to develop transportation, sanitation, education. As well as the development of the institutions of each country began. All that has required manpower, and therefore the creation of many of the jobs that the local population engaged in, which led to an increase in *per capita* income and a rise in living standards in the region. Despite the massive destruction caused by wars and revolutions, the key indicators of development in the ME became apparent to both the people and regimes alike. First led to what seemed like a new golden era, with improved infrastructure and governments systems. However, this development lasted, historically, only for a short period roughly between the fifties and nineties. The gap began to increase between the vision of the Arab people and the vision of the states regarding to the concept of development, as many initiatives and policies were formed under the guise of development but with no real fruitful results.

The UN establishment along with the US modern policies and tools in order to protect its global interests including in the ME has shifted the use of global power. This has obviously happened through the international economic, security and political institutions that followed (Mazarr et al. 2016).

The Gulf countries emerged as economic bases in the region that changed the interactions of the region and divided the region into developed "oil countries" and "development countries". The economic devision era based on 'economic classifications'. For example, the cash surplus became large and petrochemical industries began to enter the Gulf and began to invest in the infrastructure, and various financial funds were established, even Italy obtained a loan from Saudi Arabia was worth $1 billion in 1976. Here we conclude several countries in the region have achieved great economic growth in a short period. The possession of oil as a political weapon was used in several historical events as a tool to put pressure on countries and alliances. At the same time, the economic approach began to take root in the region, and consequently, the presence of other areas that represented a higher status such as Egypt and the Levant declined, and attention began to turn to the Arab Gulf as an important regional player. The question is therefore now what has prevented them from becoming competitive forces in the world?

What we can conclude from these historical events, is that this destruction and suffering have negatively impacted the '*machine experience mind*', However, such a sequence of events have now been reduced to one singular event—the Sykes-Picot agreement. This has only served to further alienate the people to their own history. At the time that similar major global forces were behind many single events that led to the societies destruction in the region. The region was not fully prepared for this kind of war as the economy was unable to bear the consequences of the war. The indigenous people in the region possessed neither an organised military nor an understanding of how to operate one. Thus, the Western military presence and what followed were the strategies supported by research and science where manipulating perceptions of everyone else on the battlefield is a necessary method, Consequently, the region turned from an open Arab World to several divided small countries claiming the protection of the security of their borders from one another. From rejecting the divisions of the map to fighting to protect the map.

Until here we have covered the main analysis of the environment that enabled different shapes of transformations to happen. The geopolitical divisions after WWI followed with economic division after WWII. Digital division is yet to come.

1.5 Summary

The common narrative of the history in the ME is a carefully selected reality, completely divorced from its original context, thereby allowing a certain narrative to prevail and shape popular perception. This has misled the decisions of people over several generations.

Europe and the ME seems to be dependent on each other longer than previously understood. The West colonialism in the region did not stop with the declaration of independence of the ME states, it was only redefining and remodelling itself under these new circumstances. It should no longer come as a surprise, that many of the major eco-political events or decisions which took place in Europe had subsequent effects on the ME. The leaders of the ME today still underestimate the teleological nature of this connection.

The MENA went through a series of events, starting just before the fall of the Ottoman Empire, that laid the foundations to shape the geopolitical borders and the contemporary ME states that we know now. This geopolitical division was only the beginning of a longer-term strategy that followed with the introduction of capitalism and increased economic divisions. Yet, the divisions do not stop at the economic level. There are new kinds of divisions yet to be revealed only in a matter of time.

References

Al-Azabi I (2020) Despotic regimes are the greatest threat to our being. https://www.ssrcaw.org/ar/show.art.asp?aid=677443

Al-Hussari S (1951) Opinions and conversations in Arab nationalism

Al-Saleh MA (2020) Managing the Syrian economy during the French mandate (1918–1946)—its post-independence effects. Presses de l'ifpo, Institut français du Proche-Orient. https://doi.org/10.4000/books.ifpo.13843

Alaraby T (2020) The Arab government in Damascus I Arabic Documentaries. https://www.youtube.com/watch?v=6CmmlUUO5M8

Aristotle (1959) Aristotle: politics. In: Rackham H, trans. London, Heinemann; Cambridge, Harvard University Press

Ashmawi M (1996) Civilisation conflict. Dar Al-Marief

Awwad T (1993) Al-Rageef. Lebanon Library

Berman H (1992) The impact of the enlightenment on American constitutional law. Yale J Law Hum 4(2):311

Britannica TEoE (2020a) Sykes-Picot agreement. Encyclopaedia Britannica. https://www.britannica.com/event/Sykes-Picot-Agreement

Britannica TEoE (2020b) Sykes-Picot agreement 1916. Britannica. https://www.britannica.com/event/Sykes-Picot-Agreement

Bsiso FH (2016) Arab economy in Palestine during the British mandate 1920–1948

Cairo NEi (2021) The importance of the Suez canal to global trade. N. F. A. a. Trade

Esemono (2008) The Ottoman Empire 1830–1923. https://commons.wikimedia.org/wiki/File:Naher_Osten_historisch_-_Osmanisches_Reich_1830-1923.gif

Harrari Y (2020) How to survive the 21st century WEF Annual Meeting, Davos

Jansen J (2010) Political and remembrance, colonialism and the Algerian war of independence in France. In: M. Pakier (ed) A European memory?: Contested histories and politics of remembrance. Berghahn Books

Johnson J (2016) The great war and the Middle East

Karatas I (2019) The Arab spring and the possibility of the success of likely revolutions. Research Gate 10. https://www.researchgate.net/publication/340810141_The_Arab_Spring_and_The_Possibility_of_the_Success_of_Likely_Revolutions

Karsh E (2020) The San Remo conference 100 years on: how the Jewish National home entered international law. Begin-Sadat Center for Strategic Studies

King C (1922) The King–Crane commission report on the near east. N. Y. Publisher, New York

Kleingeld P (2014) Kant's second thoughts on colonialism. Oxford University Press, pp 43–67. https://philarchive.org/archive/KLEKST-2

Lahav P (2015) The Suez crisis of 1956 and its aftermath: a comparative study of constitutions, use of force, diplomacy and international relations

Library HoC (2016) Balfour Declaration. UK Parliament

Malhees G (2020) The war raging on consciousness is the most dangerous war

Mansour J (2006) Historical features: the Hijaz-Palestine railway and the development of Haifa. Jerusalem Q: 5–21

Mazarr MJ, Priebe M, Radin A, Cevallos AS (2016) Understanding the current international order. RAND Corporation. https://doi.org/10.7249/RR1598

Meshrek AA-L (2019) Colonialism is between making the illusion of elites and education without education. https://www.aljazeera.net/blogs/2019/7/16/النخب-وهم-صناعة-بين-ما-الاستعمار
Nationalization of the Suez Canal Company (1957) Harvard Law Rev 70. https://doi.org/10.2307/1337813
Oakes, DFK (2009) A peace to end all peace: the fall of the Ottoman empire and the creation of the modern Middle East. Macmillan USA
Pappe I (2006) The ethnic cleansing of Palestine. Oneworld Publications
Register J (2017) Why narratives matter for social progress. In: Inclusivus. https://inclusivus.org/inpowered-perspectives/2017/4/19/why-narratives-matter-for-social-progress
Reimer M (2006) The King–Crane Commission at the juncture of politics and historiography
Rekacewicz P (1992) The Middle East in 1914. Le Monde diplomatique. https://mondediplo.com/maps/middleeast1914
Roccu MPR (2020) Imperial pasts in the EU's approach to the Mediterranean, pp 671–685. https://www.tandfonline.com/doi/full/10.1080/1369801X.2020.1749702
Saeed E (1993) Nationalism, human rights and interpretation. https://hekmah.org/13201-2/
Shaher SI (2017) Post-Sykes-Picot maps...from partition to deconstruction. In: Arab Democratic Center. https://democraticac.de/?p=44471
Studies, CfWA (2021) Colonial class: indirect colonization in the name of freedom! https://alkhanadeq.com/post.php?id=855
Theompson E (2020) How the west stole democracy from the Arabs: The Syrian Arab congress of 1920 and the destruction of its historic liberal-Islamic alliance (New texts out now). Grove Atlantic
Treaty of Sèvres and Lausanne (1920). https://www.fransamaltingvongeusau.com//documents/dl1/h1/1.1.18.pdf
UN, U. N. (1951) Review of economic conditions in the Middle East
Wali A (2013) Geographical history of exploration and drilling for oil in Iraq. J Remote Sens GIS, ISSN: 2052-5583, Manchester, UK, pp 60–75, 1, 60–74
Wezeman PD (2018) Saudi Arabia, armaments and conflict in the Middle East. https://www.sipri.org/commentary/topical-backgrounder/2018/saudi-arabia-armaments-and-conflict-middle-east
Wood J (2015) The west created this mess with Sykes-Picot, it's time to fix IT. https://calert.info/details.php?id=255

Chapter 2
Multidimensional Consequences

Warda Samara

2.1 Eco-Political Consequences

From 1881 to 1914, there was broad monetary stability in the region in general under the gold Turkish lira. But after the outbreak of the war, the Mandate authorities began implementing monetary and financial policies in the mandated territories. Although through several decisions and policies, the most effective was to increase taxes. During the Western colonial era, people's identities became public fact. One now had to find a place in a group classified to protect themselves as Sunni, Shia, Catholic or Orthodox Christians, etc. This newfound demand for identity became a deliberate strategy to exacerbate political, social, economic and security problems. The loss of minority rights and thus led to revolts and armed conflicts in many regions.

Back in 1919, the social, economic and psychological effects of famine, poverty and asylum seeking were profound on the one hand and the uprising against the monopolists from another hand who laid their hands on staple food commodities for gain and wealth, while the common people starved, scattered for a bite and died on the roads (Fawaz 2014). This prompted the Allies during the WWII to take strategic measures such as fortifying the interior areas that provide military food supplies. The ME Supply Centre, located in Cairo, was formed to avoid social unrest and revolutions in their regions and ensure maintenance of the military operations and the supported industries produced by the locals on the main front (Al-Saleh 2020). This intervention in the treatment of urgent economic and social problems in the ME, constituted a turning point of the external forces intervention where the direct economic intervention served capitalism to expand. This shaped a central authority operates to manage the economic process from one hand, and reshaped the control over some sectors in the region especially agriculture which was followed with the policy of economic control.

The start of capitalism in the region was marked by the attempts to absorb all profit from the agricultural sector, including home handicrafts. Especially as this sector was even competing on an international level (Al-Saleh 2020)! This introduced the idea

W. Samara and M. Samara, *The Power of Perceptions in the Middle East*,
Perspectives on Development in the Middle East and North Africa (MENA) Region,
https://doi.org/10.1007/978-3-030-99150-0_2

of the countryside existing to support the cities. The cities are now being considered as the centres for new industries and later technologies. As the cities continued to grow, the countryside declined with a mass depopulation of skilled people migrating to the cities. This is a direct representation of the interests of capitalism being served at the expense of the people.

Since WW1, the regional workforce in the colonies was forced to adopt a new economic structure. The labour of the indigenous people were soon replaced by large commercial units in order to provide the army with sufficient clothing and weapons. These commercial units, or factories, would then lure craftsmen away from the countryside sparking unfair competition between huge commercial businesses and the farmers. This economic transformation did not come without the help of military domination. One would be rather surprised that this economic intervention was organised by the British Ministry of War, not the Ministry of Foreign Affairs. Therefore the method of dealing with the local population with this intervention involved having a strict approval system of any economic initiatives proposed by the people.

Administrative obstacles and overlapping responsibilities have always been deliberate attempts by the Mandate Administration to delay the implementation of projects demanded by the people. In sum, the roots of capitalism in the ME are not just found in globalisation but also in military domination.

Some argue that if WWI had never happened, the world would be wealthier, trade, capital and people moving would have been much more seamless than the control on trading these days. A big scale of destruction on all life's aspects was the primary result, not peace. Across the world, hundreds of millions of lives were lost, countries and communities were destroyed and countries were redefined. Despite the Arabs having no cause for this conflict, the destruction did not exclude them and did not stop there.

Since the West ruled the region, the phenomena of the educated intellectuals and local leaders who advocated Arab unity has gradually declined. It is, for external forces, a necessary step to finally finish the collective spirit that might develop into any major political or economic system. Instead, political parties ran by incompetent elites were formed, creating a weak whole structure. Most countries have long remained under the influence of one-party rule, later several movements and political parties started to arise in the region after the fifties. Hence, why figuring out the size of the caused dilapidation is relatively limited (Khawas 2019). Moreover, Western forces have separated the Arab world from its Eastern or Oriental side by planting the Zionist entity in the core of the region and declaring Israel as a state without clearly identifying its borders. This became a security threat to all countries in the region including Israel. This has subjugated the Arabs after their fragmentation into more numerous but less capable entities, focusing on dividing or weakening the Arab "Centre States", or the so-called "confrontation states", namely Egypt, Iraq, Syria, Lebanon and Libya. Achieving this system means dissolving the Arab and Islamic identity in favour of a confusing geographic affiliation, stripping people of their former chosen identities (Ashmawi 1996).

Putting this into an eco-political perspective, several long-term issues have since emerged. The most tangled of these issues being the occupation of Palestine and the Kurdish issue on the political level. Meanwhile, further widening the gap between the rich and the poor on the economic level. All signs indicate that there is no future solution to any of these problems.

2.2 Palestine-Israel—The Chronic Headache

From 1916 until today, the common historical international reaction to the conflict in Palestine is *the muted international response* to—almost—any event that happens against Palestinians (Chomsky 2016).

In about the middle of the nineteenth century, the great economic transformation began to accelerate in the cities of the eastern Mediterranean basin like Beirut, Akko, and Haifa, through increased trade relations with Europe. This economic transformation also included the development of steam to propel ships, making it a more efficient and cost-effective form of transport. Furthermore, a branch of the Hejaz railway was built on the Palestine coast where Haifa became a major port for exporting wheat and receiving pilgrims to Mecca (Yazbak 1988). In 1918, the coastal areas in Palestine, Haifa in particular, were the strategic locations for the British military along the Suez Canal, as well as being the 'land link' between Haifa and Baghdad (Yazbak 1988).

Palestine at this time was an Arab country inhabited by the indigenous Arab Palestinian population (Muslims, Christians, Palestinian Hebrews and other minorities). In order to successfully implement the Zionist ideology, it was crucial to ensure the isolation of Palestine from Great Syria, especially as Palestinians were consulting the international Arab higher committee under the claim of borders security. At the beginning of the migration, the Palestinians initially believed they were hosting Jewish refugees fleeing persecution in European countries so they hosted the refugees and started to integrate them into the local economy especially since Palestine was a primarily agricultural society, as the amount of Arab land in Palestine before 1948 totalled to 6.3 million acres (Bsiso 2016). It is important to note that there were two distinct groups of immigrants to Palestine. The Jewish immigrant simply sought a secure homeland after experiencing persecution. The other, being the Zionist, who immigrated with a specific ideological goal.

However, the ulterior motives of the new Zionist entity began to become apparent. The British Mandate enacted a discriminatory economic and financial policy that serves its interests on the one hand, and serves the Zionism presence on another hand. The restrictions on Arab traders in agricultural sector increased and began to turn to foreign traders, which increased poverty and unemployment rates among the Arabs. Britain the greatest importer of Palestinian citrus fruits. Between 1935 and 1936, Palestine was the fifth-largest citrus-producing country in the world. Britain was the first to benefit, owing to the fact that it was the first to purchase the fruits (Yagi 1982). During the same years, the percentage of what was imported from the total Palestinian exports of citrus reached 96.3%, respectively. Britain controlled 70% of the total exports of Palestine, with the privileges of customs duties applied to all parts of the empire (Bsiso 2016). In an endeavour to support the growth of a newly developing country, Israel began to expand into Palestinian territory. This expansion took form through the establishment of settlements and the occupation of agricultural lands. All activities were made possible by British support. This expansion which continues to grow to this day, meanwhile also continues to hurt any economic growth in Palestine. Thus, when the whole world was suffering from WWI, a new financial and economic system was created in Palestine, with the acquisition of local lands and building agricultural settlements on top of it to then and encouraging Jewish immigrants to settle there as part of their call to the 'holy land' (Metzer 1998).

However, the British Army began to withdraw from Palestine and new troops and soldiers as later named 'Israel forces' began to replace them. This coupled with the fragility of the Palestinian leadership after WWII and increasing "complications" from the local population led to the official announcement of Israel as a state in 1948. What followed was brutal massacres all over Palestine, wiping out at least 530 villages and creating a sea of refugees.

While the unarmed Palestinians in this case were simply expendable and not a factor to be considered, they still are, after decades, the majority in the land. Even though the active encouragement of Jewish immigration to Palestine was and is part of demographic transformation which takes roots in the early phases of Zionism (Pappe 2006). These Jewish settlers were later used as an excuse for justification of the confiscation of more land and subsequently allowing the Zionist forces to carry out ethnic cleansing by other means (Pappe 2017).

Of course, there are many Arab scholars who seek to find more about the reality of what has happened in Palestine, but this is not discussed in this book. I found it more enlightening to discuss the perspective of several Israeli scholars and historians. Particularly those who recognise and concluded that Israel was shaped and based on manipulating the collective consciousness of three groups of people. First, the Arabs' 'collective consciousness' (regional awareness) by isolating Palestine and creating heightened borders for security. Secondly, the collective consciousness of the Jewish immigrants who were told that Palestine is an empty land without people. Even Jews, who rejected the Zionist project, were forced to flee due to tyranny, saw Palestine, the promised land by God, as an area of safety. The third consciousness is manipulation of the collective global memory, the '*machine experience mind*' through an attempt to erase the 1948 ethnic cleansing of Palestine. A relatively modern time crime has been attempted for a long time to remove it from the mass consciousness. Instead other narratives are persistently promoted with the purpose of serving external forces, especially in light of the contribution of non-Jewish Zionism in the formation of Western consciousness towards their project (Pappe 2006). Several Israeli historians like Ilan Pappe, Avi Shlaim, and Shalom Sand have questioned the current narrative about Palestine and have been remarkably committed to searching and standing for truth. This is happening on a remarkable scale for the first time since the Arab-Israel issue started. Which is important to educate both sides within where peaceful solutions can find a way. On the other hand, these historians communicating this opinion in Israel to the people, is a sign that *people to people* solutions are possible if they are locally well organised. Many peaceful tools would be implemented in order to allow this to happen. This solution needs a cooperation of people on both sides, this appealed cooperation can be done when both sides have a mutual understanding of what has happened and where the '*Machine experience mind*' was manipulated. Create long term plans to fix errors that guarantees a peaceful life for future generations.

What makes the Palestine case one of the long term unique cases are three reasons. First, its link to religion and ancient myths. Jewish religion instructs its adherents to await the coming of the Messiah to the Holy Land at 'the end of time'. The area is considered a holly place by Muslims, Christians and Jews. The second thing is the Palestinians' are still living in historical Palestine (Palestine and Israel), under several various titles. For example, Palestinians who live in the West Bank hold a Palestinian Authority ID, the Palestinians who live in areas like Akko which is under Israeli control hold an Israeli ID, while Palestinians who live in Jerusalem hold a 'Jerusalem Status' ID. Moreover, millions of Palestinians are still living in refugees camps in other Arab countries. These were replaced by new immigrants. That makes Israel the only occupation project that is still running until now without solutions and without any international political acknowledgement of the massive ongoing impact on the Palestinians. The third point is that the most powerless people—in terms of military and forces—perhaps on the planet, are rejecting and even resisting the project of the most powerful forces. Some forces obviously have something to do in Palestine, but not through the Palestinians. They rather do it themselves in cooperation with Israel.

These are mainly the points that have been preventing what so-called 'the two states' solution that proposed an independent self-administration to the Palestinians. Which has failed as Israel would not allow the Palestinians to get control over any of Palestine's borders. As a result of this stuck situation, people started to accept the con-federation system to be implemented. This emphasises on the possibility to create solutions beyond the political protocols and governments benefits.

Palestine, the cities of Jerusalem and Bethlehem in particular, as a strong spiritual metaphor for Muslims and Christians, started to disappear from the '*machine experience mind*'. Not only that, but by also re-directing the new generation to modern narratives that led them to materialism, capitalism and consumption in a way to separate them from their roots. Now, Mecca, the Holy Place of Islam has become akin to a commercial centre. The pilgrimage has become a religious, tourist and commercial season losing its original holy spirit that emphasises the advancement of capitalism as an ideology (Crooke et al. 2021).

During the transformation Palestinians, the indigenous people of the land, were subject to ethnic cleansing; rural areas were destroyed, key people in the communities were killed, hundreds of villages were wiped out and as a result, the whole economy collapsed. To benefit Jewish immigrants, a "segmented entity" in Palestine was constructed entirely separate from the Arab economy, sponsored by the British Mandate create institutions underpinning an urban and industrial economy (Schewe 2017). This was followed by provisions of education, health and welfare services to the Jewish community over the Palestinian which has gradually led to the isolation and then domination of the Palestinian economy. Now, this situation with all its policies has created two main communities (Arab Palestinians and European Jewish) sharing the same land with conflicting ideologies that leaves both communities in a continuous conflict. Since 1948, the Palestinians have lived under Israeli military occupation, where all borders and resources are controlled and resources are regulated by Israeli industries. In an attempt to emphasise on separating the two communities, construction began on a separation wall by the Israelis in 2003, a physical and psychological division for both Palestinians and Israelis where you could physically walk from one world, through a military checkpoint, into the other (Niblett 2019). Even the Israelis are not permitted to cross it except, for example, if engaged in a military operation in Palestinian territories. A hard card being played to manipulate the consciences of both sides in order to erase human curiosity and rights from the new generational awareness. As a Palestinian, after walking through the remains of the Berlin Wall during the 30th Anniversary of its fall, it strikes to me personally a symbol of the unification of the ideologically divided. Will Palestine-Israel ever witness the fall of the Israeli separation wall and the unification of the people starts where everyone lives in justice?

The decline in the Palestinian market has been remarkable in its elimination of the economic activity, but also its impact on social behaviours. As a result, many Palestinians, especially the young and educated started to immigrate to the blooming Gulf countries, causing a brain drain.

In conclusion, Palestine has witnessed a dramatic transformation, that shifted the power, one more time, from the indigenous people to a new force which keeps continuously reshaping the geopolitical map of Palestine and Israel. Figure 2.1 represents the change in the historical map of Palestine from 1920 to 2020, where the Israeli control over the area is gradually expanding over the Palestinian land. This is a clear violation of international law. The end result, Palestinians nowadays having almost no control over the land, except inside the Gaza Strip. Moreover, in 2020 the US revealed a plan to resolve the Palestine-Israel conflict. This Plan is known as the 'deal of the century'. It allowed for more Israeli annexation of the land in an attempt to expand Israel's borders, which once again reshaped the geopolitical map. The logic of this deal may be an introduction to the "*digital classifications*" described in Chap. 5. Especially in light of the Arab economic treaties that followed while the details are a well-kept secret (Asseburg 2019).

From time to time, many events happen in Palestine that could be considered an "electric shock" to revive the regional spirit and a provocation that examine the global responsibility towards history and human rights, by having the world witness this continuous tragedy. These events force the Israeli communities to distance themselves from these novel views. The whole implications of the historical consequence have left two people (Israelis and Palestinians) sharing the same dream about the same land like the same dream of group sovereignty on the same land Each claims their land for their own, while the consciousness of the majority on both sides is still committed to specific narratives about the other. This therefore leads me to question: will Palestinians face the same fate of cleansing and displacing to implement the myth of what is called 'the great Israel'? Is the rise of AI the beginning of the *people to people* solution? Both, in fact, are valid options to happen if the current

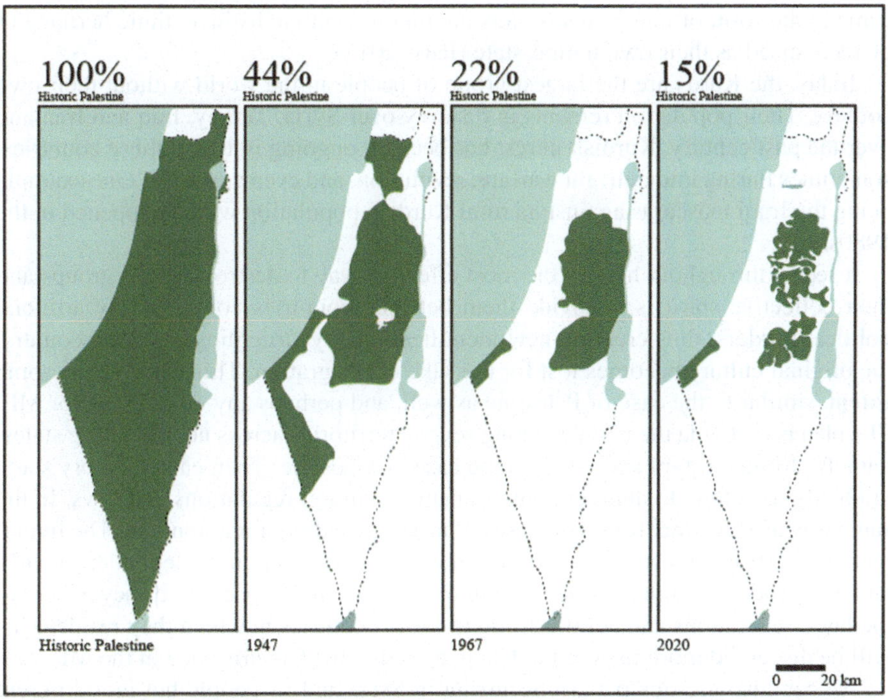

Fig. 2.1 Map of Palestine between 1920 and 2020 (*Source* Author's own design)

Israeli policy continues the same way and the international response stays mute while Palestinians continue to suffer a crisis of leadership.

2.3 The Kurdish Struggle

The divisions of the people by states did not only occur in the MENA region, but there are many examples of division and redetermining the borders in Europe. As well as in Asia which was not excluded from such divisions. In addition to dividing the Arabian Peninsula into seven countries, dividing the Indian continent, separating Pakistan from India, which is inhabited by tens of millions of Muslims, and then dividing Pakistan itself into two parts: East Pakistan, which was called "Bangladesh" and the remaining West Pakistan in its name, and the third division of the country of the Turkic Tajikistan and Kyrgyzstan.

The most remarkable was the division of the 36–45.6 million Kurds, whose homeland was now divided between four countries: Syria, Iraq, Turkey and Iran. Throughout the twentieth century, their struggles for political and cultural autonomy were opposed by the various regional governments. This opposition unfortunately came in the form of massacres for any attempt to claim a distinct ethnic heritage or be recognised as their own nation-state (Paris 2017).

Today, the Kurds are the largest group of people in the world without their own country. Their population remains in disarray over Syria, Turkey, Iraq and Iran and over the past century, Kurdish unrest has been an ongoing issue for these countries, sometimes flaring into outright warfare, revolution, and even genocide. One example being the Iraqi mascaras against its rural Kurdish population which happened in the 1980s.

It seems throughout history the most effective way to destroy certain groups and their collective spirit is to divide them between countries controlled by artificial political borders, thus creating new identification. By struggling in a new country, the original culture becomes lost for the sake of integration. This could be, to some extent, similar to the case of Palestine as well, and perhaps any other plans for ME. The plan is to divide the people among several territories across neighbouring states, namely; Jordan, Egypt and Israel in the case of Palestine. Then each territory starts gradually to belong to another country, nation, culture, regulations and laws. In the same way as Palestine, Kurds in these countries are calling for autonomy. The fundamental question persists however; does autonomy actually guarantee independence and independent identity inside the country they live in? Especially if they adhere to the laws, regulations and administrations of the countries in which they reside. This will be discussed more in detail in Chap. 5, Federalist Govern-once in the ME.

We can also see this pattern occurring in Syria and its people but in a different way, Syrian people are being divided over other countries but maintaining "Syria" itself. What purposes the land will serve in the future and will Syria be able to protect the name 'Syria' or will it change especially after losing control on many areas where more than 13.5 million Syrian were displaced and split between the countries under the name of refugees and immigrants. Becoming minority refugees in other countries adopting a new identity that likely destroys the mental health especially when children and housewives spending long times in the refugees' camps or fail to integrate with the host communities that leads to a damage in the '*machine experience mind*' and the collective spirit. The whole suffering process that individual goes through allows new political solutions in their home countries.

In 1920, as mentioned in Chap. 1, the Treaty of *Sèvres* called for the independence of Kurdistan, but the Treaty of Lausanne eliminated these aspirations in 1923, as it did not stipulate any right for the Kurds to self-rule and the League of Nations then abandoned its support for Kurdish independence accordingly (Radpey 2020). This have prove to be a common occurrence throughout history, the Kurds are promised with an independent state within different defined borders as shown in Fig. 2.2 only to have this later revoked. Referring to the Kurdish Institute in Paris, Fig. 2.2 represents the Kurdish populated areas of the ME where the Kurdish states were proposed in 1919, 1920 and 1945.

Several revolutions broke out in 1925 and 1926, both of which were suppressed. Later revolutions such as the one in 1938, witnessed brutal suppression from the Turkish army with extensive use of army used warplanes and tanks extensively, leading to the death of more than 70,000 Kurds. As planned, the Kurdish revolutions

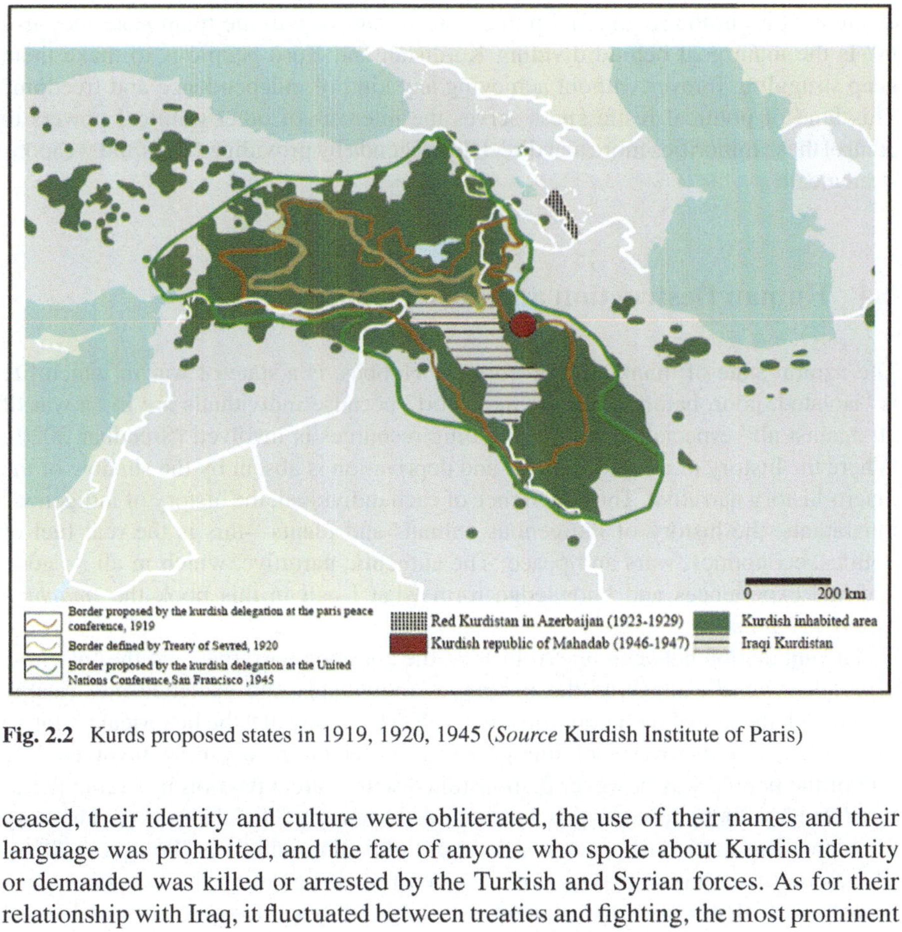

Fig. 2.2 Kurds proposed states in 1919, 1920, 1945 (*Source* Kurdish Institute of Paris)

ceased, their identity and culture were obliterated, the use of their names and their language was prohibited, and the fate of anyone who spoke about Kurdish identity or demanded was killed or arrested by the Turkish and Syrian forces. As for their relationship with Iraq, it fluctuated between treaties and fighting, the most prominent of which was a chemical weapons attack that killed about 5,000 Kurds. It became a clear change in the equation after the invasion of Iraq in 2003. The limit in Iran has reached the point of declaring jihad against the Kurds, where the rest are killed, facilities are destroyed, and people are displaced.

Kurds believe that the Kurdish nation has historically occupied a distinguished position in the map of Islamic nations, therefore their suppression is by no means arbitrary. However, by recognising their historical role and importance, it has raised the importance of the Kurdish language and culture, and pioneering a discipline of 'Kurdology'. There is now hope that this serves as a means of sparking debate and even offering a few first hypotheses through education associated with Kurds in education centres and universities worldwide (Ray and Scalbert-Yücel 2006).

There are several crucial questions resulting from the Kurdish division that should be taken into consideration. Even simply questioning about where this suppression came from, whether this is due to political strategy ad conflict or ideological reasons that are publicly not known. Are the Kurds minorities in these countries meant to create conflict in the region and political restlessness with the main state they live in? Is the main goal behind dividing Kurdistan and Kurd people is to make them keep struggling forever without achieving any kind of independence and freedom? This kind of political restlessness serves the interests of other political powers to control these minorities more and direct their agenda by providing funds and weapons strategically.

2.4 Human Destruction and Social Consequences

The natural state of mankind, according to Hobbes, is a state of war in which life is "isolated, poor, hateful, brutish, and short" because individuals are in "a war of all against all" especially when controlling resources is involved (Sreedhar 2020). Where the history of a life of hunger and deprivation is absent by the shadow of the macro-history narrative. The experience of each individual, the history of indigenous inhabitants, the history of indigenous animals and plants—this is the real fuel of politics, economics, wars and peace. The authentic narrative, which in all its good and bad experiences and knowledge form what I call in this book the '*machine experience mind*'.

The interaction between macro-history, the common narrative, and the '*machine experience mind*', concerns the history of individuals and societies inextricably linked with the fate of their countries. After WWI, we saw that the historical narrative did not focus on the overwhelming post-war burden on the countries involved. The fate of the people was however demonstrated with a great passion in Arabic literature (Dandoy 2006) however this was excluded from any official narrative. The story of colonialism determines people's sense of political possibilities (Wengrow 2018). Therefore, the common narrative is designed for manipulating the '*machine experience mind*' that transforms societies, shifting the dynamics of groups and social behaviours, affects the economic activities that impact the environment and thus affects the cumulative mind of the purposely neglected accumulative awareness. It is like a different kind of cyberattack that is hacking the mind of people as it is the main competitor to the materialism narrative (Al-Qattan 2018).

The treaties to share the Arab world were just the beginning of a radical social-economic change leading to the decline of the individual role in society, a necessary extension of the industrial and material revolution. The destruction of the "*machine experience mind*" where war destroyed entire societies through land and village destruction. Even armies of young people were simply cannon fodder fighting for battles they did not truly understand. They died amid transformational illusion. No one could ever know what kind of narrative was influencing the perception of these soldiers. The main narrative we know today was written from their sacrifices while their suffering as individuals and the subsequent destruction that affected their families and communities afterwards is barely mentioned.

The violation of human rights happens in all societies depending on the variations of social environment, it takes different and even more subtle forms. In general, this has led to the gradual erosion of human rights, by destroying the core of empowerment for their own people in the MENA—the family and the village. The first pillar of society collapses occurs upon the destruction of villages, agriculture and local industries. German-American philosopher, Herbert Marcuse has further emphasised this in his book *the one dimensional man*, by arguing that this is a necessary result of the transition to capitalism and globalism (Marcuse 1991).

Consequently, the natural development of human communities has been unwanted as it holds a common consciousness comes from the '*machine experience mind*' which allows these groups to have ability to solve problems in a unique aspect. These groups I call '*natural symmetrical communities*'. Yet, they are unexpected in their contribution to the society especially that they have their own economic and social dynamics seemingly independent of the whole system. Where certain individuals from these areas have proven to be innovators and drivers of social and political reforms on a national and even international scale. In general, these people are highly driven by a strong faith and common belief making it difficult it for external ideologies and forces to influence them to follow. They are ready to sacrifice everything they have in the name of a common collective belief. They live a simple life style and think any challenge they face is testing their faith, so they have the inner strength to overcome and survive. Even though responsibilities are distributed naturally among them. As their effort is still not organised on a systematic level, and thus far have not been viewed as a considerable player in wider society. As a result, we may have the reason for repeatedly unsuccessful change. For example, villages in the ME were productive and operated in a spontaneous cooperative manner; where men gathered the harvest, and the women would then market and store it. When the land was in common and not divided for individuals ownerships like today, the only required effort was a large workforce (Smith 1976). The villages collect the surplus for sale once ensuring that everyone in the village has enough for a year, if they were physically unable to contribute. Consequently, unemployment in these societies was almost non-existent and self-sufficiency could thrive in its fullest form. Through the introduction of the industrial revolution, the initial call for group identity through self-sufficiency was taken away. Without this common force to protect them, the ties between well-known extended families also collapsed, which represented the justice, responsibilities, and duties of all members of the family or the society. This is an example of how a whole group system was disrupted and can no longer depend on themselves. Decision making or planning has shifted from the first economic social cell 'the family' to the factories and politicians in the cities.

All of this led to an increase in the poverty rate, and then an increase of ignorance. This inevitably reinforced violence within societies, facilitated its penetration at the socio-political level in the face of civil wars and increased internal societal divisions in societies. All that has reshaped the dynamics of the main three indicators of human development: health, knowledge and income. This affects first and foremost life expectancy, level of awareness, and the level of poverty as represented in Fig. 2.3.

One must also not forget the psychological complications following scenes of repeated killing and destruction. This psychological suffering also significantly contributes to both the loss of individual and collective identity and the consequent

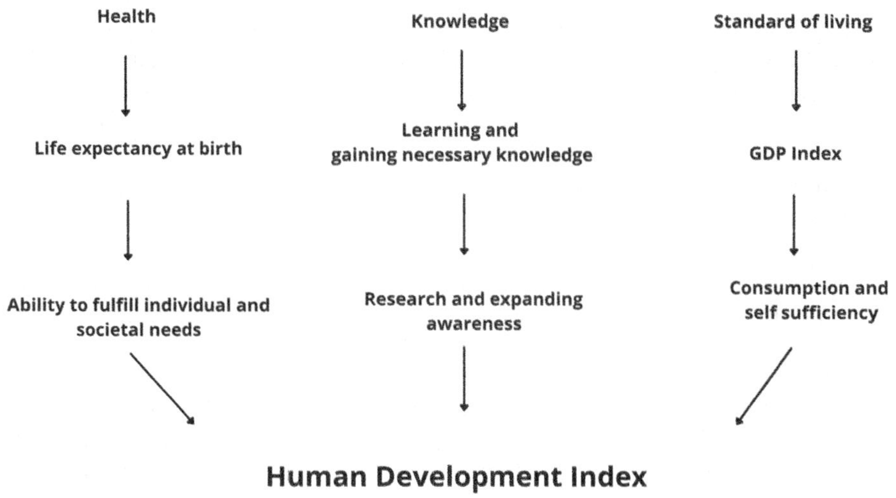

Fig. 2.3 Human Development Index (*Source* Author's own resource)

loss of the rights of everyone who has no experience in dealing or interacting with the new social order. A collective trauma has replaced the collective knowledge that fuels the '*machine experience mind*'. Children and women, including mothers, are persecuted and forced to work in highly risky fields, such as the military or warring groups. This situation is only made more complicated when adding the factor of asylum to neighbouring countries and to other countries as well, allowing the spread of diseases in the camps and the inability to adapt to the host communities.

It is clear by now that when human capital (or more simply put, the skills of the workforce) is damaged and its tremendous energy is directed towards self-destruction, it increases the collective trauma repercussions in the entire community (Goldin 2014) leading to the delusion and the shrinking of the '*machine experience mind*'. It is these personal effects of conflict which generate a negative-impact on entrepreneurs and small businesses. By witnessing an overall decline in the demand, increased transaction costs, interruptions in supply chains, many become discouraged from developing independent entrepreneurship (Bullough et al. 2014).

The effects of poverty, oppression and suffering have become a scar in the collective and individual memory of people seeking social, political and economic justice. This led to doubt among the people concerning the '*machine experience mind*' due to its inability to offer material solutions. This insecurity with the '*machine experience mind*' is considered the turning point for ideological transformation in the region. It marked the introduction of ideologies which only served the external powers rather than the people. In one way, the core of institutions that exist to defend human rights simply preserves themselves based on the continued violation of human rights. No long term effective solutions are provided, otherwise these institutions will put themselves out of work.

It has been known for centuries that contradiction such as this one is the source of thought (Perroux 1983). Thought that assures the link between philosophical ideologies, and development or underdevelopment. The narrative of the group becomes a tendency to address consequences rather than addressing the structural root causes. It is akin to taking treatment to reduce a high body temperature when you are sick without questioning what has caused this temperature change in the first place (Registre 2017).

This caused a defect in the collective awareness, and consequently, the individual citizen became isolated from their real role and lost confidence in all the actors on the ground. The first core cell of society and its active members was rendered a non-essential player in politics or society, especially after weakening all criticism or real opposition. By negating these communities own necessity, they instead can become tools in the hands of those who have the power—whether industries, political forces, or regional and international powers. As a result, there are few obstacles to manipulate the self-determination of the next generation and after a while this new generation loses the sense to be critical and simply surrenders to the current system without understanding.

2.5 Underdevelopment and Knowledge Production

We may believe that science is progressing passively toward greater technologies without resolving the flaws that are arising (Magno 2020). At a time when nations are keen to develop a knowledge-based economy, the Arab states possess little to no weight in this development. The progress of people and nations has always depended on free thought, science, philosophy and the production of knowledge, which is also the mainstay of religions and some ancient myths. Knowledge and intelligence are some of the most important pillars of the deep ideologies that have ruled the world for ages. It is the science leading to progress and further development that civilisations have always been struggling for. The race is for technological knowledge production which will determine who will be a global hegemony. Even though this understanding and importance of knowledge is very clear, it has yet to lead to increased output from the ME.

The race for knowledge is not solely understood in terms of production, but also control. Primarily by preventing others from accessing sources that might affect their own production of knowledge and therefore any progress. The ability to produce own knowledge in the MENA may conflict with the strategy of the superpowers in the current pattern, and therefore part of the current race is to reinforce ignorance when and where it suits. In the case of ME, the ancient systems were once a source of intellectual and knowledge production. Therefore, the idea of they own the resources 'yes!' but are they allowed to use to bring progress to the region? 'No!'. This then begs the question, do we, the Global forces, decide what to do with others resources? '!Why not'.

The elimination of the '*machine experience mind*' is also described as a 'mnemocide' (Alessandrini et al. 2016) and 'menticide' (Wordplay 1999–2021), the killing of memory, the killing of the community spirit and mind. Wars, throughout history, were accompanied with 'libricide' (literally translates to 'the killing of books' as an indication of 'homicide'), the killing of people, 'genocide', the killing of an ethnic group (Alessandrini et al. 2016). Emphasising on the importance of the deep level of the cumulative knowledge of the "*machine experience mind*". '-cide' in the Latin language reveals the killing (Donald 1960), even in 'pesticide' and 'suicide', it refers to death and extermination. Similarly is the death that comes together with the transforming of the core of the MENA region. This shifting of the regional core was an attempt to exterminate the unification of the people and their connection to a higher reason through the place in order to announce the death of the source beyond materialism. In fact, this makes sense from a technological advancement perspective where people have to be connected to another—materialised purpose created by the matter, decided by the masters of the materialisms, or perhaps at one point, only by the machine. Where matters is the only existing thing that really matters!

On another hand, this further creates the need to use force to transform societies. This call for 'killing' as a notion, implies that the '*machine experience mind*' must be damaged in order to transform life style and daily activities (Alessandrini et al. 2016). The moral balance between the destruction of heritage and the loss of human life is connected and very much not mutually exclusive. Weighing human suffering and personal tragedy against collective loss and cultural damage is always painful. Consequently, this enables the weakened environment to transfer to the new system.

The same approach has been followed during contemporary history in the region. In 1919, all documents of the first Syrian conference were destroyed (Alaraby 2020). In 2003, Iraq witnessed the destruction of their libraries. This indicates that it is not solely about environmental destruction, but warfare by other societal and knowledge-based means. Hence, either it works for the intellectually dominant states' benefits or they are deposed of accordingly. In the case of the ME, if libraries were burned, their old books and sciences were expatriated from the society that produced them (Taylor 2017). Moreover, new scientific advancements were introduced to align with the colonial goals, paying great attention to the preparation of the loyal elite to the control of the eco-political system in the region. This had a prominent role in the sovereignty of underdevelopment and corruption in certain countries, as well as encouraged the plundering of public resources and the increased import of goods. It allowed large industries to penetrate these countries at the expense of the local merchants and entrepreneurs. Moreover, during the formation of the modern governments in the ME, the priority was a heavy financial investment into military institutions under the guise of security rather than investing in knowledge production or any related infrastructure. It should be no surprise that this investment lead to increased inter-regional wars. Each nation employs weapons provided externally to destroy each other's societies. This is considered the mark of increased potential ideological strife in the region. This is one of the elements that feed into a mindset based on materialism, ignorance and underdevelopment.

In order to understand underdevelopment, a common sense of development must be identified. Conceived by French economist François Perrault, development is a set of psychological and social changes that enable a group to grow its real gross product in a cumulative and sustainable way. Development is also a phenomenon that is qualitative, social, and cultural in nature, while there is a quantitative and economic aspect to growth (Perroux 1983). As a result, development differs from growth in the sense that growth can occur without development. Such as in the case of discovering valuable minerals or energy resources. It is important to know that growth and development are not always aligned, This explains why in the ME, there was some growth but development remained stagnant, if not declined. This happened because growth took place without any consideration for the structure of the societies.

Sustainable development was not considered as of the same importance as continued growth from their natural resources. Underdevelopment does not simply affect the wider societal structure, but also begins on the individual level. These two aspects are not separate, but rather intertwined and both must be examined to understand how sustainable development would be successfully implemented.

Hence, the underdevelopment of the ME and its chaos has deeper roots beyond the contemporary history that further concealing the reasons or the causes of the current underdevelopment. As development depends on a nation's civilisation, it fades away gradually with accumulative consequent reasons and not one specific cause. Scientific production remains a fundamental pillar that impacts the change in societies, as it is followed by a new state of awareness that make the collective effort alert to the necessary changes. Without scientific production developed systems or societies wouldn't be able to sustain or continue to be innovative along with the new eras indicators like technology. If we look at the scientific journal production in the MENA, we find the region in the bottom among other countries. A study on scientific wealth indicates that all countries in the MENA have shown multiple cases of negative growth, which constitutes a wide gap between the productivity of the MENA region comparing to other countries at the international level see Fig. 2.4 that represents the production of scientific journals for five different regions in 2001 and 2013 (Siddiqi et al. 2016). This gap is remarkable compared to other countries like Norway whose population is only 5 million people. The gap is remarkable comparing to other countries. Moreover, when researchers seek to study the region, they rarely find suitable scientific research coming from the region itself.

Another factor for development decline is removing the Ottomans archives that directly affecting knowledge production in the MENA. These contained historical writings, legal documents and related civil right documents. These archives provided a deep insight into the eco-political history of the Arabs, one of the best pieces of contemporary evidence on civil rights in the region. Despite the great importance of the Ottoman archive, very little effort from the Arabs side was invested in it. The number of documents related to the Arab world is estimated to be between 80 and 100 million, of which only 50,000 documents have been translated so far. Neglecting to learn and study these archives creates a gap in understanding the contemporary history of the region and simply creates further ignorance and misunderstanding

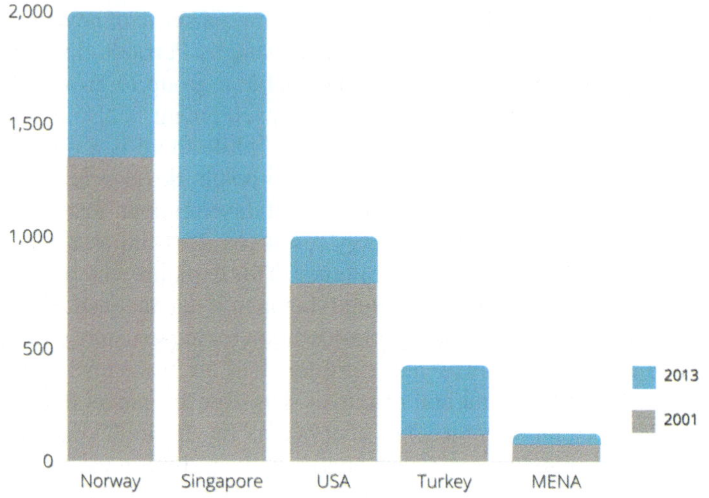

Fig. 2.4 Journal papers production in the MENA compared to other countries 2001–2013 (*Source* Author's own design)

unless the Arabs take the responsibility to translate most of these documents (Al-Khouja 2008).

Arabs to this day still praise the 'golden age'—eighth to the thirteenth century—of their ancestors and the ancient knowledge contribution. The fact that the quality of knowledge production since then has regressed must be admitted. It will not return by claiming otherwise. However, Western forces have taken advantage of this to promote their own interests. On the one hand, the West translated classical and scientific works produced by the Arabs, and were taught openly in their own curriculum at universities. By 1200, Oxford and Paris had curricula that included works of Islamic science, translated by Aristotle, Euclid, Ptolemy, and Galen (Ofek 2011). All while, the Arabs and Muslims were sinking further in regressive attitudes under a new system for the benefit of the external forces.

That situation has increased the gap that even people in the ME today underestimate, with this state of unconsciousness leading to further regression. The gap continues to expand between scientific and technological activity, demonstrating a lack of clear and specific strategies or policies in these fields. Regardless of the restrictions in intellectual research, I will also focus on who sponsors and supports any current research in the ME. Answering this question may blame the people in the region for their choices especially with the decline in the Arabic language as a foundation of the research.

Adding to this culture of development decline is the political monopoly over many sensitive state positions which has led to a climate of incompetence over-informed leadership. The regional leadership understand politics from a single perspective related to economy, control and surviving the system. This comes with underestimating the importance of local scientific research that analyses the details of current and future planning. On the other hand, developed countries are interested in attracting minds through material temptations and the offers of citizenship. Recent events in the region have further complicated this gap in knowledge production in both the short and the long term. What happened in Iraq in 2003, for instance, was the near-emptying of the intellectual pool, as well as the mass migration of many competent academics, professionals, entrepreneurs and engineers. This has created a gap in the executive positions that manage institutions and nurture future generations.

In recent decades, the conflicts in the region have arguably caused more migration of peoples, whether collective or individual, voluntary or forced than any other factors. A study revealed that nearly 20 million individuals from the ME have immigrated. Every year more than 100,000 scientists, engineers, doctors and professionals immigrate from eight Arab countries: Syria, Lebanon, Iraq, Jordan, Egypt, Tunisia, Morocco and Algeria (Batrawi 2019). This situation creates an imbalance in the societal structure in these countries, where the middle class is shrinking and leaving increased levels of poverty and underdevelopment and very few left can pass on any knowledge. Eventually, this left underdeveloped societies awaiting aid from other countries by other means.

Despite some countries in the region being resource rich like Lebanon, Tunisia, and Iraq they are considered as 'underdeveloped' because they lack the necessary control and efficient use of these resources. This classification impact how people perceive themselves and their interaction with external forces. Especially considering the absence of local scientific research that could suggest alternative use of these resources without external interference. Yet, such classification serves to groom the local people to accept outside authority regulating their lives. One could argue the public is submitting themselves voluntarily, while the other side views it as a planned outcome from the external forces to maintain control over these resources.

However, the criteria for the classification of "underdevelopment" is actually borne from global institutions like United Nations Development Programme (UNDP), the World Bank and the International Monetary Fund (IMF). According to the world Bank, the capabilities of a country to create national economic growth is the indicator of development (Nielsen 2011). Whereas, the indicator by the IMF is the degree of integration into the global financial system beside other factors. It should be no surprise that this was set by the very same external forces that dominate other countries based on this criterion. As all the external forces involved in resource management in the MENA are also heavily involved in these global institutions. In this context, why analysing the extent of damage caused by countries to other nations or people is not taken into account, as an indicator, when countries being classified as developed or development.

Moreover, several years of war have a heavy financial burden in Turkey, Lebanon, Jordan, Iraq, and Egypt alone with close to an estimated USD 35 billion in total cost, which in 2007 equalled the GDP of Syria (Bank 2016). Clearly demonstrating an investment in wars and all its related industries rather than developing societies. This contradiction shows that there are two dynamics that are operating on different directions. The first one is committed to using all means and power in order to achieve goals (the strong forces). The second one (the weak forces) is, unfortunately, waiting for the first one to decide to offer them some justice without working hard for it. Awaiting justice to come voluntarily from the stronger player in the better position would not happen, unless the weaker player was able to dramatically change the rules against the stronger player.

As a region, the ME contributes relatively little to the generation of new knowledge than other parts of the world. Although the Gulf states are small and modern, they seek to promote a knowledge-based economy through educational investment. In light of these developments, significant challenges remain in promoting and producing high-quality research in the social sciences (including business). Even though, this progress remains on the regional eco-political systematic level and not competent on a global level. The question is, what hindered the MENA region's post-war development compared to other countries like Japan which also faced tremendous destruction during WWII.

2.6 The Production of Ignorance

There is an inseparable relationship between both the production of knowledge and ignorance. The latter being defined as the result of ignoring all kinds of science that lead to enlightenment. Science, on the other hand, will also refer to all branches of knowledge including psychology, cognitive science, philosophy, sociology and history (Proctor 1995). Due to this relationship, I believe that a prerequisite for the study of ignorance is understanding how to produce knowledge. Ignorance and knowledge require each other to reproduce themselves. The forces that produce ignorance are the ones who own the knowledge and understand its potential impact should it become available for the people. The aim then in producing ignorance is to allow it to occur in an intuitional subtle manner, in order to subdue peoples' perceptions and their interaction with the environment around them. The output of knowledge or ignorance reproduction as a process shapes the "*machine experience mind*".

> "Ignorance is not just the not yet-known, it's also a political ploy, a deliberate creation by powerful agents who want you 'not to know'"
> *Agnotology*

The "*machine experience mind*" became almost completely absent in the ME. Any knowledge that is produced is often rejected due to incorrect information or even fundamental errors in the mother language. There are natural causes for this that may be tolerated by any society and there are external causes that may occur deliberately. They are intrinsically related to the extent to which an individual or group knows about the concept of life in a fundamental way, the associated cosmology and the power of spiritual power. Controlling the concepts of life is therefore the gateway to controlling the consciousness of individuals and groups (Croissant 2018). This is what has been enshrined in the world of capitalism and technology starting from the age of the first Industrial Revolution.

Capitalism continuously needs new markets for its mass production, employing all possible tools to create the required demand. By producing new industries to emphasise the marketing potential of the 'one-dimensional individual', they become products of a network of institutions working for the benefit of several industries (Marcuse 1991). This demonstrates the crucial need to manipulate or even suppress the '*machine experience mind*', because that mind can realise the illusion around these 'fictional necessities'.

A network of institutions dedicated to these industries perpetuates ignorance through thorough market research like any other product. For example, resorting to the TV programmes and the media to chart the lifestyle that must be the life of all societies worldwide. The destroyed communities without clear structure and knowledge render people vulnerable to becoming consumers to a lifestyle with potentially damaging consequences.

The depth behind any new lifestyle is not seen for the people which explains why many people follow without questioning. While the '*machine experience mind*' is unknowingly distributed and spread thin and distant across the spectrum of society. Take beauty products, for example to some extent, everyone likes them or appreciates their intended function. Simply demonstrated by the fact that the total spending in the global beauty industry in 2020 was $500 billion USD (Gerstell et al. 2020). Many people use these products and ignore the fact that not only do they look more beautiful without these products, but more importantly these cosmetics are a superficial short-term solution creating a constant demand. Beauty has been made a commodity, and a necessary one at that. Few people choose not to follow this lifestyle, based on intelligence thoughts, and not buy these products or to buy the necessary ones. The difference is attention, awareness and perception. A similar difference between ignorance and knowledge!

However, if ignorance production and creating demand is only for commercial and profit generating purposes, the discussion would be more straightforward. Ignorance as a science is used as a weapon comparable to military power, insidiously used to achieve political interests at the expense of the people.

Like all other products, promotion is a crucial step in the supply chain. There are the suppliers, the manufacturer then comes the distributers which are in this case a network of various institutions, see Fig. 2.5. Afterwards comes the retailers or the

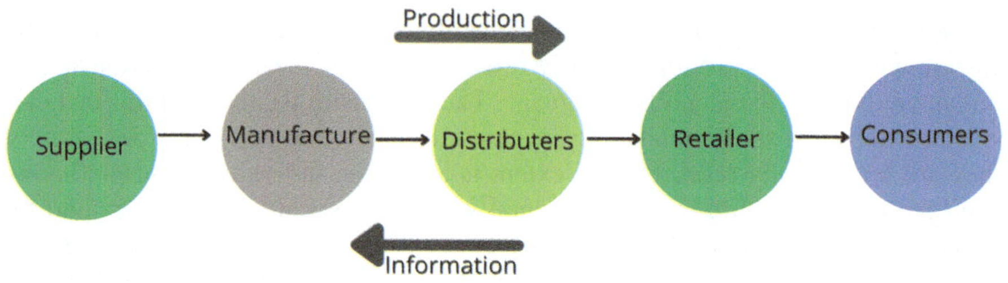

Fig. 2.5 Supply chain management (*Source* Author's own design)

pioneers who are in this case in the important positions in the local organisations like technocrats, young politicians or researchers and non-seasoned clerics. Ending, of course with the receiver who is you and I, the consumer. Here comes the role of trial and error, what is the consumer willing to buy. The only difference, perhaps between the supply chain of ignorance and of material production is the cost of the product itself. The product of ignorance is distributed free of cost to be sure to reach as much as possible of the public, there is no branded exclusion like with designer clothes that only a few can afford. In comes social media, the most fertile grounds for knowledge production. Within the aforementioned supply chain, those involved do not necessarily have the knowledge that they are distributing the product of ignorance or perhaps that are involved in this process at all. They may have reached the point that they are fully convinced of what they are doing because they do not have enough competencies or experience to understand otherwise.

On the other hand, industries are marketing their products to make a profit at the end of the day. Thus, each person according to these industries is simply an economic unit who has to be convinced to buy a certain product. In short, they cannot obligate anyone to buy a product. However, through the use of constant and pervasive marketing or advertising, many simply accept what is presented to them. While, the final decision to purchase remains with the individual, saying no to a product is not meaningful liberation from this system.

The importance of enhancing individual awareness to restore individual thought is now absorbed by communication and indoctrination that mislead public opinion and disturb the '*machine experience mind*'. This is a sign of the power of forces that prevent the realisation of intellectual freedom. The strategy of instilling unnecessary material needs by creating urgency to make them essential is the most important tool for directing thoughts that eliminates any growth and development.

Media and education play important roles where both could be used as very effective tools to combat misinformation. Accurate studies of sociology and perception and what affects them do indeed exist. For example, to change the name of the region from "the Arab Nation" and "the Islamic Nation" to the ME, itself pertains to a strategic significance and goal, created for a long-term strengthening of the military bases. Afterwards, these bases are planted in the centre of strategic areas where the illusion of manipulating people's identity is being emphasised where the higher reason is replaced. This includes employing the language to make this illusion real to the public (Saeed 2018). The reproduction of language and the re-creation of societies in a form that destroys the human resources that has been for decades neglected and oppressed in the whole region.

While the MENA region was one of many countries that were left destroyed following both world wars, there were some countries who were able to bloom following this period. Japan, for example, paid an unforgivable price during WWII namely the atomic bombings of Hiroshima and Nagasaki that put the entire nation in a black tunnel a 'lost decade' (Yoshino and Taghizadeh-Hesary 2015). Yet, 40 years later, the GDP of Japan had increased to 1.065 trillion US dollars. In fact, in 1980, Japan became the third largest economy in the world after America and China. This rapid economic growth resulted from a set of comprehensive cooperation, sound government policies and the cumulative effort by the people. Their highly skilled population demonstrated an ability to innovate and improve the system that follows with inventions and low-cost mass production. Hence, the unemployment rate in Japan is lower than that of the main advanced countries in the ME. Based on World Bank data, Fig. 2.6 represents the unemployment rate in Japan between 1999 and 2019, where in 2018 the unemployment has reached the lowest percentage, which is 3.89% (O'Neill 2021b). By openly allowing the public open knowledge, Japan had the necessary ingredients to develop into one of the most advanced and sophisticated nations. Hence, Japan poses an interesting comparison than to the MENA region due to their significantly differing post-war trajectories. Instead of the MENA region being allowed to develop their own post-war policies, they were subject to follow external forces to neglect the structure most beneficial for the people.

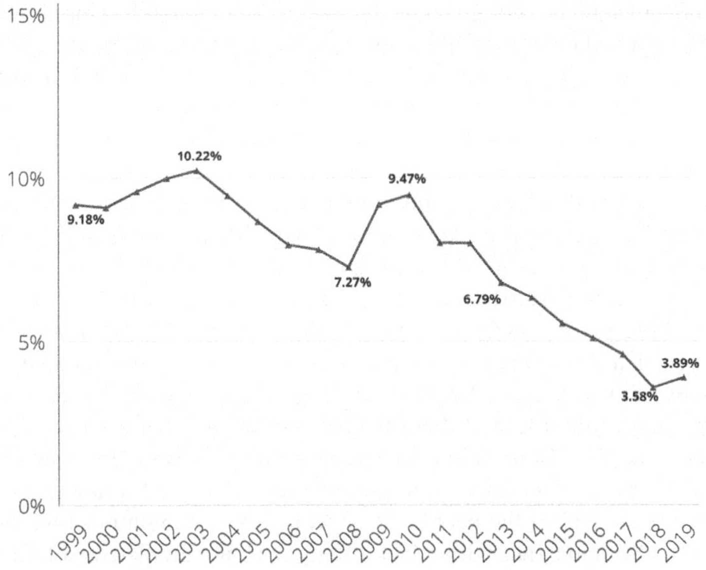

Fig. 2.6 Youth unemployment rate in Japan (*Source* Author's own design)

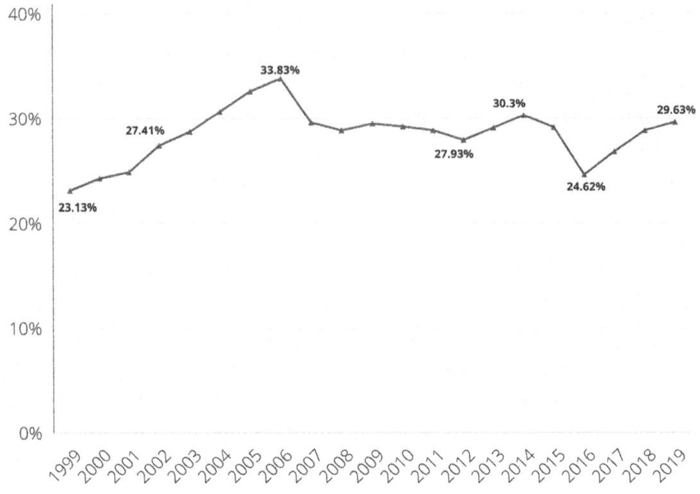

Fig. 2.7 Youth unemployment rate in Saudi Arabia (*Source* Author's own resource)

Economic growth has happened in countries like Saudi Arabia while a comprehensive development is still struggling with an ineffective system in place, society, in general, became unaware of the changes required to deepen certain knowledge that leads to innovation. Thus, the unemployment rate remained high. Based on World Bank data, Fig. 2.7 represents the unemployment rate in Saudi Arabia which reached 28.84% in 2018. This indicates that there is a deep analyse of the economic requirements in Japan which are not given the interest in Saudi Arabia. This shows that the ME has to learn and cooperate. Japan is a modern example where the ability of the people of the nation has successfully fused in order to understand the knowledge and competencies gained from external forces in order to achieve progress. When the population is aware and willing to feed and learn from the '*machine experience mind*' the progress starts.

Chomsky argues that fears are the foundations to keep control. Unstable public relations were created to promote ignorance on a systematic and strategic basis that keeps the population unaware (Comsky 2005). This is intended to raise doubts and cultivate bewilderment from the abundance of conflicting information, where rational decision-making gets lost in the mix. The leaders of the local community are ignorant about their own affairs, increasing their own psychological and mental burden. They realise there is manipulation but they are not equipped with the necessary data, knowledge, and tools to allow them to find the balance between the community needs and the rapid transformation in the region and worldwide. In other words, they still struggle to find organised ways to present themselves as a competent local force that represents the will of the people. Meanwhile, the communities find themselves convinced by the status quo with a lack of any feasible alternative solutions on the ground. Thus the only solution becomes the one proposed by the external authorities which surround the region with a set of rules and decisions that only serve their own agenda.

Where Japan issued governmental policies creating a culture of promoting public knowledge, we see a myriad of insidious forms of ignorance production in the MENA. This has become ingrained in the region in the form of deliberate or adverse neglect etc. (Proctor 1995). What this all ultimately illustrates is the power to transform systems from rubble to progress using their own population, rather than using the system to serve them.

The worse is when the effect of transitions turns the mind into submission to the realities of life and motivate the ability to reproduce a similar kind of Ignorance and more fear. With the absence of the '*machine experience mind*', individuals find more connection with the material things 'made' their daily life; therefore, they simply accept the law of things and the laws that reshaped their societies.

What has been happening in the ME for a century has created in the minds of the public that they have certain rights unrelated to their basic freedoms. For example, the right of a citizen to a passport means that they must acknowledge the borders they are in on paper in order to travel. By accepting this, they are now accepting the existence of a state that was neither agreed to or actively sought after. By accepting these borders, the next step for a government would be to 'protect' its citizens from any dangers outside. From here on, policies in public relations began to form the interaction with other states and nations. This acknowledgement of borders has only served to further muddy the waters of the already complicated social identities. This left the people misinformed about their own identities and culture, playing an important role in assuring the continued production of ignorance.

2.7 Institutional Corruption and Its Extensions

When discussing corruption, people tend to emphasise on financial and administrative corruption, unaware of its other more insidious forms. In this case, I argue that ideological corruption is a real threat to the economy, impacting the political position, ruin social values, manipulate the purpose of Education and learning, all leading to the creation of ignorant people—further gambling on the '*machine experience mind*'. Arguably, this ideological corruption sets the groundwork for financial and administrative corruption to flourish (Jakhotiya 2019).

When the so-called 'Arab Spring' emerged in 2010, people revolted to address corruption not only as a phenomenon but as an ideology that destroys societies. They began to fundamentally question the existence of these systems that were never designed to the people's benefit since their establishment. While the middle class and the poor people challenging tyranny and injustice as results of 'ideological corruption'. Perhaps one would argue that people must be highly conscious to recognise this level of corruption! Nonetheless as mentioned before the 'naturally symmetrical life' allows the domestic communities to somehow have a strong sense of any external ideologies. Those communities are naturally connected to the collective awareness even though they might not be aware of it. And therefore, they are able to detect any errors. As with any self-sufficient communities, it is usually challenging to integrate and control them with the centre of the external rules and forces. However, it does not matter if these revolutions creating positive changes or not. This was a clear objection to the manifestation of capitalism in the region, demonstrating that collective awareness can still play a critical role. As mentioned in the abstract of Crony Capitalism in the ME these popular uprisings were also a "rebuke to crony capitalism" (Diwan et al. 2019). A strong outcry for higher solutions, believing that the whole structure stands out for a positive change.

These systems have to be declared as ill systems where a comprehensive new structure in demand. Why have people then lost faith in the current systems? How do they interact with the illusion created by these systems? Most of the systems in the ME have taken the current shape as an extension for two external forces in the region, the Ottoman Empire and Western colonisation. When the West left the region they supported the monopoly of the power within the political elite and their unlawful advancement to the top. An absence of transparency of public institutions, and low trust in public institutions in the less fortunate countries in the region such as Palestine (Warf 2019). The colonial tradition is closely related to levels of corruption (He 2016) where leaders and elites deal with the system as they own the country and the rest of the citizens have no rights.

What we see of practices that people consider as corruption do not fully reflecting the whole concept of corruption. These practices are the results of deeper causes. However, I highlight here some of the practices that impact people most directly: nepotism, which became a common fact of life in most Middle Eastern countries. To the point where it has gone beyond politics, you may need nepotism for treatment in the hospital. In its most subtle form, personal contacts are used to obtain public services rather than face the bureaucracy. In Jordan, Lebanon and Palestine, more than one in three people (38%) with access to public services have used nepotism. On the other hand, there are unfortunately an alarming number of instances of citizens who are coerced to provide sexual favours in exchange for public services, 'sexual extortion'. For the first time in Lebanon, Palestine and Jordan, it was found that one in five people experienced sexual extortion, when accessing a government service, or knows someone who has. This applies to all genders (Warf 2019). Research show a high prevalence of corruption around elections. Nearly one in three people was offered bribes in exchange for votes at a national, regional or local election in the past five years. In some countries, citizens are also threatened with retaliation if they did not vote a certain way (report 2019).

Connections and the ability to use nepotism for one's position is a highly sought after professional asset and represents valuable social capital (Doughan 2017). The unpleasant fact is that people tend to get what they strongly believe is theirs through practising corruption. They feel satisfied with it and consider it reasonable even though these practices are destroying the mind. However, on a more Machiavellian note, 'the end justifies the means'. This unanimous acceptance of corruption has created social disorder leading to a lack of trust with the regimes (He 2016). Fortunately, corruption and nepotism have not managed to infect all communities and some have remained independent of this entirely. These are the groups that are being counted on, one day, to lead to change on a societal level.

Corruption has also reached the land sector has been mismanagement for the political, military and tribal favour elites. It is remarkable in Morocco, Jordan, Libya, Egypt, Bahrain, Sudan, Turkey, Jemen, and the complication of the land sector in Palestine (Nolting 2015). This type of corruption restricts people's access to land resources and encourages natural resource exploitation, which undermines food security and social stability, and hinder economic growth and sustainable development (Nolting 2015; report 2019).

Due to the diversity of historical experiences and political cultures in the region, it is important to view the impact of corruption practices of each country in the MENA individually rather than as a regional collective. For example, in less developed countries who are dependent on external aid, the phenomena of illicit wealth are increasing among politicians (Schoeberlein 2019). Moreover, it can be said that the vast majority of the people of the region live under corrupt regimes. Many regional governments simply do not comply with the separation of powers, especially the judiciary, which are directly dominated by implanted regime loyalists in critical institutional roles. Thus, only increasing the loss of confidence in the legal body and thereby increasing the gap between the rulers and the people. Until this gap just degenerates into further chaos (Khairallah 2015).

There is a causal relationship between corruption and human rights on the ground. In essence, once human rights have been compromised, or even outright denied, the people lose trust in their supposed "democratic" authorities. The systems that are not even helping them guarantee their rights or keep them out of poverty. Some analyses have argued that since the resources come directly from the people who manage them, they must receive a fair distribution of the revenue received. If these resources are sold by the corrupt authorities who retain the profits for themselves, these sold resources should be considered as stolen from the people. Based on this logic, other states are then importing stolen resources. Regardless, there will be continued cooperation with these authorities and even maintaining their power, which will ensure that their populations continue to suffer (Pogge 2002).

In social philosophy, corruption is a dialectical concept. It indicates the death of a community and collective awareness. Petty tyrants arise who possess all of the vices of a single dictator. The remains of freedom gradually become insignificant and unable to justify where a single dictator emerges to rule the people (Baron de Montesquieu 1751). Some studies show that poverty and injustice are some of the indicators that encourage rising corruption practices. For example, the rich are more likely to view practices of corruption as a way to facilitate their services and to preserve their interests as a protective measure for themselves. People do not support corruption blindly, but they believe they have no power to prevent it. This environment contributes nothing except to widening inequalities and increasing discrimination for marginalised groups like women and children (You 2005, pp. 136–157). This attitude of tolerance and apathy towards the problem of corruption stems from the two levels of manifestation of corruption. There is the network on the systematic level, but also on an individual basis which has become part of an accepted social life. This applies to what Adam Smith indicated "corruption perception is not the reflection of an absolute situation; it is a social phenomenon" (Smith 2010, pp. 120–131).

People have been witnessing these corrupt practices for such a long time, that the different forms have now become accepted and commonplace. However, this leads the people to have a clear perspective on corrupt regimes and even possibly become aware that it leads to unavoidable results and long term consequences. At the same time, and more commonly, they believe that some practices are necessary to obtain better quality, especially in education and health care. The popularity of this perception among the people makes individuals resort to more corrupted practices such as securing an academic seat for their children to obtain a quality education. In this example, parents believe that this certificate will enhance the position of their children and enable them to eventually live without the need for the corrupt system. But soon enough, the children graduate from universities and find themselves in the circle again, often in need of nepotism to get a job. More generally, as these corrupt practices facilitate obtain necessary services, it becomes an accepted and more common-place societal practice. It simply becomes a vicious circle that one cannot break out alone, the only solution would be systematic change. It is adding fuel to the fire even knowing oxygen is the solution (Jain 2011).

These practices reflect only the tip of the iceberg, the output of the ideological corruption after generations of societal conditioning. It begins with the acceptance of several powers creating a role model to the people afterwards until it became a life style and a strong attitude many in the population. At least this was certainly the case until the Arab Spring Revolutions in the early 2010s.

While some analysts may argue 'Arab spring' had failed in its original intentions, whether or not it was hijacked by politics, others see it as a mark of social change. Namely, the beginning of a new level of societal awareness. This argument has gathered more traction since the increased examination of cumulative awareness and the power of communities. Especially the role of women and youth in recharging the '*machine experience mind*'. Increased collective awareness will lead to no change if the system remains incompatible.

2.8 Summary

The disastrous consequences of the shift from the Ottoman era to Western colonialism had multidimensional repercussions on all aspects of life. This led to an atrophy of political maturity in the region, demonstrated by the response to the Palestinians and the Kurds' fight for national recognition. These two cases still persist today with ever-increasing complications.

In addition, local corruption, unwise leaders and the systemic production of ignorance among the population made it difficult to find solutions for any sustainable development. A century of destruction and underdevelopment created a weak image in the minds of the people and governments of the ME, leading them to prey on larger forces under the premise that they are unable to help themselves.

Eventually, successive military interventions in the region displayed a clear retreat particularly in access to knowledge, Hence, a massive decline in the collective consciousness has happened and thus demonstrates how the ME have been unable to escape from this black tunnel.

While there are countries, despite suffering total destruction from war, have demonstrated high levels of development and can compete even at the global level like Japan. This has not yet to be the case in the ME and thus shows that the ME has to learn the importance of an empowered population in development and growth.

References

Alaraby T (2020) The Arab government in Damascus. Arabic Documentaries. https://www.youtube.com/watch?v=6CmmlUUO5M8

Alessandrini J, Bethany Anderson AA, de Guevara M, Breemen V, Butterworth J, Anderson B, Assmann A, Butterworth J, Collier M, Cullhed P, Derez M, Duffy C, Fabian C, France F, Garside P, Ovčina I, Claudia A(2016) What do we lose when we lose a library. German Commission for UNESCO. https://www.goethe.de/resources/files/pdf94/streamgate.pdf

Al-Khouja K (2008) History of the Arabs in the Ottoman Archives [Interview]. Awsat. http://www.turkishculture.org/general/museums/ottoman-archives/history-of-arabs-772.htm

Al-Qattan N (2018) Literature (Middle East). Frei Universität Berlin. https://doi.org/10.15463/ie1418.11235

Al-Saleh MA (2020) Managing the Syrian economy during the French Mandate (1918–1946)—its post-independence effects. Presses de l'ifpo, Institut français du Proche-Orient. https://doi.org/10.4000/books.ifpo.13843

Ashmawi M (1996) Civilisation conflict between Arabs and Israel. Dar Al-Maref

Asseburg M (2019) "The deal of the century" for Israel-Palestine. https://www.swp-berlin.org/publications/products/comments/2019C20_ass.pdf

Baron de Montesquieu CS (1751) The spirit of law

Bank TW (2016) Economic effects of war and peace in the Middle East and North Africa. https://www.worldbank.org/en/news/press-release/2016/02/03/economic-effects-of-war-and-peace-in-the-middle-east-and-north-africa

Batrawi H (2019) The brain drain, and its economic effects. https://arb.majalla.com/node/70426/هجرة-العقول-النابغة-ها-آثار-و-الاقتصادية

Bsiso FH (2016) Arab economy in Palestine during the British Mandate 1920–1948

Bullough A, Renko M, Myatt T (2014) Danger zone entrepreneurs: the importance of resilience and self-efficacy for entrepreneurial intentions. Entrepreneurship Theor Pract 38(3):473–499. https://journals.sagepub.com/doi/10.1111/etap.12006

Chomsky N (2016) Who Rules the World. Penguin Random House UK

Comsky N (2005) The manipulation of fear. https://chomsky.info/20050716/

Croissant J (2018) Agnotology: ignorance and absence, or towards a sociology of things that aren't there. Soc Epistemology 28(1):4–25

Crooke A, Kinninmont J, Rogan E (2021) GSF Middle East roundtable: the changing dynamics in the region [Interview]

Dandoy JFR (2006) Chaos theory and its application in political science. IPSA World Congress, Fukuoka, Japan. http://hdl.handle.net/2078.1/176425

Diwan I, Adeel M, Izak A (2019) Crony capitalism in the Middle East: business and politics from liberalization to the Arab Spring. Oxford Scholarship Online. https://oxford.universitypressscholarship.com/view/10.1093/oso/9780198799870.001.0001/oso-9780198799870

Donald JB (1960) Dictionary of word roots and combining forms. Mayfield Publishing

Doughan Y (2017) Corruption in the Middle East and the limits of conventional approaches. German Institute for Global and Area Studies GIGA, Hamburg
Fawaz L (2014) A land of aching hearts: the Middle East in the Great War. Harvard University Press, Cambridge
Goldin C (2014) Human capital
He N (2016) Rethinking the causes of corruption: perceived corruption, measurement bias, and cultural illusion. Chin Polit Sci Rev 1(2). https://doi.org/10.1007/s41111-016-0024-0
Institut kurde de Paris (2017) The Kurdish population. https://www.institutkurde.org/en/info/the-kurdish-population-1232551004
Jain A (2011) Corruption: theory, evidence and policy. In: Econstor, p 9
Jakhotiya G (2019) Capitalist corruption leading to global socio-economic collapse. Munich Personal RePEc Archive. https://mpra.ub.uni-muenchen.de/95771/1/MPRA_paper_95771.pdf
Khairallah D (2015) Corruption and impeding change and development in the Arab World. The Arab Center for Research and Policy Studies
Khawas M (2019) Political corruption in sub-Saharan Africa
Magno C (2020) Evidence, rationality, and ignorance: agnotological issues in COVID-19 science. Rev Soc Bras Med Trop 53
Marcuse H (1991) One-dimensional man: studies in the ideology of advanced industrial society. Routledge & Kegan Paul, London
Metzer J (1998) The divided economy of Mandate Palestine. Cambridge University Press
Niblett R (2019) Why we build walls: 30 years after the fall of the Berlin Wall [Interview]. https://www.chathamhouse.org/2019/11/why-we-build-walls-30-years-after-fall-berlin-wall
Nielsen L (2011) Classifications of countries based on their level of development: how it is done and how it could be done
Nolting M (2015) The land and Its people: civil society voices address the crisis over natural resources in the Middle East/North Africa. MENA Land Forum—The Housing and Land Rights Network of Habitat International Coalition (HIC-HLRN)
Ofek H (2011) Why the Arabic world turned away from science. The New Atlantis 30:3–23
O'Neill A (2021a) European Union: gross domestic product (GDP) from 2016 to 2026. Statista. https://www.statista.com/statistics/527869/european-union-gross-domestic-product-forecast/
O'Neill A (2021b) Unemployment rate in Japan 1999–2020. Statista
Pappe I (2006) The ethnic cleansing of Palestine. Oneworld Publications, London
Pappe I (2017) The biggest prison on Earth. Oneworld Publications, London
Perroux F (1983) A new concept of development, vol 224, 1st edn. Routledge, New York
Pogge T (2002) World poverty and human rights, 2nd edn
Proctor RN (1995) The cancer wars: how politics shapes what we know and don't know about cancer. Basic Books
Radpey L (2020) The Sèvres Centennial: self-determination and the Kurds. https://www.asil.org/insights/volume/24/issue/20/sevres-centennial-self-determination-and-kurds
Ray ML, Scalbert-Yücel C (2006) Knowledge, ideology and power: deconstructing Kurdish studies. Eur J Turk Stud. https://journals.openedition.org/ejts/777
Registre J (2017) Why narratives matter for social progress
report G (2019) Global corruption barometer: Middle East and North Africa 2019—citizens' views and opinions of corruption
Saeed S (2018) The science of ignorance and the engineering of ignorance
Schewe E (2017) Post-war economies (Middle East). International Encyclopedia of the First World War
Schoeberlein J (2019) Corruption in the MENA
Siddiqi A, Stoppani J, Anadon L, Narayanamurti V (2016) Scientific wealth in Middle East and North Africa: productivity, indigeneity, and specialty in 1981–2013. PLoS ONE 11:e0164500. https://doi.org/10.1371/journal.pone.0164500
Smith A (1976) An inquiry into the nature and causes of the wealth of nations, vol 1. Liberty Classic
Smith N (2010) The perception of corruption. Int J Pub Opin Res 22(1):120–131

Gerstell E, Marchessou S, Schmidt J, Spagnuolo E (2020) Consumer packaged goods practice—how COVID-19 is changing the world of beauty. https://www.mckinsey.com/~/media/McKinsey/Industries/Consumer%20Packaged%20Goods/Our%20Insights/How%20COVID%2019%20is%20changing%20the%20world%20of%20beauty/How-COVID-19-is-changing-the-world-of-beauty-vF.pdf

Sreedhar SLS (2020) Hobbes's moral and political philosophy

Taylor A (2017) The most important libraries that were destroyed throughout history. https://www.noonpost.com/content/19574

Warf B (2019) Spatiality of corruption in the Middle East and North Africa. In: Global corruption from a geographic perspective. University of Kansas, pp 83–109

Wengrow DGD (2018) How to change the course of human history. Eurozine

Wordplay (1999–2021) Cide words

Yagi I (1982) التطو ر الاجتماعي الاقتصادي. مجلة الجامعة الاسلامية بالمدينة المنورة.

Yazbak M (1988) Arab immigration to Haifa during the Mandate period: a historical, economic, demographic and social study. Al-Qabas Library

Yoshino N, Taghizadeh-Hesary F (2015) Japan's lost decade: lessons for other economies. https://www.adb.org/sites/default/files/publication/159841/adbi-wp521.pdf

You S (2005) A comparative study of inequality and corruption. Am Sociol Rev 70:136–157

Chapter 3
Chaos and Ideological Strife

Warda Samara

3.1 Global Floundering and Regional Chaos

Chaos is by no means modern and has appeared in many different ancient accounts that discussed the origins of the world. Chaos as an "ancient" concept is seen as "a metaphor cosmogony". It is defined more closely in Hesiod's *Theogony*, as an empty space or matter which is not yet shaped (Gündüz 2006). It is described in Genesis as a coarse yet homogeneous structure that is feasible. The nut was the formless world that gave birth to the sun god in Egypt. The dragons in China arose from a single homogenous and undivided realm, imposing yang order on the four corners of the matter Yin (Plaza et al. 2006). The philosophy of chaos is a fundamental player in the research of mathematics, astronomy and various sciences. It included the social sciences and the restructuring of the holistic environment system that began to take up more space in research. The rationality of capitalism and globalisation is one of the most confusing aspects of the current era because of its progress in such an irrational manner. In order to support its productivity and efficiency, as well as an its ability to increase and spread amenities; there must be an unnecessary urgency on the demand. This turns the people into part of the system design and renders individuals into commercial units. Machine models and profit become more important than the people it should serve.

If we consider perfection supposedly as order, we find chaos operating in opposition within the same space. The similarity is deep in its roots while the difference is the indicators in each environment and therefore the employed tools differ. If I ask, what differs the chaos in Iraq from the chaos in the US? You may instantly laugh. It is the attention in our minds. We are accustomed to the global echo of incidents that is reported from the media so that we are busy with the outside chaos forgetting that it can appropriate several forms and appear in a monotonous attitude that becomes unrecognised on a wide scale. Perhaps because people have reached a stage of coexistence with this chaos it is now an unquestioning part of their daily life. Exactly like strict adherents to an Orthodoxy. Everything is taken for granted and no doubts or

W. Samara and M. Samara, *The Power of Perceptions in the Middle East*,
Perspectives on Development in the Middle East and North Africa (MENA) Region,
https://doi.org/10.1007/978-3-030-99150-0_3

questions are allowed to arise—this is the core where chaos thrives, especially the '*quiet chaos*'.

The ripple effect of the '*quiet chaos*' started to be realised worldwide upon the outbreak of the COVID-19. Due to the new uncertainties caused in daily life, it was now impossible to ignore the unobserved chaos within. Prior to COVID-19, one may argue that what is happening in the MENA region is, to direct public attention to a chaos happening elsewhere for the sake of suppressing '*the quiet chaos*' at home.

Whether this is happening in a structural way or not, it causes traceable confusion in the actions and reactions of global, regional and local players. Watching the news on the TV channels where people in the West are losing their minds; fighting for and hoarding necessities in the supermarkets, one would think it *truly* is the end of the world. This was a clear indicator of global floundering from all governments accompanied by publicly unprecedented cooperation among several authorities worldwide. This complex situation has produced several major challenges, that cannot be resolved without a paradigmatic change and international cooperation and leadership. This worldwide cooperation referred to the lack of the MENA region players' capabilities to tackle these challenges by themselves or, for other reasons, it wanted to show the public this image. Quite justifiably, people have tended to overlook the potential brought about by the COVID-19 pandemic. If people could see past the whole image of the negativity, they would notice the historical opportunity to create social change. It became more obvious than ever that the local interaction with the major forces and vice versa is more interconnected and holistic and necessary to happen the way it happened in order to reshape capitalism as an ideological system that we knew until the pandemic. However, the voices who are against the very structure of capitalism and its extensions themselves are not calling for a complete over-through of capitalism because they are aware of the unwanted consequences that might put the whole world in a dark age without an alternative system (Varoufakis 2021). Capitalists themselves realise that their system is in a troubled state and may be undergo a necessary transformation resulting in new eco-political dynamics. It would not be capitalism anymore, but the driving main forces remain the same.

What happened in Beirut in August 2020, for instance, demonstrates a huge confusion has happened on both official and popular levels. Many condemned the incident as an unforgivable mistake from the side of local parties and urgently called international support to save the country from further disastrous consequences. On the other hand, one could also consider what happened as undermining the political structure and the economic social life in Lebanon and its deep interaction with the international forces. This consequently offers a great environment for the international forces to interfere under the guise of "support". It maintains the French economic interests in Lebanon, where French investments in 1914 accounted for 66% of the total foreign capital invested in Ottoman public funds. That is, a total amount of 1.15 billion French francs with France obtaining 80% of the shares of the port of Beirut (Al-Saleh 2020). Hence, many Lebanese have expressed their concerns about Macron's visit to Beirut as viewed as an external interfering in the main economic pilar where the port total revenues amounted to about $290–350 million in 2018 (Berger 2021) but are not operating any more. The crux of his visit served as a historical emphasis of France being responsible for the region by employing different tools to promote the necessity of their role. Although Lebanon is considered as an independent entity, it is seen, in some context, as an extension for the "Greater Syria" where some analysts saw that chaos coming to Lebanon was in order to offer the reconstruction of the whole system that fits with the new era order and maybe a new ME. In any case, however, the whole situation has left a devastating economic loss in Lebanon where the physical damage alone was estimated to be between 3.8 and 4.6 billion USD (Berger 2021).

Hence, people believe that without the active involvement of the people themselves as the model in Japan, the whole ME region will deteriorate to darkness with heavy bloody prices and humanitarian suffering. The violent practices of chaos will not be stopped here, it might even reach Europe and the rest of the world and undermine the values system of the free and enlightened world (Michael 2015).

Following the Cold War, the concept of "creative chaos" was developed from the US (Ahmad 2011), representing a major turning point in foreign policy and the debate against what they described as external terrorism. The concept means the deliberate creation of disruption in specific countries in order to prepare them for a new economic and political order. However, the concept of "creative" also pertains to a second meaning. Creativity is complex, and can lead to an abundance of possibilities. With no systems in place to support such creativity, only chaos has resulted. This is the second level in creative chaos.

The US was funding systems in several countries in the region like Iraq, but later declaring war on them after they became allies. This is a clear example of the unexpected results of creative chaos. In addition, the US military appearances in these countries for decades and its constant interference created several co-dependent states within the state. As a result, one could observe the destruction in these countries but could not imagine an end to this chaos. In the case of Iraq, it led to comprehensive destruction of the national economy in addition to loss of infrastructure. This has increased poverty especially with transforming the Iraqi market to a consuming state rather than self-sufficient where national return became exclusively dependent on oil. Even the return on oil is used to recover the imported products that are no longer produced locally. On the American side, this war cost the US the average amount of \$3.5 trillion between 2003 and 2017 which is one trillion more than the US Congressional Budget Office (Schumer and Maloney 2008). These numbers emphasising the importance of people's perceptions who are trapped in financing part of these wars. Referring to the 'silent chaos' during 2003, the US national poverty rate increased to 12.5% to about 35.9 million people (Labor 2005). That is even more than the population of Iraq. This \$3.5 trillion could have been invested for the prosperity of the people in both countries.

Yet, chaos in the region has been like a dance on stage demonstrating the actions and reactions of the US and their allies as institutions and elite leaders. When the US leaders declared war against Iraq they expressed their concern of the 'external threat' and then bombed cities without thinking of the people's suffering as a worthwhile consequence. The destructive war was described as "the error" when the Americans finally admitted to their brutal but unintentional consequences. But it only killed over half a million and displaced over ten million Iraqis, which Tony Blair views it

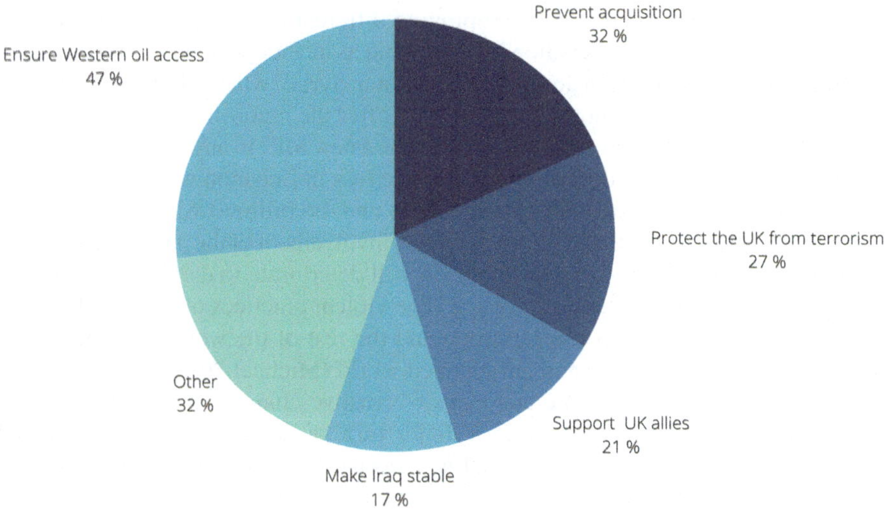

Fig. 3.1 UK public perceptions about war on Iraq (*Source* Author's own design based on UK study)

as "good planning for the conflict" (Stewart 2016). "We thought there was a nuclear weapon in Iraq". US intervention in the region was ended with the withdrawal from Afghanistan in 2021 after declaring that the inside terror was the only real threat. This marks a clear beginning of the US military decline in the region.

Moreover, a study conducted in 2011 about the UK public perception towards the war on Iraq and Afghanistan showed that one in five people disagreed with British involvement in both the wars in Iraq and Afghanistan. Figure 3.1 represents the public perception when asked about the purpose of military intervention in Iraq (Gribble et al. 2015).

Authorities seek to obtain public support therefore the perception of their citizens is important for them in order to achieve their certain goals, not necessarily to get direct approvals, especially when political and military missions are involved. The study concluded that those who were thinking that the war happened for personal benefits, which is the oil narratives on Iraq, were those who are likely to educate themselves about the external missions (Gribble et al. 2015). Public perception and manipulating reality while emphasising on the crime in the state of mind is still happening, those who are aware of the fact whether they are not interested to make difference, or they do not have access to the right tools and methods to be used. Worst case, they might view these war forces as a non-ending fact of existence. The resulting chaos in Iraq was described as. The increasingly strong presence of international corporations in the region for oil, communication and transportation networks is an obvious indicator of the reality of these military missions. Highlighting the fact that Iraq contains greater than 112 billion barrels of oil reserves with the daily production before the war estimating to be around 2.5 million barrels (Kaysen et al. 2002). In short, this demonstrates a strong emphasis on the fact that it is all required to produce desired interest regardless of the heavy consequences but under the name of the people whose army was fighting there.

John Locke (1632–1704) had deep concerns about the sovereign power of authorities and argued that Hobbes "social contract" which concerns limiting personal freedom versus protecting the state from chaos, should include a certain level of living for the public. Including the freedom of choice to remove "unwanted governments" (Greenbank 2014). The Arab uprising, the call for freedom of choice, was subject to an unprecedented trend of "creative chaos" as a tool of opposition. Opposition against the superpowers' interferences in some countries justified their chaos into the social fabric. The idea very much misappropriated aspects when declaring that: "victims deserve their fate" and destruction is justified as long as it makes a change (Afifi 2011). The greed of global forces and the rapacity of the local forces. For people to revolt against the latter is a tacit objection to the greed of the former. These local regimes refused to respond to the demands of the uprisings and were met with repression depending on external forces. What resulted was an increase of the interventions of Western countries in the region—especially from the US, France and Russia—through economic pressure and divestment, and extended support to certain groups that increase global competition to maintain their own interests in the region.

Without forgetting the current influence and the strategic position of Iran, Saudi Arabia and Turkey that have themselves contributed to the increased chaos in their own region. Under all these implications it becomes too overly complex as a task to create an eco-political balance between internal and external forces. Regardless of whether governments in the countries of the region are loyal to their people or not, in order to maintain their security, the local players must collaborate through various alignments in order to counter the external pressure of global forces. Thus, local powers must choose whether to find a desirable balance to interact with all forces or step down from their position of power. Especially external forces are able and willing to distract any regional attempts for local reform if it goes in any direction that conflicts with their interest in the region.

"Creative chaos" could result in an unsolved maze where all players find themselves trapped inside with undesirable side effects. A fact that the relationship between this chaos input and output are neither certain nor predictable, the possible results can get out of control (Régis 2006) as we witnessed in the aftermath of Iraq. It is true that the global hegemonic forces having the ability to create chaos, a monopoly of knowledge, advanced weapons and technologies, but these are all tools that are used to obtain certain results under certain conditions. Otherwise, the sides effects could easily spiral out of control. What is important then for these forces is to maintain security over the regions where their corporations are operating and transporting the resources. It is somewhat exaggerated to describe these forces as extremely powerful, it is necessary for them to have the public perceive them this way, even though chaos could be a spot in many areas. The perception from Western people of not supporting the military missions in other countries; the perception of the people in the MENA region of not accepting the status quo; and the complexity of some cases in Palestine and with the Kurds. Furthermore, the contingency like in Lebanon and the global COVID-19 crises are indicators of the limitation in the ability of these forces to use the right tools that help to negotiate with the others (no matter who they are) to create a balance between their interests and people's needs. In both Syria and Iraq, all the conflicting parties, agree that the output is in favour of construction and creating a positive change in the region, however, conflicting on the fundamentals of this construction remains the major issue.

The chaos in the MENA did not start with the wars in the last two decades. Rather those wars are understood as a direct result of a continuous process of long-term events, maybe going back centuries in human history. The ability of the regional societies to reproduce ignorance, mentioned in the previous chapter, has led to the emergence of some local groups, equal to the main and the opposition parties, to adopt some strange ideologies to the region. This has led to not only increased complexity of the local structure but also left these countries devouring themselves from within. What is new is that all this horror only became clearer to the public after the destruction from the wars on Iraq, Yemen and Syria and the emergence of the Arab uprising followed by the COVID-19 pandemic and ending with the port explosion in Lebanon. More will come.

3.2 Ideological Strife

The British historian, Hubble said "in order to cripple societies, first, their collective memory must be erased" (Kahlah 2021), to allow the deactivation of the '*machine experience mind*'. This collective memory is then primed to be replaced by another narrative. This forms part of the prevention of knowledge production leaving people unable to distinguish reality and facts from deception.

> Force has always been on the favour of the ruled; rulers have nothing but their own opinions to count on.
> David Hume

One prerequisite for civilisation is the accumulation of knowledge and experience as a part of the '*machine experience mind*' on an intellectual level. It interacts with the materialistic products and the general attitude of people until reaching general prosperity that we call "civilisation". This formation is complex and includes historical and ideological foundations linked to an understanding and interaction with science and cosmology. This requires a fundamental interconnection between intellectual and material production that produces prosperity on all levels. I believe if the relationship between intellect and material could not achieve a balance in the way they interact and the activities that are produced then civilisation begins to lose its power and decline. Intellectual production alone therefore cannot be called civilisation and likewise for the sole presence of material production even if it reaches high technological progress. The accumulation of the intellectual and philosophical experience and its interaction with the material creates the '*machine experience mind*' that reflects the way of dealing and producing material objects. This interaction can differ from one civilisation to another, potentially leading to outbreaks of conflict. Otherwise, there could be cooperation and exchange of their output that could lead to higher production and prosperity for all as well. But in many cases, they would rather shift to its control goals where materialism dominates and the intended balance with intellectual production is set to the wayside. Various conflicts, therefore, arise from ideological bases such as the years-long war between communism and capitalism. In order to understand the roots of such conflicts and what drives them, we need to understand the roots of these ideologies and the reasons behind their ideological strife.

Some researchers and politicians see the contemporary ideological strife as only limited to five or six civilisations, the main Global forces (Huntington 1996). While this book argues that ideological strife is too comprehensive to simply recede into only the world's well-known economic and military powers. The current strife is characterised by the whole surrounding environment and it differs from all the previous conflicts with the presence of AI. This specifies the strife between the mind of AI and the '*machine experience mind*' which raises the alarm for potential great risk in the future. The current technological advancement is growing fast in a way where machines are more efficient and can soon replace and improve the performance of many jobs. In technologically advanced countries, this started to grow right after WWII when factories had to cover for the great losses of lives from the workforce. While I do not wish to underestimate the role of women here, they were not in charge nor made the decisions regarding the sophisticated jobs. In short, the developed countries were the first to replace humans with machines out of necessity due to the substantial losses creating a huge gap in the workforce. The MENA while in its early stages is a fertile ground for machine-based factories to expand there. The difference in technological evolution stages will exclude entire countries from the market in favour of '*digital classifications*'. While on the one hand reducing competition, it also increases a greater clientele pool for greater market forces to profit from.

Thus, there is also in advisable ideological argument about the relationship between AI and humans. It is not only about the 2.7 million Robots that work in factories as of now (Robotics 2020), it is about how we will have to change our perceptions of the principles of life.

While some nations today lack some of the expected technological or militarily advancements, this does not mean they did not reach a certain status of intellectual production. They simply lack the ability to access this specific knowledge or they have to compromise to access part of it. Even though media nowadays favours marginalising intellectual production in favour of promoting materialism, the global forces are aware of the reality of the power of these nations. These go beyond religion, race or economy but are more linked to human civilisation and the cosmology that is producing the '*machine experience mind*'. The basis of this ideological strife is not only to control this mind but to somehow imitate this in AI as an extension of the Natural Intelligence (NI). This technological race determines who is ruling the world. This technological advancement thrives on the wars of human minds for national dispersion and lost identity, both crucial for the victory of this kind. Kurdistan, for example, is a nation that has been exposed to deep ideological strife in various forms. Starting from preventing the practice of their mother language, to then displacing them to many countries around the world, with the hopes of distracting the new generations from their roots that might lead them to develop an extension of the ancient science. Why then are the global forces insisting on preventing the unification of a nation if it does not possess a potential powerful ideology? Cooperation and ideology are key, unsurprisingly that media, education, law and even film industries have been weaponised against the individual mind. There are several indicators that capitalism, is facing severe conflicts with the indigenous nations who do not deny the human potential to transcend the world of matter and nature.

Wars no longer unfold in the obvious fashion involving military invasions and tanks (one would be hard pressed to find the kind of physical military campaigns like Napoleon nowadays). The rules have changed and with that, so have the methods of manipulating minds, creating the "one-dimensional man" as the one who is either cooperating or competing with machines. The most prominent event of the ideological conflicts that occurred in the ME was against the Levant and Egypt. The systematic cooperation between science and the military began by, for example, excavating ancient Egyptian (Pharaonic) antiquities, extracting them and shipping them to France. Prior to this cooperation, Egypt was a landmark country for culture and scientific work. Various industries and education even expanded in Egypt despite British occupation and a royal autocracy in place. What the Egyptians continue to lack since 1919 is the holistic long term planning that would have secured this sustainable development.

As Zionist ideology began to take root in Palestine, which became the philosophy of the axis of political, economic, social, technical, cultural and religion in an attempt to demonstrate superiority over all others in the region. In particular, Zionism is a political ideology that has created a state in the heart of ancient civilisations and established research and centres of study because they were always aware that information, data and knowledge are the bases of the future conflict with the entire region (Ashmawi 1996).

As for the two-armed advantage of the ME, it is the core of several ancient civilisations, and it is also the geographical location of the struggle of these civilisations over the ages, but with different tools that adapt to each era. The region demonstrates in a phenomenal way the ingredients of both intellectual and material that makes it a fertile ground for potential civilisation. One could argue this is one of the causes rendering the ME as an arena of a conflict of global forces over time with different tools.

The Zionist-Arab ideological strife is not limited purely to the Israeli–Arab conflict as popularly envisioned, it is only a fraction of the overall conflict between materialism and spirit. Materialism manifests itself strongly through Israel presence as an extension of the production of Western enlightenment that follows with capitalism. Especially since Israel is now home to several major technological industries. I am concerned, that at some point, there might be no need for the crowd of citizens on either side, where AI and its developments replace everyone in favour of a new version of capitalism. That can at one point classify people based on digital criteria and digital divide. When the Zionist project started, the first immigrants to Palestine were those who greatly prioritised ideological thought, especially as almost all of them were either professors or highly educated, and therefore believed in the necessity of applying their ideology and transferring it to the future generations (Oz 2005). Then the mass immigration followed to balance the demographical change with the Arabs. Especially until the year 1915, the percentage of immigrant Jews to Palestine was only 6% of the total population. A new wave of immigrants was organised between 1919 and 1923 that included more than 35,000 which increased the Jewish population in Palestine to 12% of the total (WAFA 2014). That was not enough to create any demographic balance. Nonetheless, in 1984 more than 531 Palestinian villages were completely wiped out, thousands were killed, 44% of the population was displaced, and 67% of the Palestinian lands were occupied by Israeli military troops at that time (Pappe 2006). Meanwhile, more Jewish immigrants were welcomed at Haifa port as "new inhabitants" of the land who were escaping ideological tyranny, they themselves escaping one ideology to become masters of the other. Two nations were in a way taken advantage of by suppressing their holy stories with an idea that is likely to be heading towards the employment of AI which could be not in the favour of both people at one point. A people-to-people solution remains an option if both sides started to educate themselves with the intention towards finding solutions.

Consciousness and physical matters are strongly present in most ancient religions, where spirituality is a way of experiencing material life. The power of Islam, especially in the ME, persists as a universal icon for the Arab people. The core of the conflict of the current forces is not only the ordinary people who manifest Islam and practice it in its organised stereotyped form, but it is on a profound level. Yet there also is a great intent to manipulate the people's collective memory, the '*machine experience mind*' specifically in this region to split it from the true ideologues of the so-called "*Ahl Al-Theker*". These are the scholars, the seekers, the scientists and the intellectuals who are specialised and can analyse the interdependence and complementary nature between matter and consciousness. These who are highly aware of the matrix of materialism and at one point were able to lead people in the region. The dramatic demographic changes in the region and displacement of the population of the MENA is one of the indicators of the ideological strife, maybe more to come. What stands in the way of creating prosperity in the ME are the ideologies that have authorised themselves to act in the name of religion and modern science that abort any reforms of a nation civilisation (whether or not they are supported by external forces to work in the opposite direction to mislead and confuse people). This has been happening since television became a popular knowledge source, and continued through other media channels with social media now allowing space for every entity. With each entity, there are huge quantities of data uploaded with the effort to re-identify concepts and mislead peopled to benefit technological advancement without thinking of the people. Especially because accurate data is hidden from the people in the region which even obscures understanding of the local leaders themselves.

Liberating people from their cultures, traditions, religions, and even their mother languages under the name of freedom, democracy or fighting terror, is an attempt to preaching to the "Supreme man". This is the individual who is so dependent on technology, they care purely for the material and nothing of the spiritual. It is the ideal state to have someone in order for them to submit to rules and a specific order. This eventually leads to the establishment of a global state united under one form of culture, tradition and language to name a few. This is a prelude to the deterioration and the dissolution of the nations and the collective mind. Perhaps it is the completion of the phase of the Western Era of superiority where the current global floundering pervades states at this stage which is related to this decline and deteriorating (Hassna 2001).

The ideological strife has also appeared in the attempt to hollow out the MENA from its people. In particular, Arab Christians who are a natural part of the region. Encouraging them more than other people through immigration programmes or less opportunities in their home-countries. However, their heritage, thoughts and culture are still shape the distinctive identity of the Arab Christians, forming part of the regional ideology and when religion was not a means to divide the people.

3.3 Power of Perceptions

Capitalism has left people owning no assets having no purpose except as a working force selling their skills, competencies and time to get make a "living" in return (Kelly 2020). Even these might be at risk of being replaced by AI for the 4IR favour.

A man believes that he is obligated to do a job, really an unessential role in an unimportant department in a useless institution. Imagining himself as a small entity within the whole structure. The reality is this man in the core of the circle, the one who has the first-hand experience, putting his indigenous experience in a huge system. He supplies his department with his expertise and skills, his department collects data and report it to the higher supervision where this data is then processed. Processing data that reproduce knowledge, which is kept within the forces, 'the masters', who refrain from repaying the individual with the output of the produced knowledge or inventions. The output is, in many cases, used against this man and best-case scenario, the knowledge simply remains hidden and exclusive in the hands of certain people. This process assures that there is no new knowledge is returning to the first circle that could feed the '*machine experience mind*'. Essentially, the information in the communities is going one way and never returns to enhance the skills and the competencies of the first-hand individuals. Institutions and authorities, in this case,

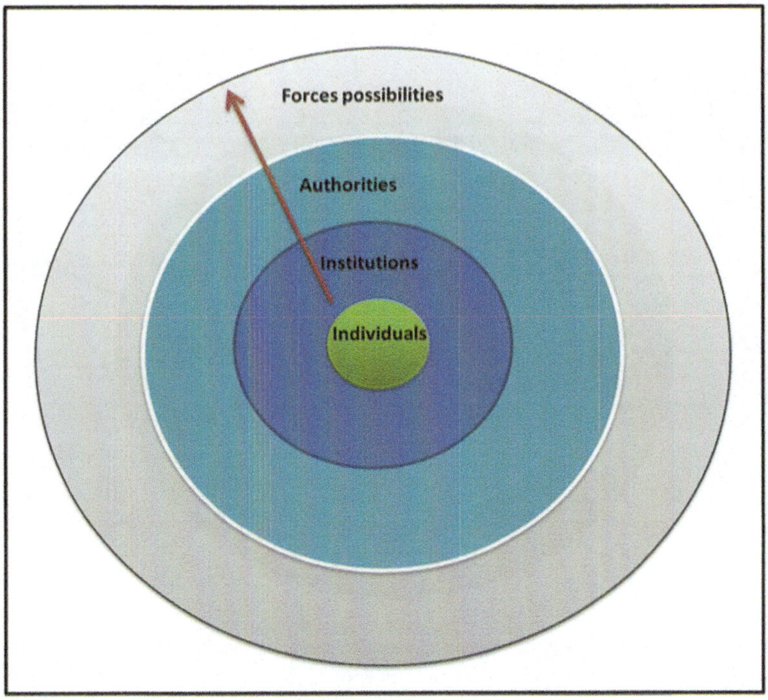

Fig. 3.2 Dominated perceptions and data flow (*Source* Author's own resource)

are gaining more power than their real power which leads to tyranny, oppression, and loss of human rights. Figure 3.2 represents the one-way data flow.

This structure limits the general ability to consider more possibilities because these forces are using the data for their own benefit, even though they are depending on the man to provide this data. When people surrender to this perception, they become the 'ideal' citizens of this kind of system.

The origins of democracy and elected leaders, which are, as concepts, promoted by the West and the US, are practically conflicting with that structure. Figure 3.3 explains the real power of a group of individuals as humans, nations or groups. Where popular governance is adopted, and institutional departments and authorities are no more than cogs that are created to take care of administration and processing services to the benefit of the people. The relationship between the small circle and the bigger circle becomes highly interactive flowing in both directions. Where self-learning, knowledge reproduction, and the expansion of prosperity is assured while the people can access more possibilities in all directions rather than being limited and controlled by certain forces. One would argue that by allowing people to access all possibilities it has a 90% chance of leading to the same control by certain forces. This is also one of the possibilities and the choice is always in the hands of the many, the people as one piece, not only one group or specific forces. Perhaps, this was the case with the

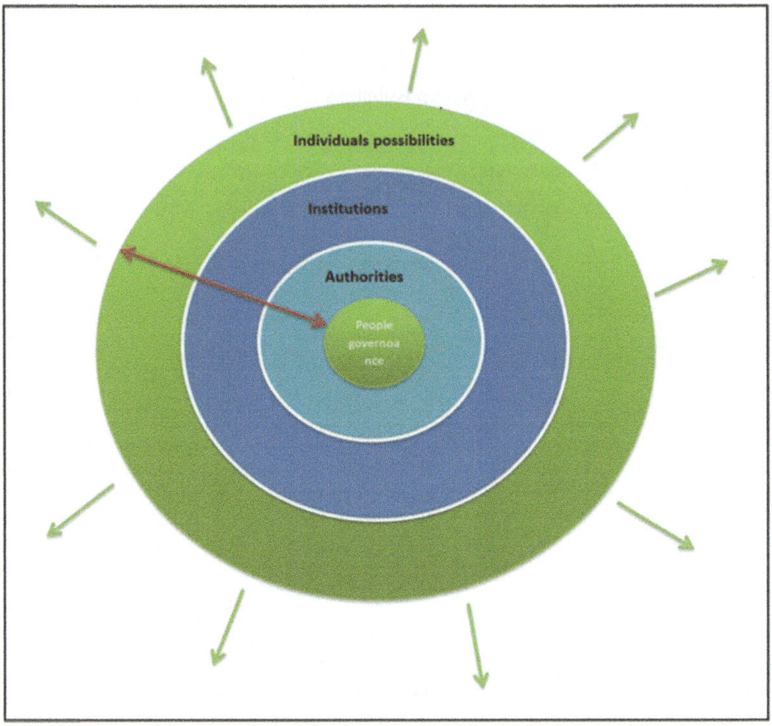

Fig. 3.3 Enlighten perceptions and their wide possibilities (*Source* Author's own source)

ancient civilisations who reached the peak and started to decline specifically for this reason.

There is a great difference in both positions, where man, in the first model perceives himself small and neither contributes nor influences any change. The same man perceives himself as part of civilisation or prosperity that occurred when communities reach a peak of cumulative knowledge that interact with societal enlightenment for higher possibilities. Obviously, if you were part of those authorities, you would stand by the first model denying people the ability to take care of their own benefits. Even fear-mongering the people under the pretext of their inability to maintain the status quo. When the system of these forces fail, they would rather reset it than continue to consider any serious negotiations with the people.

This what is happening on the ground everywhere, not only in the MENA region, where people have already separated themselves from their real roles and responsibilities and stop thinking of any higher purposes. People, or rather "the one-dimensional men" are mainly divided into two groups of people. Those who became machine-like by following a certain kind of lifestyle that is promoted, international or not, by several industries. He spends long hours working for fewer wages, spending these wages on high standard living expenses, taxes, insurance with the rest disappearing within the massive tourism industry. The case in the MENA is taking exactly the opposite approach yet yielding the same results. The man became like a faulty machine, occupied by the conflicting environment and its sorrows, losing his power even as a working force, this group of people either killed or displaced, the rest of them are being paid or fed under the name of foreign aid. The human mind, in this case, is put under extraordinary pressure and therefore unable to think otherwise. Both societies are in different modes, and are asked to do nothing except for accepting the status quo. Societies therefore require enlightenment that filters and processes data the natural way, and this cannot occur without the interaction that feeds the collective perception as explained in Fig. 3.3. This changes the scales from the inside sparks that spread all over.

Nowadays, in both cases, the man (male and female) is unable to play his role in the society, the family (the main productive cell) is unable to afford the new living standards, the community is re-shaped and a complete nation is totally subject to the capitalist machine and no one has time to remember or research the original idea behind anything anymore. It then keeps moving towards the same destructive direction and reproducing itself, with less external effort required from these forces for the benefit of the system. Being on the side of these forces who perceive reality as it is, it must be very joyful to watch.

For these forces to continue existing and enjoy watching the manipulation of the '*machine experience mind*' the perpetual control of mass perception is essential. We see global forces, authorities, governments, political parties and even individuals, manipulating perceptions through propaganda in order to achieve their goals. This is a necessary method to be used in any case to influence internal and external decisions there. Both players have their interests and therefore have populist support that strengthens their positions. Therefore, we see people that are divided into several cognitive levels of perceptions.

Materialism, a consumerist lifestyle and technology are engaged in each the activities of each individual which has facilitated the process of manipulating perceptions. Even though a huge effort is still needed that costs huge financial resources to maintain the manipulation of the 'machine experience mind'. Jakhotiya (2019) in his article *capitalist corruption leading to global socio-economic collapse* explained the manipulation forms of capitalism shown in Fig. 3.4.

All the aforementioned events that took a place in the MENA region were driven by perceptions. The perception of man, the one of the authorities and of the external forces. The elimination of the democratic council in Syria in 1919 was in part to eliminate the perception of the people in the region.

Promoting perception that presents the MENA as a region of "terror", a product shaped by the influence of Islam and by later groups claiming to be 'Islamists'. Though the latter is wholly unfair for the regional rationality and any minorities, but more on this later. This perception is not only promoted on the international level, especially in the West, it is also promoted among many groups in the region, who are more likely to believe what they witness on television and social media.

The reality is smoother, rational, and naturally organised, where Judaism, Christianity and Islam are the major religions that have been contributing to the output

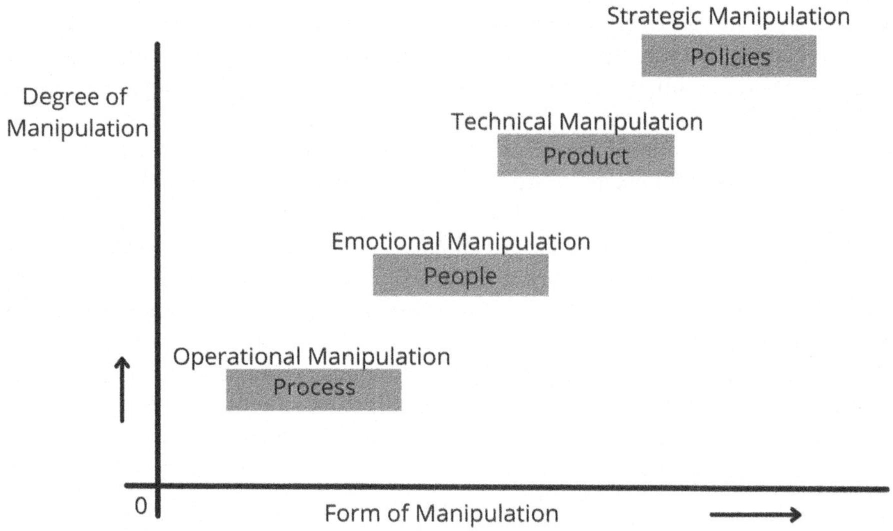

Fig. 3.4 Form of manipulation (*Source* Author's own design)

of the region (in addition to other small minorities). For example, in Egypt alone, more than 10% of its population is Christian which is almost 10 million. The original Arab Jews in Morocco numbered about 300,000 before the founding of Israel. Jews, Muslims, and Christians were sharing a diverse environment in the MENA together and no religious discrimination was involved. Until the emergence of the Zionism movement that has changed the religious demographic distribution. While the Jewish population were called to immigrate to Palestine, the number of Christians (around 25% of the population) began to face too many challenges. This was due to various conflicts and fewer opportunities so they were encouraged to leave the region much earlier than Muslims. As they had better connections and scholarships through the network of churches, their immigration was easily accommodated. Therefore, it was both Jews and Christians themselves who first paid the price of the irrational advancement of capitalism. The difference is that Muslims are paying the price now. The ME has deeper roots than being confined and enclosed to one element. The envision of the region by external forces, through history, have left more consequences on people's lives as discussed in Chap. 2.

3.4 Summary

It would be too easy to describe chaos in the MENA as beginning with the wars in the last two decades. Rather those wars are understood as a direct result of a continuous process of long-term events setting the stage of chaos. Chaos has now become so omnipresent, it exists even in more developed societies as 'quiet chaos.' However, this quiet chaos by its very nature is delicate and can betray itself easily, the most recent example bing from the COVID-19 pandemic. Watching the world leaders flounder in response to an unknown, inhuman threat revealed the thin layer of calm hiding the chaos underneath.

Nonetheless, other forms of chaos are manmade and form as part of deliberate strategy. "Creative chaos" is a concept developed by the US in order to groom the environment in other countries to adapt to a pre-planned eco-political order. The US and its allies' war on Iraq is a clear example. Despite the disapproval of their own people both on the Iraqi and the US side, new forms of communication and understanding have to be created to justify their course of action. In face of increasing disapproval, manipulation of the mind or its understanding of reality is now crucial.

In the ME, this allowed the permeation of ideological strife and in some cases, people authorising themselves to act in the name of religion and modern science that abort any reforms of ME states. This saw an increase, for example, once television was accepted as a source of knowledge, and thus now only worsened in the age of social media and the internet and social media where conflicting and ideologically charged information are displayed on mass. Further digitalisation and the gradual integration of AI, despite holding great promise, will ensure to maintain increasing complexities and chaos for the benefit of those leading the Global digital strategy.

References

Afifi F (2011) War of creative chaos: the central tendacy in the globalized Arabs revolutions. Al-Mustaqbal Al-Arabi

Ahmad K (2011) الخلاقة الفوضى نظرية تنفيذ يجري كيف.

Al-Saleh MA (2020) Managing the Syrian economy during the French mandate (1918–1946)—its post-independence effects. Presses de l'ifpo, Institut français du Proche-Orient. https://doi.org/10.4000/books.ifpo.13843

Ashmawi M (1996) Civilization conflict

Berger R (2021) Joining forces for a new Beirut port area

Greenbank J (2014) The key ideas of the Western philosophy. Philosophy Now, a magazine of ideas

Gribble R, Simon W, Susan K, David A, Christopher D, Nicola F (2015) Attitudes towards Iraq and Afghanistan: British public opinion after a decade of war has implications for the viability of future mission. https://blogs.lse.ac.uk/politicsandpolicy/british-public-opinion-after-a-decade-of-war-attitudes-to-iraq-and-afghanistan/

Gündüz G (2006) Ancient and current chaos theories. https://www.indecs.eu/2006/indecs2006-pp1-18.pdf

Hassna N (2001) The Arab–Israeli conflict within the framework of the dialogue of civilizations

Huntington S (1996) The clash of civilizations and the remaking of world order. Simon & Schuster Ltd.

Jakhotiya G (2019) Capitalist corruption leading to global socio-economic collapse. Munich Personal RePEc Archive. https://mpra.ub.uni-muenchen.de/95771/1/MPRA_paper_95771.pdf

Kahlah A (2021) Historical review from the first centuries to the fourteenth century. In the case of our Aramean Christian people. Retrieved 2021, from http://aramean-dem.org/Dr.Andre_Khale/2.htm

Kaysen C, Miller S, Malin M, Nordbaus W, Steinbruner J (2002) War with Iraq costs, consequences, and alternatives

Kelly K (2020) What 'capitalism' is and how it affects people. https://www.teenvogue.com/story/what-capitalism-is
Labor UDo (2005) A profile of the working poor, 2003. https://www.bls.gov/opub/reports/working-poor/archive/workingpoor_2003.pdf
Michael K (2015) Superpowers in the turbulent Middle East and the potential Chinese contribution? An Israeli perspective
Oz A (2005) A tale of love and darkness. Penguin Random House UK
Pappe I (2006) The ethnic cleansing of Palestine. Oneworld Publications
Plaza F, Joan P, Dandoy R (2006) Chaos theory and its application in political science
Régis PFJPD (2006) Chaos theory and its application in political science. IPSA World Congress, Fukuoka, Japan. http://hdl.handle.net/2078.1/176425
Robotics IFo (2020) IFR presents world robotics report 2020. https://ifr.org/ifr-press-releases/news/record-2.7-million-robots-work-in-factories-around-the-globe
Schumer C, Maloney C (2008) War at any price? The total economic costs of the war beyond the federal budget
Stewart RMAAH (2016) Tony Blair: 'I express more sorrow, regret and apology than you can ever believe'
Varoufakis Y (2021) Indigo festival [Interview]. https://www.youtube.com/watch?v=XIgFnfHhcRc
WAFA, PNaIAC (2014) Jewish immigration since the beginning of Jewish settler colonialism in the late Ottoman rule. https://info.wafa.ps/ar_page.aspx?id=2213

Chapter 4
The Ancient Middle East and the New Middle East

Warda Samara

4.1 Who Rules the Middle East

To investigate who owns decisions in the ME, there is some historical basis that should be taken into consideration: firstly, the historical differences and the roots of each country and nation considering their current global and regional positions adding each country's complex internal structures. Secondly, understanding who even rules the world—'the driving forces'—and how they interact with the ME authorities and institutions. Third, human history and the ancient civilisations that influenced the environment in the ME.

In this book, however, I will not be discussing the ancient ME civilisations and their link to today's events deeply. I am referring to it on a level that induces minds about the vital link between ancient civilisations' productions and today's output, that might help in planning for a better future. What sounds bizarre though is that the geographical location of the first human civilisations core has become the same epicentre of chaos in the present day. Murder and war stand exactly where the first human civilisation thrived and was described in the 70s as a "human extermination in the land of ancient civilisations" (Perknis 2016). This indicates the long process to reach where we are today. This may open several questions about any possible connections which have been a focus for many researchers.

The Ancient civilisations have a wealth of foundations for all subsequent civilisations. Hence, all the achievements that we are witnessing today is a result of accumulated human knowledge, including trading, law, public relations and others that have influenced both Western and Eastern philosophy as well. These civilisations, as they stretch so far back in time, they carry mysterious details concerning their prosperity and the exact causes of its decline. Some researchers attribute that either due to a lack of documentation or due to natural disasters. Some other researchers consider it an unknown forces that refrain from sharing ancient knowledge, wisdom and cosmic science with the people, fearing the '*machine experience mind*'. Therefore, we see all civilisations bear both good and evil. No society has been without

W. Samara and M. Samara, *The Power of Perceptions in the Middle East*,
Perspectives on Development in the Middle East and North Africa (MENA) Region,
https://doi.org/10.1007/978-3-030-99150-0_4

wars, bureaucracy, patriarchy, slavery, literature, art, science, philosophy, sociology, trading and public relations (Wengrow 2018).

For example, Iraq, the country located in the southwest of the continent of Asia, was called by the Greeks "*Mesopotamia*" which means 'between the two rivers', the Tigris and Euphrates rivers. This region became a large part of the so-called fertile crescent that led to the beginnings of the ancient ME including interaction and cooperation with neighbouring nations like Iran. This quickly turned into a valuable part of the larger imperialist policies, including the Persian and Greek dynasties where philosophies arose to the rest of the world from the eastern Mediterranean that enhanced the ideological development and the emergence of philosophers and scientists who had great input to the intellectuality and enlightenment (Sağlamer 2021). After the seventh century it became an integral part of the Islamic world, and Baghdad became the capital of the Abbasid Caliphate in the eighth century. It was one of the most important centres of power that changed the shape of the region, as it had military and political power and cultural influence. This emphasises that control was a primary feature of ancient civilisations (Flegel 2018). The recognition of the whole grid of cosmos intelligence which is already engineered perfectly since it was created, learning from this natural order is the foundation of the ancient civilisations that followed with other civilisations as well. Some civilisations have left great evidence like the Great Pyramids of Giza in Egypt, built from 2550 to 2490 B.C. A mysterious design that has been challenging human intellect until now, which is enough to think that ancient people have reached certain kinds of advanced knowledge, and not necessarily the ones we know of today.

With the rise of humanity in the "the birth of the living" era referred to *Renaissance*, world problems have increased. Hence, reliance on reasons rather than spirituality as a justification for these problems became more commonplace. The means of illusionary had to therefore exist in order to organise societal activities. It originated in redirecting attitudes towards dealing with knowledge (Greenbank 2014). Thus, the divide between spirit and matter is what I believe distinguishes the advancement between ancient civilisations and the current era. A transition to matter is the beginning of vanishing of synchronisation of spirit in the societies and systems. However, the Mediterranean region began to lose central power, while Europe and North America gained influence. Therefore, the development of modern philosophy, science, technology and control has moved away from the most ancient civilisations through Greece to the West.

I am concerned if we can call the current era a 'civilisation'! the eco-political system and its institutions' web is not a civilisation, it is much more than that. This is only a manifestation of what we can or cannot call a civilisation. For more than a century the world is set in a constant state of war, whether declared or undeclared, the effects of this are felt through tremendous destruction, poverty, terror and fewer learning processes. It reflects less of a golden age and more of an era of decline, if we believe the self declared status of the US as the last force of the extension of the Greek and Roman empires. Many civilisations have stayed for thousands of years before they disappeared and even experienced several stages until they came to an end. The US has emerged as a democratic force supporting people's rights, soon it immerses itself in several conflicts worldwide with a particular focus in the last decades on the ME. Over time the image of America as an influential global force started to fade from popular opinion. Shortly after, it became news on media all over the ME.

What we learn about the knowledge produced by ancient civilisations opens more space for seekers to learn. Otherwise, it is not possible to suggest solutions to people without understanding the implications behind any era's prosperity or failure, especially the more influential civilisations. The further we go back in history we find huge similarities in human behaviours where empires were expanding and controlling people.

When we think, for example, of the transfer of powers in the MENA, we find that the region has been continuously under the rule of external powers. In contemporary history, the power has moved from the Ottoman Empire to the British Empire and then the caliphate of American intervention after the West. One would ask why these external forces have emerged and expanded always along with violence, wars, and scientific involvement.

The current eco-political systems are not separated from the philosophy of ancient times and civilisations where cities, politics and governments have started. Everything is a stretch. It does, however, take a turn that corresponds to changing data over time and to the cultures of various populations. No doubt, the people who rule the world now (and I do not mean the politicians who we know and see on the television), who still remain illusive in the form of deep states or other entities, have reached acquaintances that formed the deep philosophy that enabled them to sort of control the world and its resources. The indicators of their powerful philosophy that are seen in almost all global activities and attitudes yet eludes our common understanding. They are relentlessly committed to their mission regardless societies destruction, they tempt to hold a massive power worldwide by employing all the available possibilities in order to apply their own law to the world through several institutions and channels. However, their power ultimately rests on the ignorance and apathy from the population. Unfortunately, this popular apathy also extends to fewer people standing for justice and coordinating efforts to stop this power monopoly.

'Democracy' and language use have been employed as a strategic indirect weapon. Its promotion has allowed the US and their allies to invade other countries and participate in a war against countries like Iraq, Syria, Afghanistan and Libya. This caused unforgivable devastation. There were always differences on how to identify 'democracy' which finally explains why people in even the most advanced society have misunderstood the basics of democracy. This even leads to the destruction of their own democratic rights while under the impression of practising democracy. 'Democracy' as a concept holds very positive indicators, sparking images of equality, various rights and public engagement across all demographics to name a few. But there are many forces reforming and re-defining concepts in order to gradually chip away at the understanding of good democratic practices. Further, creating a dependency and even want for stricter authority.

What does the average middle American know about promoting democracy in the ME by the US while they themselves, for example, suffering from discrimination in the heart of what is described to be a ‘democratic country’! Do people even truly understand what is being done under their name by the forces that represent them?

The conflict between capitalism and communism goes beyond eco-political reasons. It is a fight for world domination. Especially that China’s undeclared methodology is shaped with a determination of implementing the BRI. China’s focus is to enhance their foreign relations and geographical connections in order to sustain economic growth through closing the global infrastructure gap that currently constrains trade. This is also connected to several other geopolitical goals (OECD 2018). Meanwhile the US has been fighting in several wars and asserting its military prowess in many countries. This assertion, however, has led to a major draining on its military and economic resources from their policy of the war on terror. The last of these wars are still going on in the ME, perhaps, against *illusory or created enemies ‘creative chaos’*, essentially announcing defeat against people who possess neither military nor technology power. This is covered with huge propaganda and sanctions against several countries and groups in the region. Yet, these sanctions have never affected the intended ruling parties, it always left devastating consequences against the people with no say how on they are seen by other countries. As *Denis Halliday*—the former assistant secretary-general of the United Nations served in Iraq—said ‘We Kill People with Sanctions’ and described the sanctions in Iraq as a genocide against the people there (Davies 2021).

Now, China is using different kinds of soft strategic tools to achieve their specific goals, through enhancing trade and economy with cheap labour and quick delivery at the core. Now, the Chinese GDP has reached proportions that surpass that of the US (Orlik 2021) particularly through its increasing acquisition of corporate assets and resources in Africa, Latin America, Europe and Asia. China has made a remarkable change in the military structure, through improving their weapons and techniques that became also available in the market to whoever wants to buy, unlike the US. This makes China the world’s third-largest country in terms of military power, and it appears that only in a matter of time, it will become the most powerful military force. Where military roles will be adjusted for the protection of various external interests. In brief, while the US was fascinated with domination through capitalism, China had successfully combined both aspects of capitalism on the global space and communism on the local space for their greater purpose! Moreover, Russia, an ally of China, has been increasingly placing itself as a major external influence in the region. Issaev and Zakharov (2021) argues that Russia is legitimising its leadership activity in Syria where the new order would depend on Orthodoxy—a fundamental element of modern Russian identity.

The decline of the US in the ME, the return of Russia intervention and the attempt of France to keep domination on some areas in the region are indicators of global power repositioning. Moreover, Chain is rationally penetrating the region. Hence, the new world balance in which China and the US divide themselves across spheres of influence—essentially dominating together might find a new balance from the perspective of both poles. It demonstrates a major transformation in US diplomacy and foreign policy. This leads to great consequences in the ME.

The US is currently finding itself in a position having to acknowledge the following circumstances: further political divisions following Trump's loss in the 2020 elections as well as increased apprehension from both Russia and China as a rising global threat. Considering also the way the US reports on MENA affairs by focusing on Iran, Turkey, Saudi Arabia and Israel. The world is facing too many new problems to confront, let alone from the ME (Crooke et al. 2021). The ideologies on different sides of the spectrum remain essentially conflicting. This will form the basis for understanding how to approach the ME in the future. The region is important for the security of the West, especially the US, which has engaged in several wars in the ME. China, on the other hand, has been focusing on trading and exchanges trade with the ME through the last decades without assigning any security sources in the region.

For many decades the western powers have continuously pursued full access to whatever they need in the MENA not only to natural resources but also ancient knowledge and monuments. Their increasing demand leading to further military intervention to maintain access to any possible resources. Freeman (2012) argues that the military interference for 'democracy' has failed in the ME and the events in Iraq have been a remarkable witness to prove this failure. What happened was a deep tampering of the Iraqi realities and its common narrative. It should be known by now that the greatest impact of these military interventions and economic pressure was the destabilising of the internal structure of many countries.

The ancient Chines philosopher *Sun Tzu* (495–551) a major influence on contemporary Chinese war strategy, states that all war events are based on deception (Zu 1910). Assuming that all countries are in a perpetual state of war, even if there is no physical war is happening on the ground. As discussed in the previous chapter, this war is one "on minds, the ideological strife, and manipulation of the *machine experience mind*". Channelling perceptions through inexperienced groups in the local space is the best example of undeclared wars, as an effective way to eliminate any impulse to change people's painful reality that has been in place for decades. These local groups operate within a certain frequency as they believe they have an impact on the decisions of the authorities or certain situations through their genuine local efforts unaware of the harsh reality. It is inconceivable, how many Trojans would be required in the region to understand the comprehensive formula and manipulation tools for their own protection.

It should be unsurprising to find political leaders perceiving the whole global system differently from their own people. However, the gap is even bigger and scrawled in the MENA. In general, the choices and decisions of the political leadership are heavily influenced by the "internal concentrations of power" (Chomsky 2016) and its external extensions to the entities who had the access to that knowledge. Where the general population remains within a limited range of fraud knowledge that limits their perception about the whole environment. Consequently, the mass population is losing their influence in their own countries' policy making. This applies even to societies, that consider themselves highly democratic.

4.2 The Emergence of the "Middle East" Term and the "New Middle East"

The creation of terms is rarely arbitrary but is rather the result of changes in our collective understanding. This is then followed by the reproduction of political terms as a sign of the embodiment of a new reality. New signs took a place in the political and economic narrative whose main purpose is to change the social-related narrative that affects popular perception. The dominant force, whether regional or international, can impose these changes within their tricky ideological systems (Voloshino 1973).

By using the power of concepts as a tool to create new common sense, we can detect what contributes changing reality (Bourdieu 1991). Hence, why new terms become familiar and fit the mainstream narrative. This applies to what is called the 'Middle East'. The term Middle East came to light in 1902 by the writer *Alfred Mahan* to refer to the western and Northern routes leading to India in the face of Russian activity in Iran and was used to denote the region between the Near and Far East. Since then, there has been wide disagreement on how to really define the ME. For instance, with the recognition of Israel as a state in the heart of the region, it became urgent to dispense with the term 'Arab World' to replace it with the more general term, 'Middle East'. Although the term ME varies geographically between international organisations it remains widely used. On the other hand, despite its neutral appearance, the term has been used to obscure Arab nationalism and its movements.

The Arab uprisings demonstrated the serious need for new systems and comprehensive change for the people. All people across all social demographics agreed that there are rights that should no longer be ignored. Sparking a debate about the whole issues of the ME as a region and the necessity of its own "renaissance". What remains at the centre of the debate, however, is how change should happen and in favour of whom.

Many people in the ME still have in their memory what is maintained in the '*machine experience mind*', the old terms that are signs of nationalism and struggle against colonialism. Thus, these people do still use the terms, 'the Arab World' and 'the Islamic World'. Most authorities in the ME ignore these constants and are directing the attention on politics, security and the military fields while moving a new economic and trading dynamics in the region. Therefore, many countries represented with their leaders have quickly fused into the plans of the global order and its terms to maintain their interests and influence in the local markets. It is therefore no issue for them to employing and promote imposed terms on the region as long as it is in line with their benefits.

The apprehension is not from using new or different terms, sometimes it is necessary to adjust and reproduce terms when it is based on realistic research, science or public need. The point is about what influences the reputations of the nation, instead of letting the people in the region as nations gain visibility and put themselves on the world map as distinctive entities by drawing on various cultural or national symbols.

The whole region is branded by external forces for their benefits which eliminates the identity of each country as a separate entity.

With radical global change and rapid transitions, national reputations are accompanied by new methods and mechanisms of modern advanced technologies and international lineups. It is quite possible that the geographical division of the region may no longer be at the forefront of the discussions. This will be discussed in detail in Chap. 5. The tools for domination have shifted dramatically, to the point where in the future we may never see a human soldier on the ground.

The new world is equipped with different knowledge and different kind of weapons that change any former scenarios that we ever knew. Is humanity about to witness a virtual federalism system? Living in the era of technological development, the internet became the new standards of progress and monitoring the world. The new division between people is now technological advancements rather than natural or political borders. If this field is studied and analysed widely by the less fortunate countries in the MENA, it might give them new kinds of strengths that offer newfangled solutions to the benefit of their own people. This is, again, emphasising the importance of knowledge production.

What we know is a new world structure that is designed by the great forces while the MENA countries have no fundamental role to play in this level. Particularly in a strategic game that is getting more complex, while the region is more branded with conflicts and terror. Once the era of the COVID-19 pandemic ends, the whole world will have to cooperate and work together to rebuild the destruction of this economic and health deficit. The ME could play a role in this, despite the destruction, there are all the necessary resources and it has a large potential market for several industries expansion. It has strong potential for investment and trading opportunities for the future. The only challenge is creating conditions for these projects to grow and flourish (The World Bank 2018). However, the ambiguous nature of the new treaties between the Gulf and Israel could be the indication of a new era. Perhaps even a new world structure, particularly as the terms and purpose of these treaties have not been announced fully to the public. In any case, the 'new Middle East' has been strongly introduced by both regional and international forces, where many leaders suggested an economic field different from the current one.

This vision intended for the ME is inspired by the EU economic experience that allows trading to be open among 27 states while each state stays independent. The main EU Institutions—the Commission, the Council of the EU and the European Parliament—work together to create and approve a common policy and a common ground in light of the EU aspects of sustainable development represented in Table 4.1 (EU 2021). Some economists view this kind of cooperation in the ME as a great opportunity that allows economic growth in the whole region. As well as a beginning to end the regional conflict and will give people opportunities to exchange knowledge and develop their competencies at the individual and at the institutional levels. As a result, this will bring social, human and economic development for the whole region and for all the ME countries. Furthermore, this development will increase and improve interaction and relationships with other countries beyond only the ME which

Table 4.1 The EU aspects of sustainable development

Aspect	Description
People	• End poverty and hunger in all forms and ensure dignity and equality
Planet	• Protect future generations from environmental destruction and resource depletion
Prosperity	• Ensure prosperous and fulfilling lives in harmony with nature
Peace	• Create peaceful, just and inclusive societies
Partnership	• Implement development work through global partnership

Resource Author's own design based on EU data

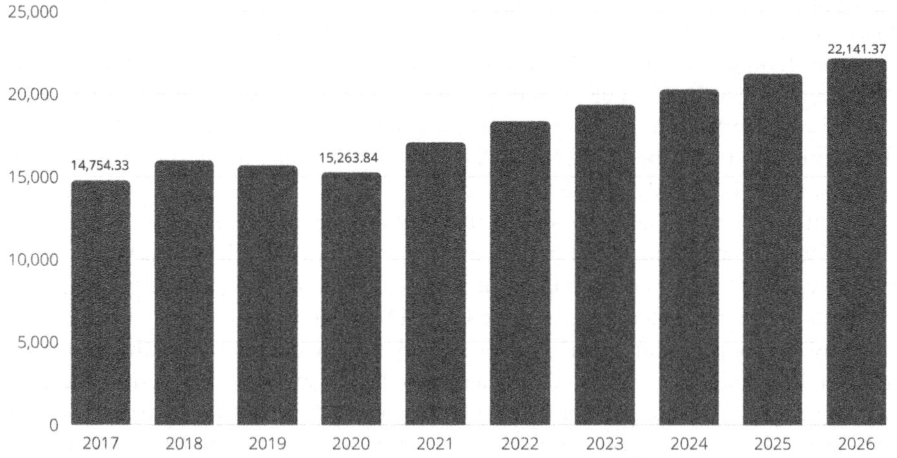

Fig. 4.1 European Union: Gross Domestic Product (GDP) from 2016 to 2026 (*Source* Author's own design)

will allow more cooperation at different levels and different files such as agriculture, industry and trading (EU 2021).

Despite the fact that the EU as a model has shown promising progress on the EU GDP, as shown in Fig. 4.1 (O'Neill 2021), the federalism model is still viewed as not a suitable solution for many parties in the ME as long as enough trust is not there. For these, proposing any new economic solutions might be an introduction of the 4IR's output where the region might be subject to '*digital classification*'.

In all the federalism experiences, sharing knowledge remains a crucial aspect. Moreover, in the case of sharing knowledge personal views and assumptions play a role in the understanding and analysing process. In light of this, there are three intermediate forms of knowledge: external knowledge, shared knowledge, and common ground (IPSF 2021). See Fig. 4.2 that represents the process of constructing knowledge. Sharing knowledge aim to find a common ground that allows negotiations and integration. This remains very challenging to be seen on the ground in the case of ME. Thus, a regional trained workforce is required to deal with such a complication

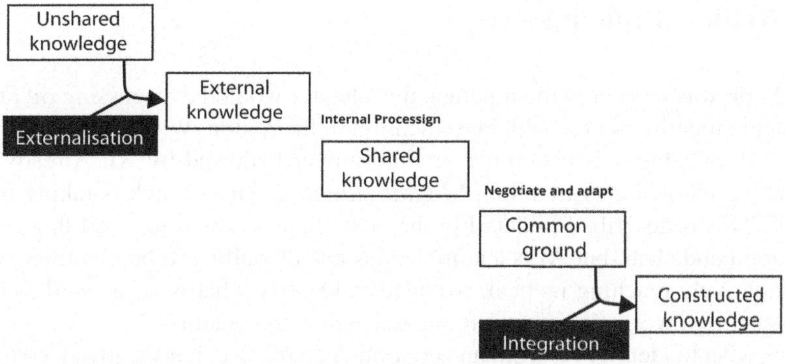

Fig. 4.2 Unshared knowledge (*Source* Author's own design)

in the ME, these who are able to deal with high implications and finding a common ground for long term visions (Beers et al. 2006).

There are conflicting perceptions about the position of the regional forces in this scenario, some perceive the new project in the ME as a strategy that opens the region to economic prosperity and political solutions leading the region to a new era. On the other hand, others view is this as a tool that will soon be in the hand of external forces for further domination. Using it as an opportunity to get out of the crucible of 'security' issues, they cannot retain it the same way any longer, subsequently replacing national security reasons with regional economic reasons. This may be the cause of a regional economic structure that limits the range of flexibility in taking national decisions.

The US is in its own state of constant fluctuation leading to further neglect of the countries in the region. Meanwhile, China maintains its neutral relationships with all the major countries in the region. This interest in the region might enhance the economic cooperation especially after China announced a new trading road that will cross the ME. Superpowers race to maintain a presence in the region while the intended output for a new ME remains vague and unannounced and continues to be uncertain under the shadow of COVID-19. Predicting it in terms of all the indicators seems to be *the abstinent plain* that appeared easy to be implemented but it is almost impossible to make it happen. However, it remains within the framework of the global scheme for a new world order that aspires to achieve global governance. The way people act, interact or respond to the manifestation of reshaping systems remains the fingerprint that will shape the future and perhaps even reproduce new terms like the 'digital ME' where people can interact and operate their businesses beyond the geopolitical borders.

4.3 Artificial Intelligence

If this book was written in the nineties, this chapter would be discussing oil and gas as strategic identifiers in wealth classification in the region. While oil in the current era is still valuable it is becoming gradually overshadowed by AI. Already AI is introducing its own classification: '*digital classifications*', which is taking hold in the ME. This is described in detail in the next chapter. The role of oil in general is understood and clear, but AI is a complex issue still waiting to be identified. As AI is progressively reaching its peak we need to identify what is AI as well as how it affects security, work, decision making, education and health.

If we wish to identify AI from an economic perspective, it is an advanced tool for opening opportunities and challenges in a growing economy (Wang 2019). Whereas on the political level it is viewed as the ability of the machine to sense, reason, learn, make decisions and dominate. Thus, since the beginning of the first industrial revolution, there were always groups who were concerned with the state of technological progress which could increase domination by governments. It is even more contradictory at the community level, because AI lacks a clear approach to determining which types of AI systems are even convenient. I perceive AI as a network of machines designed by humans for analysing and then simulating natural intelligence. It became a vital extension for human activities and its accelerating needs. Currently, designers are focused on creating AI with an updated mind (Bringsjord and Govindarajulu 2020), which to me is an attempt to artificially create advanced copy of the '*machine experience mind*' where the human mind becomes gradually a file of information inserted in the AI system.

In AI and the increasing digitalisation, we see a decrease in the importance of materialism and an increase in the power and potential of AI. It introduces even the potential of a knowledge-based economy, where people are no longer simply economic units but form part of the greater knowledge unit. Moreover, AI is learning by trial and error (Copeland 2021) as it needs as well to learn by experience. This is a huge risk especially when operating on a global scale. Currently, data entry is still dependent on certain groups who are responsible for feeding and teaching the AI all the required information. Figure 4.3 shows, the inability of AI to distinguish bias, intention or emotion hinders its ability to really make effective decisions. Perhaps, after the IoT, the human effort would not even be needed to "teach" the AI. What distinguishes natural intelligence (NI) is the ability of "sensory learning", which AI is now trying to imitate. This is called the Internet of Things (henceforth, IoT).

Nowadays, the institutional structure of AI is under challenge during the global transformation to digitalisation. Especially that the current economic and social dynamics are governed by a complex set of institutions, are accumulative historical forms of the basic social and economic relations of capitalism adopting to each era accordingly. Under 'normal' conditions these rules ensure regular growth (accumulation) and the continuous reproduction. When the structures of these institutions become inefficient and are unable to produce the expected outcome it becomes reasonable to destroy it and start a new one. In order to allow for a reconstruction of the

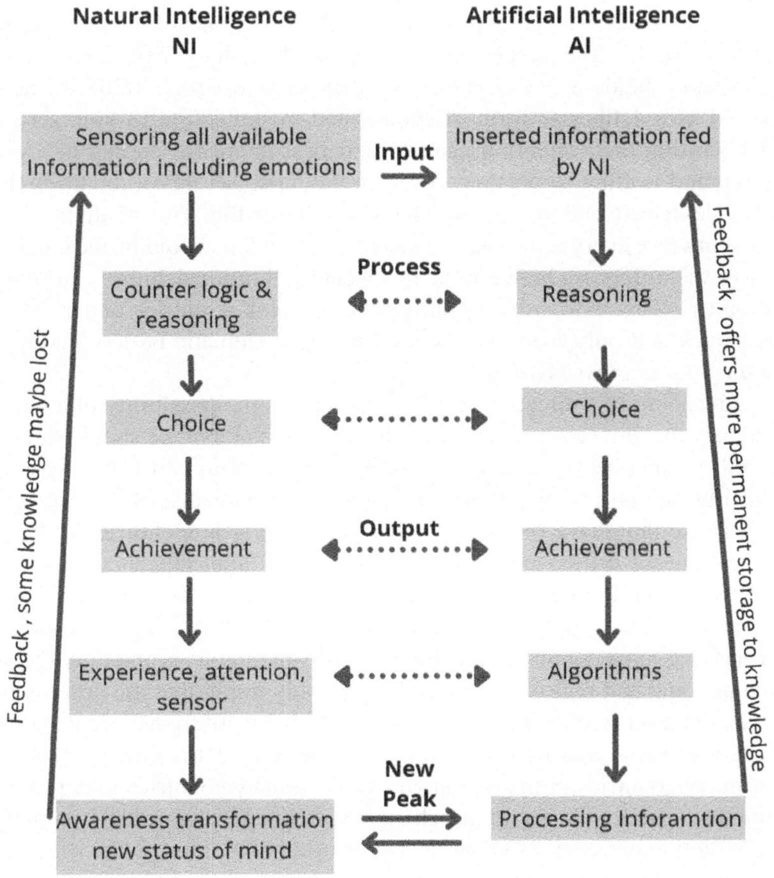

Fig. 4.3 Natural intelligence and AI (*Source* Author's own design)

global system, there needs to be a review that includes the roles of these institutions. This is akin to the World Economic Forum's (WEF) initiative, breaking with the old system known as the great re-set. Originally introduced as a response to the COVID-19 era as a reimagining of the world independent from the old system. The term became popular at first within intellectual conspiracy circles, and has since received more attention in academia as part of a serious revision of the political economy (Umbrello 2021). The founders of this initiative see it as a rare positive event that holds a unique opportunity (Schwab 2020) essentially a re-"conceptualisation of the GDP" as a feature of well-being (Umbrello 2021). However, as explained in Chap. 3 some analysts assure that GDP growth does not necessarily guarantee development.

Despite the conflicting opinions about the progress of AI, the same question is asked by all; what can be done differently? Those argue that this is a historical event to end capitalism and shift to a new global system. Additionally believing that changing the face of the economy is necessary together with a fundamental reshaping of societies. The great reset is seen by those as one of the most significant consequences of AI. The advancement that could be achieved through automation by AI in various fields would be almost unimaginable (Suzuki 2020). While others perceive AI as a deliberate form of control and manipulation of younger generations. By shifting their attention against their best interests, leading to a growing wealth gap and leading to poverty—even in the most advanced countries (Harrari 2020) has described one systematic change of AI as the "rise of digital dictatorships" that observe every individual's existence. From this would be the creation of a futile class; the difference between the few wealthy "high-tech hubs" and "exploited data colonies". This extraordinary shift puts the weak countries under the danger of dependency and only worsens already existing systematic issues. A very fertile ground for '*digital classifications*'.

AI is advancing in a direction which even enables the possibility of a one-world state under global governance. The idea itself is not bad, but we should think about all possibilities involved with this concept. Is such a central power liable to misuse? Many institutions have been authorising themselves to launch a wide world structure simply because they have the means to do so. Leaving few choices to the people who are calling for justice and civil freedom. As the latter repeats the necessity of avoiding the competition with AI in favour of societal security. A universal transformation contains many confusing aspects, especially the huge difference in national capabilities like most countries in MENA. This is the main argument in the region, in which national and regional actors will inevitably imply that the development of the implementation framework is attributed to global institutions, accusing them of confusing unrealistic and irreconcilable goals (Bissat 2018). The national incapability of many countries in the region will subject many countries to dependency if they continue pushing the region for change without any supporting structure.

All conflicting perceptions about the new world order agree on the necessity of a thorough change in the current world structure. In this view, I observe three groups who could impact future trajectory. Those who adopt the implementation of the AI agenda perceive the nature of modern concepts differently, where for them prosperity is extorting human labour for maximum profitability. Wiping out the structure of the current market system is basic for transforming markets themselves and birthing a new economy. The second group consists of those who are questioning the ethics of AI and raises awareness of the consequences of weaponising AI. This could lead to disasters that could put even the most advanced countries in unpredictable danger. If this kind of technology is putting societies under such massive threat, what is the point of using it? What is called 'progress' by leaders is advancing to shape a monopoly of the economic sector and are used to prioritising a company's profits over social benefits. These benefits contradict with the struggle of the people who perceive prosperity only as a result of social justice and an environment sustainable development. The third opinion is, those who call for a comprehensive and dedicated effort to find a mutual ground between the current system and societies in order to minimising the potential destruction through comprehensive cooperation like the suggested model of Public Private Society Partnership (PPSP) and explore other possibilities.

Regional leaders have stalled innovation by not allowing the monopolising of certain industries. This is a case of a reverse Public Private Partnership (PPP), where the corrupt public sector is involved directly in the private sector profits hindering any serious actions toward the monopolies. For example, by not allowing new companies to enter the telecommunications sector, they prevent any change that leads to lower prices and an increase in quality. In the end, they reconcile with any direction provided it assures maintaining the running system without any urgent consequences. Despite this challenging environment for any external forces, there is always the ever present opportunity to subject the region to their strategic planning and long term control.

If the transition to the digital economy is inevitable, then there are more unique opportunities and challenges facing the MENA. More details about this are discussed under the *fourth industrial revolution chapter*. A report issued by the World Bank indicated the main pillars for establishing the new economy; investing in women's role in the new markets, enhancing smart agriculture, using technology in conflict resolutions to name a few. The report focuses on the fact that incremental changes are not feasible. The MENA region needs a new economic reality, where the current stagnating economy cannot hire the most educated and productive workforce. Therefore, the reform of the current regulatory system in the region is imperative. All agree there are no easy ways out of this vicious cycle, especially with the new implications of Covid-19, where humanity is pushed to pay a huge price for this necessary transition. All opposition forces are standing exactly on the same slim rope but each one is looking in a completely different direction. The main difference is the purpose of the transition whether for or against humanity.

At a time when the most advanced communities and developed capitals are facing fundamental difficulties to cope with the evolution of AI. One requires extraordinary capabilities to reimagine how the phoenix will come out of this fire to redefine the ME, considering all ongoing chaos and conflict. With this great re-set, we are crossing the buffer zone now, where the global system is keen to establish their own novel structure in the ME. This finishes a historical era and opens a new epoch that carries various challenges and opportunities. I am concerned that the final word here becomes totally out of the local space decision. Where AI might manufacture new solutions along with previously unheard of terms in an effort to reproduce the ME, perhaps in form of 'digital ME'.

4.4 Summary

The study of political development in the ME has usually been defined by three dimensions: understanding the emergence of states in the region, understanding the dynamics of the forces who rule the world, and finally analysing human history and ancient civilisations. However, when analysing for the future, this methodology proves ineffective due to the increasing number of new concepts with no previous analogue for analysis.

Moreover, in the wake of increasing AI presence and the influence of IoT, we can see how this would affect control in the ME and perhaps reshape it. The 'new Middle East' has been strongly introduced by both regional and international forces, where many leaders suggested an economic field different from the current one.

With the 4IR we are crossing the buffer zone now, where the global system is keen to establish their own novel structure in the ME. This finishes a historical era and opens a new epoch that carries various challenges and opportunities. I am concerned that the final word here becomes totally out of the local space decision. Where AI might manufacture new solutions along with previously unheard of terms in an effort to reproduce the ME, perhaps in form of 'digital ME'.

Particularly in the wake of various digital initiatives, the countries with weaker infrastructure and limited capacity to support this, will have to once again turn to external forces for assistance.

References

Beers P, Boshuizen H, Kirschner P, Gijselaers W (2006) Common ground, complex problems and decision making. Group Decis Negot 15:529–556. https://doi.org/10.1007/s10726-006-9030-1

Bissat LM (2018) Implementing agenda 2030 in the Arab world: contextualization, action areas and policy planning. Public Sect Econ 43(4):459–476

Bourdieu P (1991) Language and symbolic power (trans: Adamson M; ed: Thompson J). Polity Press, Cambridge

Bringsjord S, Govindarajulu NS (2020) Artificial Intelliegence (ed: Zalta E). Metaphysics Research Lab, Stanford University

Chomsky N (2016) Who rules the world? The standard convention for answering this question often misses the point

Copeland BJ (2021) Artificial Intelligence. Encyclopedia Britannica. https://www.britannica.com/technology/artificial-intelligence

Crooke A, Kinninmont J, Rogan E (2021) GSF Middle East roundtable: the changing dynamics in the region [Interview]

Davies N (2021) An interview with Denis Halliday. The Progressive Magazine

EU (2021) Development and cooperation. European Union. https://european-union.europa.eu/priorities-and-actions/actions-topic/development-and-cooperation_en

Flegel P (2018) Does Western philosophy have Egyptian roots? Philosophy Now, a magazine of ideas

Freeman CW (2012) Change without progress in the Middle East. Remarks to the National Council on U.S. Arab relations 21st annual Arab-U.S. Policymakers Conference

Greenbank J (2014) The key ideas of the Western philosophy. Philosophy Now, a magazine of ideas.

Harrari Y (2020) How to survive the 21st century WEF annual meeting. Davos

IPSF (2021) Common ground taxonomy—climate change mitigation. https://ec.europa.eu/info/sites/default/files/business_economy_euro/banking_and_finance/documents/211104-ipsf-common-ground-taxonomy-instruction-report_en.pdf

Issaev L, Zakharov A (2021) Federalism in the Middle East: state reconstruction projects and the Arab Spring. Springer

O'Neill A (2021) European Union: gross domestic product (GDP) from 2016 to 2026. Statista. https://www.statista.com/statistics/527869/european-union-gross-domestic-product-forecast/

OECD (2018) China's Belt and Road Initiative in the global trade, investment and finance landscape. https://www.oecd.org/finance/Chinas-Belt-and-Road-Initiative-in-the-global-trade-investment-and-finance-landscape.pdf
Orlik EZT (2021) When will China rule the world? Maybe never. https://www.bloomberg.com/news/features/2021-07-05/when-will-china-s-economy-beat-the-u-s-to-become-no-1-why-it-may-never-happen?cmpid=socialflow-twitter-business&utm_medium=social&utm_campaign=socialflow-organic&utm_content=business&utm_source=t
Perknis H (2016) The new confessions of an economic Hit Man. BK Berrett-Koehler Publishers, Inc.
Sağlamer G (2021) The Mediterranean: cradle of civilization. United Nations
Schwab K (2020) The great reset. weforum.org
Suzuki K (2020) AI: a new open access journal for Artificial Intelligence. AI 1:141–142. https://doi.org/10.3390/ai1020007
The World Bank (2018) A new economy for the Middle East and North Africa. World Bank
Umbrello S (2021) Should we reset? A review of Klaus Schwab and Thierry Malleret's 'COVID-19: the great reset.' J Value Inq. https://doi.org/10.1007/s10790-021-09794-1
Voloshino (1973) Marxism and the philosophy of language, vol 1 (trans: Metejaka L). Seminar Press, London
Wang P (2019) On defining Artificial Intelligence. J Artif Gen Intell 10:1–37. https://doi.org/10.2478/jagi-2019-0002
Wengrow DGD (2018) How to change the course of human history. Eurozine
Zu S (1910) The art of war

Chapter 5
Federalist Governance in the Middle East

Warda Samara

5.1 Federalist Governance in the Middle East

When discussing geo-political borders, we inevitably find ourselves at the same question each time. Do borders even exist on a material level, or have we all bought this into this social construct fortifying its existence? In either case, what defines borders still must be agreed upon. During both world wars, people worldwide including the ME fought under the call of freedom (and later under the security of the nation) to create and reinforce the current borders, which are now the roots of the contemporary borders worldwide that we know today. Currently, in the ME, despite the high price paid for these initial borders, the same people continue to fight for border reconstruction, includes the modernisation of ancient concepts in the region such as 'con-federalism'.

Reshaping countries is a recurring topic that has happened many times throughout history, particularly following a period of heavy destruction. Different divisions were adopted and implemented throughout history in order to facilitate administration between the main areas and the centre or the capital. Some of them carry complex background from ancient myths, theories and concepts, which are still vital to understand in order to imagine how tomorrow would look like. The "end of days" referenced in the Bible is for all intents and purposes (Leonhard 2010), a world confederation or coalition of all states, each preserving its own integrity while accepting a common Divine covenant and constitutional order. This order will establish appropriate covenantal relationships for the entire world (Brian 2018).

The pre-modern federal system before the seventeenth century had a strong tribal. This essentially means that individuals were inevitably defined as members of permanent, multi-generational groups, whose rights and obligations were entirely or mainly derived from that group membership. Modern federalism has since rid itself of this model, emphasising a regime that is mainly based on individuals and their rights. It has little space to recognise or legitimise intergenerational groups (Althusius 1995).

W. Samara and M. Samara, *The Power of Perceptions in the Middle East*,
Perspectives on Development in the Middle East and North Africa (MENA) Region,
https://doi.org/10.1007/978-3-030-99150-0_5

Recently, there has been a growing public discourse in many states about the proposals of new border divisions in the MENA. Even though serious discussions are taking place among grass-root movements, regional forces like Saudi Arabia may say this will open floodgates that cannot be closed and will affect stable countries in the region. Furthermore, those calling for a federal system have been met with acceptance even by some nationalists, as if federations will be what finally ends any regional conflict. In several countries including Iraq, Lebanon, Libya and Yemen, federalism was put forward under different methods and mechanisms. This chapter argues that considering such an option is not a new proposal. Rather it is marking a return to—*Vilayet*—the system of states and administrative divisions was already implemented during the Ottoman Empire. Where a ***Vilayet***, is a term derived from the Arabic language and was used to represent the administrative division. It was implemented during the later Ottoman Empire referring to regions or districts, introduced with the promulgation of the *Vilayet Law* that were being enacted throughout the empire (Wikipedia 2021). One could go further and even trace it back to the pre-dynastic era (before 3100 BC), where nome "districts" served as a territorial division in the era of Pharaonic Egypt. Each nome was ruled by a Nomarch, and these districts originally existed as independent city-states, but later began to unite.

While the concept of 'divided states' was also applied by Alexander the Great (356–323 BC), the Persian and the Roman empires among others, the greatest adherent to the national division was the Islamic state. At least until it was reshaped under the Ottoman Empire *Vilayet*. As for modern Western political concepts, both the US and the EU are examples of "leagues". In theory, a "League" approach is based on political forces participating equally within a designated economic bloc. However, this has been only successful in the case of an open economy. In the case of the EU many local and regional challenges emerged especially after Britain's exit from the EU. In the ME, there are many difficulties that prevent the people in the region to build common ground and structure that allows all to feel the belonging of the regional political structure (Hindawi 2021). Moreover, reshaping the administrative structure among the region requires a new structural model for each federal state that includes new policies, legislations and new institutions able to sustain long-term developments.

After WWII, there were several attempts to frame the region beyond the geopolitical boundaries. In particular starting with the Fertile Crescent federation and then Egypt's attempt to lead the Arab world through a league, not federations. However, these positions and other similar projects were rejected or failed as some players were given a secondary place in them (Issaev and Zakharov 2021). Eventually, in March 1945, the Arab League was formed in Cairo with Egypt, Iraq, Transjordan (renamed Jordan in 1949), Lebanon, Saudi Arabia and Syria the initial members. However, the Arab League was not seen by the people of the region as an entity capable of solving outstanding problems. The founding states hardly attained their independence and their officials did not have sufficient political experience to manage their local or regional entities. Thus, the Arab league role remained very limited.

However, con-federations that are discussed in their current form, in the ME, are not necessarily an inevitable separation from the current states or authorities. It could be an administrative restructuring to allow renegotiations among the regional players, and therefore maintain the relations with the international institutions as required. As global bodies are working in the direction of re-ordering and maintain their access to resources.

All kinds of administrative divisions require a process undergoing continuous modification to fit the peculiarities of the environment in which it is being practised. Where societal needs differ from the state as do the needs of the individual. Yet, in the federal system, the focus is indeed the individual. Thus, the main feature of the 4IR is "to change who you are as a person". A 'federation' as a term has two dimensions; the dimension based on the individual ability to learn and cooperate, and the dimension of independence that protects each administration from external forces (Hamilton et al. 1987 [1788]).

Since 2003 the valid examples are increasing in the region where con-federalism and new administrative divisions were developed through a sequent of events. A decade of war caused havoc, where half of the pre-war Syria population was displaced internally or as refugees in other countries. Moreover, the economic growth has shrunk by more than 60%, a human death of 400,000 is yet subject to increase (CSIS 2021). By using the image and language of autonomous administration in the region, the external forces can re-position themselves as supporters of reconstruction in the region. This suggestion to divide the country into independent 'con-federations' that are connected to the central government responsible for finance, public relations and military. This assures to sustain access to health care, education, housing, and sustenance. How to create a system to manage all the existing complications remain the main challenge especially that this might mean some groups might be living under the rules of a party they do not support increasing political tension and possibly leading to more conflicts in the future. In 2021 the Vice-President of the Joint Presidency in the Autonomous Administration of North and East Syria, Badran Jiakard, called for the recognition of the Autonomous Administration of the areas under their control, expressing that it is not a division of the region, but an effective proposal to end this crisis, in which all parties must be open to the dialogue. Where Russia considers this as this as "a positive step towards a solution" despite the fact that the Al-Asad government still rejects the idea. This did not prevent the region from focusing on building local security and governance infrastructure in the meantime.

In the case of Iraq, we see divisions are rising due to the rapid sequence of events since the US war on Iraq. These events arguably happened intentionally to prepare the country for these new divisions. One could then potentially expect the new structure in Iraq more than elsewhere. Especially where federalism has become an increased demand by the Kurds as an ethnic group. The Kurdish protest is not necessarily a complete separation from Iraq but, at least, demands a certain level of independence that guarantees more rights for the Kurds.

In Palestine, the situation is more complex because of the spatial dimension. Con-federalism might be seen as a reasonable approach to resolve the Palestine-Israel issue for the benefit of both people without impinging on either side. However, this remains challenging due to the demographic distribution of Palestinians, and the fact that federalism might not offer solutions to the fundamental issues. The Israeli-Palestinian Confederation Committee believes that one possible solution involves electing a confederation government comprised of Israelis—both Jewish and Arab—and Palestinians (Avesar 2021).

Since Oslo, Israel has permitted various measures of Palestinian security agencies to operate, but only on the condition of what Israelis imprecisely refer to as "security coordination," which Palestinians regard as delegating the occupation. Considering the security institutions able to operate across Israel-Palestine are the demands of major Israeli political actors (Brown 2018). Furthermore, internally the Palestinian autonomous administration experience did not succeed in leading the first civil conflict in Palestine when Hamas won the elections for the Palestine Legislative Council (PLC) over Fatah. Even though they formed a coalition government, violence between their organised groups escalated and Hamas took control over Gaza. With the annexation of Israeli settlements in the West Bank, the number of settlers in there has increased by 42% compared to 2010 (Hareuveni and Etkes 2021). According to a report prepared by the Israeli Information Centre for Human Rights in the Occupied Territories, this is a clear violation of international law referring to article 49 of the Fourth Geneva Convention (UN 2015). Hence, the con-federalist model became more complex to assure political, social and economic rights for the individuals of all parties.

In the case of Lebanon, federalism as a paradigm suggests self-government in distinct geographical zones where constitutional bodies are based on main religious factions. This means that each of the major sects runs its affairs in accordance with their beliefs and culture, perhaps even resulting in minority sects in some instances. On a national level, the interaction of opposing external factors with each individual federal state exacerbates strategic conflicts. As a result, there is never a dull moment in the federal government, especially when it comes to foreign and defence policy and checks and balances.

This scenario recalls the breakdown and demise of federal Yugoslavia following the collapse of the Yugoslav Communist Party with a stable central framework. The internal struggle led to the state's disintegration and destruction (Sulaiman 2021). The major problem remains that the sects in Lebanon do not make enough effort to act independently of external forces and explore the common ground to the benefit of Lebanon as an independent state.

The proposed political divisions are based on eco-political dynamics which do not empower the people, rather akin to the aforementioned Sykes-Picot deal in 1916. Upon reflection, it is though astonishing how people forget the consequences of historical events. People of the region are accepting new borders to be negotiated at the time of great failure of the currently defined borders. Neither political nor economic progress has happened in the region. The social suffering did not cease since WWI. Therefore, I focus here on two points: the names that are used for any of the new border divisions themselves no longer have any significance. The most important point is to understand what these terms encapsulate and their implications on the ground. The second point, in order to avoid repeating history, divisions should not be seen as the only solution. Tools, methods and mature discussions about constitutions should be discussed rather than engaging in careless border defining.

Any outsider observing the region on a wider landscape, would probably assume that the confederate League is already operating on the ground in the region. However, these divisions are simply unspoken facts that have existed longer than popular understanding. They operate from the perspective of different symbolic roles which remains a mystery to the public. Therefore a different structure could be only envisioned by the designer of this system—the external forces. In fact, the development of con-federalism in the region did not suddenly happen where many local players eventually accepted the dialogue. The environment had to be shaped through a sequence of events in the last century, not only in the region but also in many countries worldwide. Divided people in multiple regions was fertile ground for conflict. The ideological concepts that encouraged and strategically divided various groups and sects to be in an endless cycle of conflict (Panella 2017).

Any forces trying to yield popular influence in the region by suggesting new divisions might lead to further devastating consequences for the people. For example, in a new divided region, Turkey, Iran or Israel may develop a hegemonic role and indirectly rule some other nations as a proxy for other major powers. We have witnessed this with the annexation of the Golan Heights by Israel in 2019 followed by the necessity of establishing relationships with more countries in the MENA. That all contributed to a general government that might represent the so-called "Great Israel", where one witnessed a league of territories or federalists emerge in its final shape. Where Iran has been supporting different allies in the region, for example, in Syria and Lebanon. Turkey is putting its hand on more lands in several countries and increasing their exploration of resources outside of its borders. Then who is the power is above the powers of the autonomous regions and self-administrations?

The anti-federalists, like John DeWitt, emphasise the role of suspicion (DeWitt 1786–1800); even though some type of federal union is necessary, citizens should exercise some suspicion of the government due to the permanent danger of a government protecting the few at the expense of the many. This contradicts democratic governance where more citizens actively participate in decision-making and the public sphere, by debating and negotiating issues vital for the community. The anti-federalists saw dangers in centralising the power of a federal government, with a constitution possessing too much power to request taxes and to control trade (Frausto 2019).

Federalism demonstrates the susceptibility of such regimes to tyrannical disorder. Therefore, when discussing the possibilities of the future of a region like the ME, one must remember that wars and chaos are connected to several events; the new world order, the way the region will interact perhaps with the multipolar system, and the AI involvement. We would have to proceed carefully if con-federalism was to be introduced officially into the region.

5.2 Perception on Geopolitical Borders and 'Digital Classification'

Borders are subject to intense political contestation and persist based on national interests. Borders therefore acquire their social relevance only as a result of political processes that normally follows wars or even negotiations. The borders in the ME are viewed from the point of their political function of originally dividing the people in the region. Whereas its symbolic purposes are more crucial for the forces who conquer the region.

For instance, the contemporary worldwide borders we know today were produced and protected for economic reasons, where the trade ultimately forms interaction between the symbolic and the functional political borders.

Open markets impose a significant influence over the regional political structures which reflects the contemporary economic motive. Where symbolic borders can triumph over the functional ones, this interdependence between the modern economy and the wide geographical place naturally transcends the current political borders of states and seeks to dismantle these borders. Even if purely to facilitate its movement and increase its flexibility. This has been emerging in the MENA region since the decline of Egypt as a referent in the global arena and the emerging of the Gulf countries as an economic regional power. By using whatever means at their disposal, the economic development of the Gulf led to the introduction of a new economic classification.

The increasing presence of AI also raises the question of why borders are perceived as the only solution. The digital era also brings a new category of classifying nations and people, under '*digital classification*'. This allows divisions to be made on the digitally rather than geographically. This classification has been lobbied by the financial system and soon will become a prerequisite for businesses going forward. I believe once this digital classification becomes accepted, this will only serve to harm indigenous groups. AS these groups possess neither the means nor understanding to obtain technological progress. Furthermore, as such classifications operate on a criteria of 'technological progress', justice and equality are not considered criteria, potentially leading to increased harm against these indigenous groups. Hence, I think, it is no longer matters how the new geographical map will look like, what matters is to what effects the ME borders are going to be classified and digitalised. As well as who will govern the new classification.

Functional borders have proved it is not in line with the construction of societies, as indicated by Benedict Anderson. Societies (or nations or cultural groups) are part of larger spaces and refer to mutual historical-cultural symbols that cross state political functional borders. In the ME, this was the common perception until the existence of Israel. The state of Israel demonstrated the function and applicability of political borders together with the tight security industry that rendered movement and interaction between the MENA region more difficult than ever before. This coupled with a different internal structure for each state in the region also complicated legal systems and the policies of public relations. This means that people accepted the borders as fact rather than a social construct defined by the people outside the region. Over time, the space of mutuality across borders has been eliminated and became a feature of social life that is accepted by the public. Thus, thinking about a new form of borders became kind of unthinkable. However, I see a high opportunity for advanced solutions in what I call '*geo-tech*' where people in a very early stage of 'digital classifications' know how to employ technology for their own benefit. This, of course, increases the requirements of skilled and competent people. Thus, the role of borders, AI and IoT should require more attention from academic and security research centres in the region. People in general should be more conscious about the function and symbolic nature of political borders, the purpose of their existence and how to cooperate beyond these borders through innovation in the AI era.

Many unexpected responses may appear in the middle of this radical progress. China BRI is actually enabling a new type of economic classification to emerge. This opens up the possibility for economic and technological cooperation that goes beyond the political borders. Other unexpected responses could stem from the social movements and influencers who could manage to lay an organisational foundation that could be no longer ignored by the regional player.

The economic bloc in Europe (either eastern or western), for example, is an expression of the desire to find a *zeitgeist* for the coexistence of the economic and political structures (Hindawi 2021), where borders could be perceived as a "historically contingent processes" (Sendhardt 2013). The EU, on the other hand, is increasingly relying on AI programs such as these to monitor people before they even arrive at its borders.

The ME states are only one of several non-sovereign agents in charge of coordinating the region and its borders, without final authority (Althusius 1995). This became obvious in the last two decades. When the attention of the ME domestic players is occupied with redefining the region geographically, busy how to name the new divisions: states, con-federations or *vilayet*. To maintain their benefits within any new system proposed. Whereas global forces have been operating their activities based on their own symbolic division which now is visioned to be the 'digital classifications', this might be the future of borders.

5.3 Summary

Despite the potential that AI brings, political models such as con-federalism and sovereignty are still pushed as genuine solutions for reconstruction in the region. Even though, AI has already been demonstrating its power to change structures on the global stage.

AI is an incredible tool, capable of many things, but it is also incredibly complicated and still eludes the understanding of many today. While the extent of its capabilities rest in the hands of forces who can afford this, other countries are subject to their adoption and their use of AI. Without the structure in countries to support knowledge production, new tools like AI remain outside of understanding on the ground and remain shaped by external forces. As technological progress becomes a bigger indicator of national image, we start to see the recognition of countries under '*digital classifications*' affecting the national identity and branding.

Despite all these complications, what remains the most important is that the people of the region do not fall prey to externally defined divisions in their societies. This strategy must operate beyond geographical borders and traditional tools like 'geo-tech' borders. In fact, there are countries in the region, such as the Gulf, where they possess the capabilities on a material level to pressure the global forces to renegotiate. Not simply within their own borders, but the region in general. This also concerns the role of the leaders, who could either allow another Sykes-Picot treaty to take effect, or genuinely search to find solutions for their people. Otherwise, the promise of true independence in the digital age remains a laborious and implausible goal.

References

Althusius J (1995) Politica. In: Carney FS (trans). Liberty Fund

Avesar J (2021) The Israeli-Palestinian confederation proposal. Palestine-Israel J. https://pij.org/articles/1073/the-israelipalestinian-confederation-proposal

Brian C (2018) Johannes Althusius's politica and the idea of federalism

Brown N (2018) Federalism in Israel–Palestine: fresh ideas, old problems. https://www.lawfareblog.com/federalism-israel-palestine-fresh-ideas-old-problems

CSIS CfSIS (2021) Syria's economic collapse and its impact on the most vulnerable. https://www.csis.org/analysis/syrias-economic-collapse-and-its-impact-most-vulnerable

DeWitt J (1786–1800) To the free citizens of the commonwealth of Massachusetts. Retrieved from http://www.let.rug.nl/usa/documents/1786-1800/the-anti-federalist-papers/john-de-witt-essay-ii-oct27-1787.php

Frausto O (2019) Federalist and anti-federalist: two divergent concepts of politics, 1. https://doi.org/10.19195/1895-8001.14.1.9

Hamilton A, Madison J, Jay J (1987 [1788]) The federalist. Penguin Books, New York

Hareuveni E, Etkes D (2021) This is ours—and this, too: Israel's settlement policy in the West Bank. https://www.btselem.org/publications/202103_this_is_ours_and_this_too

Hindawi Io (2021). Frontiers in geopolitics. In: General origins in political geography and geopolitics: with an applied study on the Middle East

Issaev L, Zakharov A (2021) Federalism in the Middle East—state reconstruction projects and the Arab Spring. Springer

Leonhard R (2010) Visions of apocalypse. What Jews, Christians, and Muslims believe about the end times, and how those beliefs affect our world. https://www.jhuapl.edu/Content/documents/ApocalypseVision.pdf

Panella J (2017) The divine secret garden series, vol 2. Create Space

Sendhardt B (2013) Theoretical perspectives on borders. In: Borders and border regions in Europe: changes, challenges and chances, pp 21–44. https://www.jstor.org/stable/j.ctv1fxhcq.4

Sulaiman I (2021) Federalism in Lebanon is a problem, not a solution. https://www.lebanon24.com/news/lebanon/841071/الفيدرالية-في-لبنان-مشكلة-وليست-حلا

UN (2015) *Israeli settlements in the occupied Palestinian territory, including East Jerusalem, and in the occupied Syrian Golan* (Annual report of the United Nations High Commissioner for Human Rights and reports of the Office of the High Commissioner and the Secretary-General, Issue)

Wikipedia (2021) Vilayet

Chapter 6
Fourth Industrial Revolution

Warda Samara

6.1 The Fourth Industrial Revolution

In the vision of 4IR, outcomes cannot be predicted due to the uncertainty of the nature of new technologies and its consequences (Kimura et al. 2019). Thus, the consequences in a region that have been constant warfare and political conflict is not too optimistic. The region was not able to take advantage of the former worldwide industrial revolutions to bring changes to their countries. This obviously led to a lack of substantial progress, either locally or globally, that was worth mentioning in the historical record. Even today as the world advances towards a 4IR, most countries in the ME are still unaware or unable to catch up in the procession even from the previous "revolutions". This atmosphere is highly expected to leave a 'disruptive' on all the economic sectors in the local and regional spaces. Thus, a holistic approach is needed to develop the far-reaching strategy of the MENA on how to utilise new technologies for economic development and not only growth. Not forgetting the possible digital domination risk when being dominated by external tech giants (Feridm and Rabah 2019).

The wealth and the technological disparity between the Arab countries has affected the ability of states to respond to this transformation based on several factors; including the levels of diversity in current economic structures, the ability to attract investments, the availability of knowledge capital and the enabling and supportive environment, This would require reforming policies that currently favour incumbents and establishing competitive economies based on innovation in order (Feridm and Rabah 2019).

For example, let's imagine how will the different countries in the region interact with the fibre optic networks that connect one network to another? This is one of the most important components of technological progress and its installation is in fact located in the ME. Through technologically seaborne cable infrastructure, it connects

W. Samara and M. Samara, *The Power of Perceptions in the Middle East*,
Perspectives on Development in the Middle East and North Africa (MENA) Region,
https://doi.org/10.1007/978-3-030-99150-0_6

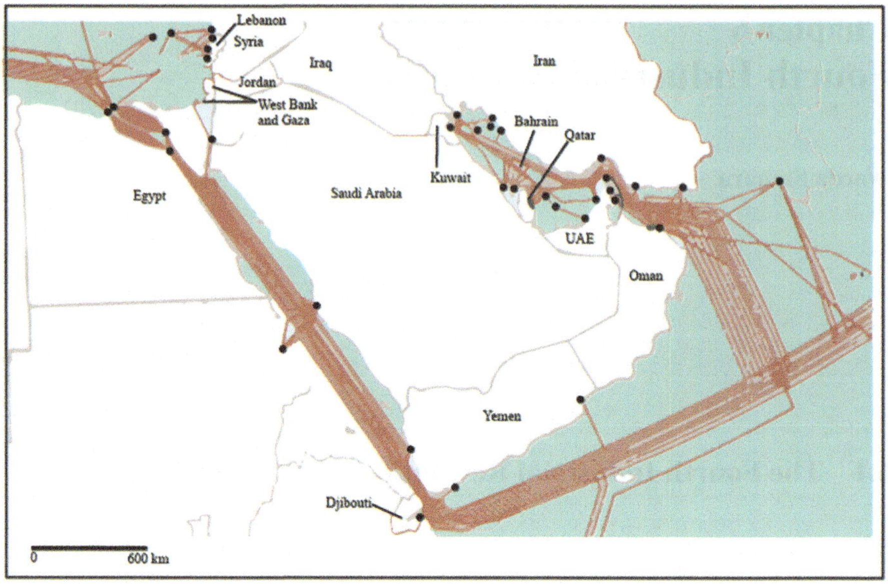

Fig. 6.1 Submarine cables and cross-border connections in the ME (*Source* Author's own design based on World Bank data and TeleGeography map)

Europe and China, the Sinai Peninsula, then the Red Sea and the *Bab Al-Mandab* strait between Yemen and Djibouti to reach the Arabian Peninsula and the Indian subcontinent as highlighted in Figs. 6.1 and 6.2. This infrastructure is complemented by strong ground networks that cross the Orient, providing alternative high-speed routes. The infrastructure of the future relies on fibre to serve its needs. Therefore, if it is invested without any external dominance, it can change the geography of the global internet infrastructure where at least some of the MENA countries have control over and thus obtain some control and even some influence. This might go beyond any original expectations.

The 4IR is characterised by great processing power, storage capabilities and access to mass data. It is the new interaction between the physical and digital worlds as one force including all advances in AI, robotics, genetic engineering, quantum computing, and other technologies (McGinnis 2020). This revolution bears radical transformations in all industries so that all aspects of the life that we know are being reconstructed (Schwab 2016). This happens as a result of technologies and industries cumulative impact on the world. Figure 6.3 represent the transformations since the first industrial revolution till the 4IR.. This includes all sectors that affect the workforce requirements.

A report issued by The Arab Monetary Fund in 2021 about the economic indicators of the 4IR, indicated that countries are moving towards a change in their economic

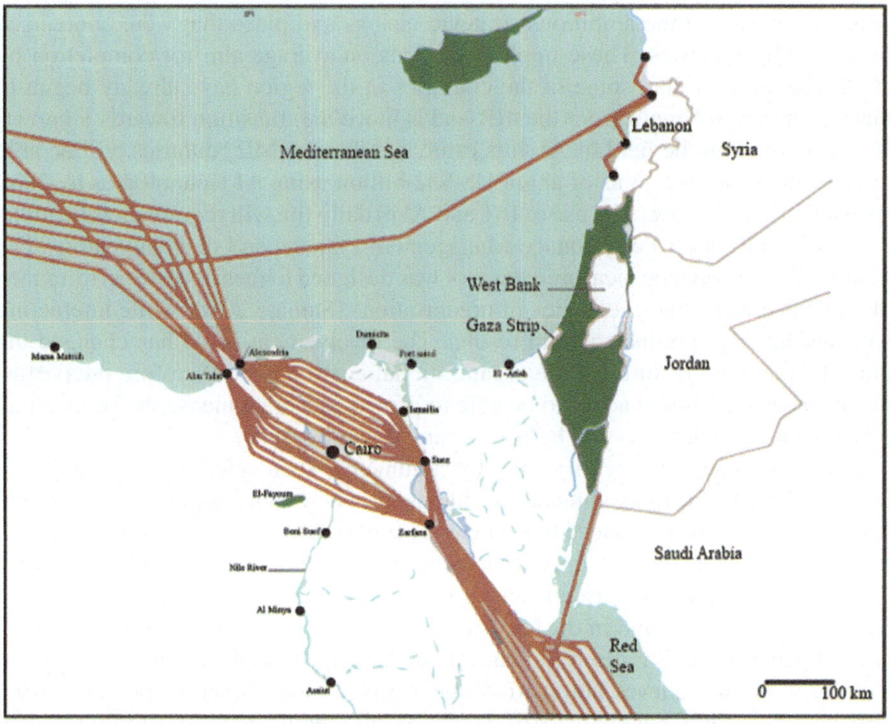

Fig. 6.2 Submarine cables and cross-border connections in the ME (*Source* Author's own design based on World Bank data and TeleGeography map)

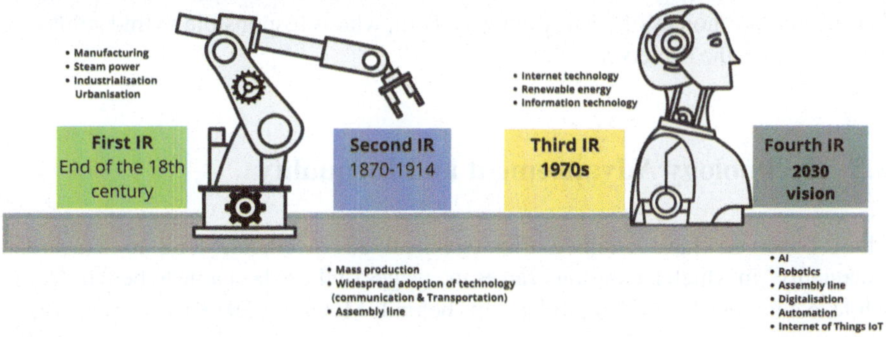

Fig. 6.3 4IR (*Source* Author's own design)

structures based on the ambitious strategic visions and plans that were announced in many ME countries. These implementations on average aim for completion by 2035. Having said that, some of the countries in the region have already begun to make progress to benefit from the 4IR and achieve the transition towards a knowledge economy. In the field of AI, it is estimated that the ME countries will be able to generate economic gains of about US $32 billion using AI technologies by 2030 (Ismael 2021). However, the use of IoT and AI in daily life will require modifications to the currently used Performance Management systems and their indicators. The traditional performance measurement tool was designed to measure the performance of humans towards the excellence of organisations (Samara 2018) while interacting with machines to produce certain results. The involvement of AI has changed the indicators and the features of the organisational environment; therefore the performance measures should adapt to be able to provide accurate measures for machine performance and detect errors before causing crisis.

Social resistance is accompanied by arguments, even scientific, rejecting this direction largely due to heightened suspicions from new technologies. The argument is that IoT is a shift to smart cities where sensors collect a huge amount of data on every possible thing in its vicinity. That means any small failure in the whole network could lead to disastrous consequences, such as a misuse of confidential information that could easily be found in the hands of hackers. Moreover, they argue that robots will surpass and then replace human labour leading to increased unemployment. Current thinking believes automation could replace more than 30 percent of the human workforce (Chui et al. 2016). However, this should be motivation for people to expand their knowledge, skills and abilities to be competent to get higher tasks which is sort of privileged for these skilled people (Mckeon 2018). What if these people who are doing the low-skilled jobs are not able to adapt? Since AI and the IoT are not the choices of society anyway, then, who is responsible to find solutions? The system or the society?

6.2 Technology Advancement and Inequality

Many observers have claimed that technical advancements tend to exacerbate 'inequality,' in which technology raises the wages of those best able to benefit from it while leaving other less powerful groups behind (McGinnis 2013). There are contradictory discussions reflecting whether that is true or not. Some argue that the "information revolution" has opened almost, an equal opportunity to people from the same community, referring to women and men, to reach information, access data, and enhancing individual skills and competencies. In this regard women in areas where are technology is easy to access were almost offered an 'equal opportunity' to catch up but many have simply chosen not to. Although many policies and development projects were enhancing inclusion for women, it was more of a superficial effort in order to increase their purchasing power. It is true that many women still face "economic inequality" or inequality in "living conditions" (UN 2015) such as the

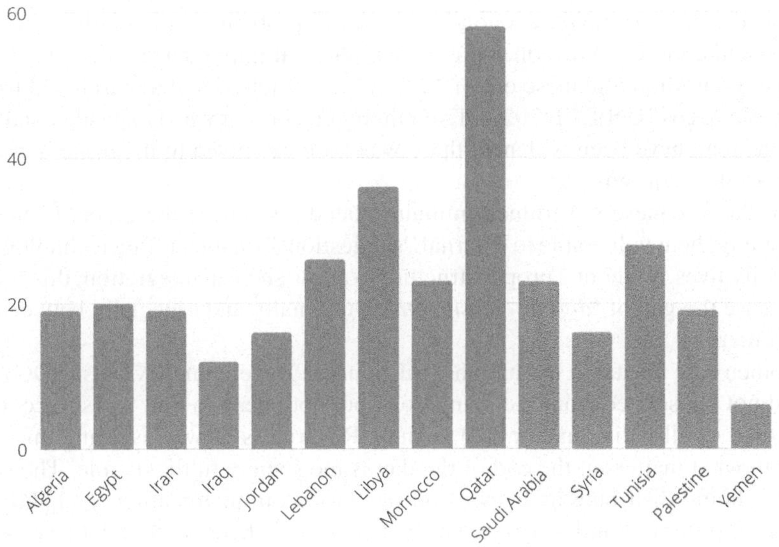

Fig. 6.4 Percentage of female labour force participating in MENA countries 2019 (*Source* Author's own design based on World Bank data)

engagement in the domestic political system. In order to suggest sustainable solutions for such an issue, all comprehensive factors must be analysed, including the willingness of women to compete as part of the workforce by enhancing their knowledge and skills. Furthermore, there should be an investigation as to why women are likely to be 'customers' for industries and technologies products rather than being innovative to improve their living conditions. Although in many countries in the ME, education is advisable and obligatory for all genders but women participating in the workforce is still low. Figure 6.4 represents the percentage of Female Labour Force Participating in the MENA in 2019.

The gender gap is already expanding as women are usually employed in traditional jobs that are likely to be at risk (industry, agriculture, construction, traditional and handicraft industries). According to a study held by the Arab Monetary Fund in 2021, women will lose three million jobs in exchange for gaining 0.55 million (Abd-Almenem and Ismael 2021).

One should not forget that the MENA as a region is a large area encompassing vast different cultural, traditional, and religious behaviour. Some countries are highly engaged in technology and others are still living without any interaction whatsoever. However, during the last decade women in entrepreneurship is remarkably increasing in some parts of the region (more in Chap. 8).

In countries like Sudan, women live under injustice circumstances where the political instability and continuous conflict over decades caused a dramatic increase of a national poverty that primarily affected women and children. There are great contradictions in this case, after the Sudanese were deprived of technological imports, they continued to suffer greater economic and social problems particularly concerning women and children. Now, once these technological imports were allowed, we still see that 3.4 million Sudanese out of 12.7 million required humanitarian aid to meet their basic needs (UNICEF 2020). Even though technology had expanded and some horizons may have been widened, there was no focus given to the basic issues that create a safe environment.

Yet, the Sudanese government remain fixated on closing the global technology gap leading them vulnerable to external "suggestions" on integrating technology into their daily lives. Without a proper structure to allow such an integration, this is likely to increase the gap of '*digital classification*' internally and especially between men and women.

Women role is vital in the nations' Sustainable Development Goals (SDG) but it should not be isolated from the man's role, but both need to find ways to cooperate for justice of all individuals in that society. Regardless of who is doing this job or that job, what matters at the end of the day is the society fulfils its role. The role of society should distribute its responsibilities based on qualifications and skills, not gender, in order to build a strong nation. Otherwise, there is an underdevelopment of a massive portion of society and further divisions.

Dividing the features of well-being into conflicting segments serve to distract from the whole purpose and vision. Inequality, poverty, nepotism, corruption cannot be solved when we segregate one individual society or when we create feuding societies. This is an essential direction to be focused on as AI and further technological advancement come into play if we want to work toward sustainable development and prosperity.

Coined by Adam Smith (1723–1790) the 'division of labour' has become simulated in other aspects that divide all life into segments that lost the connection between each other. This could be products, family members, wealth etc. Consequently, the human mind became very limited to focus on a steady income. This division of the whole existence has approved its efficiency for industries and technology advancements towards growth whereas the people in society are left behind. The 4IR should be an invitation to all to prepare for this post transition era. Is everyone on board?

6.3 Is the ME Ready?

I would prefer to discuss the positive side of AI, my fascination with IoT, and the enjoyment of living in smart cities where the public facilities are intuitive, yet advanced—irresistible. That is until I remember the malicious part of it; the forces that are likely to abuse this technology and the potential misfortune of the more vulnerable societies. This is the neglected "dark side" of the new era (Soni 2019) that is likely to create an '*AI divide*'. The non-participation of many countries in the ME will widen the current gap even further than what had resulted from previous industrial revolutions.

When global leaders sit together on the global round table, discussing suitable paths towards SDG, it is believed that every state has full sovereignty over all its resources and economic activities (Nations 2015). The questions that I ask; Is this including the less fortunate ME states as well? Or have they already been relegated to the 'digital colonised' states? Is the world subject to witness more destruction, more refugees, and wars in the region?

In order to investigate if the ME is ready for a transition to implement AI programs, we would need to define what that even means. Particularly when even the most advanced societies are not really sure how to be ready for the post transition era or even what to expect. All that can be declared for an era with unclear characteristics is a transition. As for the ME right now, again there is no one answer. During the last century, several transitions had took a place in the MENA. The region has proved its inability to achieve social and political transitions, for instance, the 'Arab Spring' transition eliminated any chance of democracy in many countries. It also caused a great loss in many sectors and increased levels of poverty in many countries where there was a struggle to even form a stable government.

A distinct methodology was developed to measure government preparation for AI in the form of ten dimensions and 33 indicators. The main dimensions include: innovative capacity, human capital, infrastructure, data availability, and accountability. Where the main pillars are: the government desire to be willing to adopt AI, the extent of development of AI technology in the country, and the availability of the a competent workforce to deal with the AI infrastructure (Shearer et al. 2020).

Due to the lack of individual technological infrastructure (i.e. not everyone owning their own smartphone), there is very little demand for AI and technological innovation from the people. Even if there are initiatives to promote technology, there are too many barriers. Consequently, this implementation rests entirely on the government. This is already a significant challenge, with many in poverty and already questioning the role of their governments. Alternative solutions to this must be found, otherwise the region will be subject to '*digital colonisation*' from other stronger, more technologically advanced countries.

Some countries like Algeria, Lebanon, and Yemen, are still under an ongoing complex political atmosphere with almost no means of establishing a foundation for a transition. Some countries like the United Arab Emirates have already made multiple steps to be competent on the global level and welcome AI into society. The more destruction a city has experienced, the more appropriate it is for a smart city model to be considered as it is completely open to a new infrastructure. For instance, the city of Damascus would benefit from the new architectural developments brought about by AI. Reconstruction is not limited to infrastructure, it includes comprehensive fields that assure the implementation of governance and healthcare while eliminating corruption, poverty and inequality, unemployment and above all reducing foreign interference.

The local population raises several questions about the repercussions of these technologies' implementation on their lives and those of future generations. Although several Arab start ups and businesses have already used some of these new tools in their operations. This was part of a programme by the WEF to promote the 4IR in the region. While a good initiative on the surface, this serves as another example of external foreign agents determining the technological progress of other countries. This might reflect the intention of the whole programme. Concerns remain on who is representing the MENA region in taking the fundamental decisions on firsthand. Those who are promoting the agenda are nothing more than a mouthpiece for the external powers' agenda.

If the ME has to be part of a new global order from the perception of the global institutions, there are two possible directions, and both depend on the decisions taken by the ME countries themselves. Due to the lack of competent and stable leadership, the most sensible decisions cannot be expected (see Chapter 4).

If the ME has chosen to go through another path rejecting the technological advancement the way it is suggested, well-organised alternatives have to be suggested along with the tools to negotiate. There should be no inter-group fighting, there should be cooperation, rights for indigenous people, and reduced harmful consequences on the environment caused by the 4IR. The driving forces cannot implement whatever they wish without clearly addressing the risks that could be caused by the 4IR beforehand. Technological discoveries should ultimately learn how to advance in the right direction that serves humanity. If AI is capable to double the world GDP why it is not able to find solutions to the main problems on the planet such as poverty and unemployment? Is it a lack of human mind or emotions? Or a lack of systematic understanding not considered by the algorithm as human environmental issues were considered a minor issue? This then being the crucial question—who is teaching AI?

It does not matter how 2030 or 2050 will look like, the ME has no choice except to be responsive to the current changes and learn how to adapt accordingly. A new status of outlook is needed where mature decisions are taking place. The good indicator 'now' is that the new global order is not balanced yet between the global forces, which optimistically speaking could open a new channel for negotiations to gain some benefits to the region. Mind you, benefits that should be in line with popular demand and not only the local forces. Imagine if domestic leaders find a way to re-negotiate the use of the region's resources, not only oil and gas but including the communication lines for the internet as well. This would be a kickstart the economy in the whole region that creates more jobs, and enhance the standard of living of people, support entrepreneurs and innovation that finally brings transition to the region. However, would global forces even agree to negotiate with states who possess less military power? Perhaps cooperating with new global forces could change perspectives and open new possibilities. In all cases, however, without the cooperation of the locals, the transition would not be possible. Correctly educating the public and empower the "*machine experience mind*" as what happened in Japan case after WWII is an essential foundation to rebuild or, if you like, to restart and transit.

For example, China is now following an unusual strategy through expanding and increasing its global role through its BRI through the ME. What are the benefits for the ME in return? None!

Not everything on the negotiation table should be physical, but leaders must find a way to expand their attention to a higher awareness that allows them to see more possibilities for negotiation. Perhaps finally some regional forces will cooperate to find solutions and plan to move out of this chaos. This needs a consistent multi-dimensional effort locally and regionally. Institutions are being reshaped, as well as education, healthcare and transport systems.

6.4 Knowledge-based Economy

Discoveries were, throughout human history, in the core of nations and civilisations, some still present today and others lost to time. Due to the nature of the data in the past, in a way, it was easier to process the data based on discoveries, research, including discovering missions and so due to its smaller scale. These days a tremendous amount of data is being collected each second further challenging the solution for suitable and sensitive data processing. Creating a product based on activities dependent on knowledge and expertise that contribute to the creation of scientific and technological progress is what is called the knowledge economy that depends on the intellectual abilities of humans (Kotuliĉ 2020).

Achievement of a knowledge-based economy requires a transition from a material understanding of the economy to one that exploits innovation potential, human capital, knowledge, and new technologies. The intellectual potential, supported by the constant development of people and the appropriate skills of the workforce, as well as the growing competition in the field of innovation, significantly influences the sustainable development of today's economies. In order to facilitate the transition, companies need to develop more extensive on-the-job training programmes, along with supporting employees in obtaining further training. The actual task is the response of the education system to the needs of the stage of social development (Pakhomov 2018).

Knowledge-based economy is the ability to enrich the economy through scientific innovative discoveries, applied research, and knowledge production. In most developed countries this represent a large component of the economic activities. While the less fortunate countries face a huge gap to have a knowledge-based economy. Many countries in the MENA do not seriously invest in knowledge and innovation as bases determine dependency and competitiveness rather most of their economies still service-based economy. Figure 6.5 shows the elements to allow the knowledge-based economy. AI and automation are transforming information work, which means that people's employment, roles, and responsibilities will significantly change (Ofori 2003). The workforce will be combined to meet AI's capabilities and handle its limits (Diakopoulos 2019).

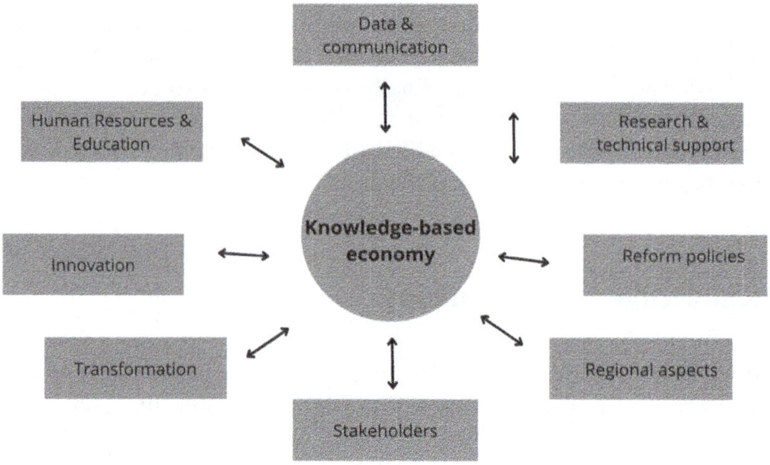

Fig. 6.5 Knowledge-based economy (*Source* Author's own design)

6.4.1 *Transition Economy and Transition Management*

The 4IR requires a competent workforce that has the ability to deal with problems, the flexibility to interface with multiple disciplinary areas as well as the ability to adapt to changes as opposed to moving or crafting physical objects in a conventional manufacturing-based economy.

> Transition is a reality, so either do it your way or it will happen to you their way.

Crises are normally perceived as an unwelcome event that forces organisations to adopt a new direction or disappear entirely from the market. Or this could be considered the wake up call to address changes that were delayed for a long time. This represents the deficiencies that were manifest in the system prior to the COVID-19 pandemic. Therefore, crises can either be a disaster or an asset and turn into an opportunity. The COVID-19 pandemic and the transition to AI is not like any event prior, it is not only changing the lifestyle but it is also changing individuals. This could then be perceived in two conflicting directions.

Change and modifications are not enough, a comprehensive shift is essential to sustain modern organisations, including those who operate in the information and communication technology sectors. The essence of change is innovation, creativity and the ability to introduce new models which have not been used before. This also requires a quick response and shift in laws and policies (Dankbaar 1993). For many agents, the fundamental correspondence could be considered as a birth for a network of institutions completely replacing the old ones.

The required transition in the current era is unique in its inclusivity. It is not an internal transition for institutions or industries. It is a transition that turns all aspects of the external environment upside down, and on a scale that humanity might be dealing with for the first time. It is exactly like your own computer, when overloaded with faulty applications and unneeded data, it runs slower in order to process all running activities. Or sometimes, like my old fashioned mobile, it starts to type messages by itself or refrain from turning on and so on. In the end, you decide to ask an IT specialist to delete all your activities and induce a hard reset on the device. Of course, lots of data could be erased within the process but the physical device with the basic features are still there. Anyway, not an issue if the old apps no longer serve your current needs since there is always the next update waiting for you in the play store. You might think, it is still the same mobile. I say, think again.

The decision to reset your phone with all your accumulated data and images may not be easy. However, the longer you wait, the longer your device would be at risk of losing much more or switching off before you had the chance to save anything. In short, the decision should be yours before someone or something else makes it for you. In all ways, a comprehensive transition is needed while adopting your internal process to external indicators.

Organisations are already shifting from one model to another while being linked to a new financial system. A comprehensive shift that requires efficient correspondence to manage the transition after the crises. Yet, one needs efficient transition management with the assistance of technology where intelligent choices are made and problems must be identified to produce new efficient models to reflect the new economic order.

The current era of transition includes all fields including all its axes, this means that the internal and external interactions must be reset, the internal structure of the organisation and its connection with the external structure must be reset. Even the individual attitude and behaviour must be shift to adopt with all these updates.

We are not discussing a transition of a company that might affect hundreds or thousands of people if it fails, the discussion is about the whole structure transition (the human made universe system) so to speak. Hence, here I illustrate transitions into macro, intermediate and micro levels: the transition from an eco-political, financial and societal level. The industrial networks transition in the middle and the entrepreneurs transition including individuals on the micro level. This analyses the foundations that links the micro and the macro systems. See Fig. 6.6.

In regard to the global eco-political systems transitions, we notice the change must happen in the lower two levels, from bottom to top which allows at one point to meet the macro level vision. The remarkable distance point that the decision is already made on the macro level and is awaiting the lower levels to submit. If they do not submit the vision will not be derived on the ground.

Thus, the current global transition attempts to generate economic growth on a macro level. This could be possible by changing the activities and the interaction of

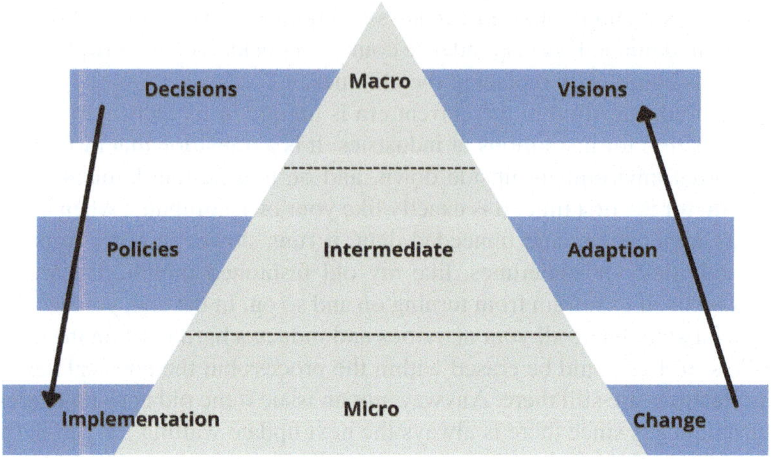

Fig. 6.6 Transition levels (*Resource* Author's own resource)

the lower levels, which has been remarkably happening since COVIDE 19. There are few institutions on the macro level that makes the overall decisions where companies on the intermediate level in cooperation with governments interoperate them to policies, rules and regulations under the form of Public Private Partnership (PPP). On the micro level the daily activities of social economic attitudes have to change as a necessary response.

When the activities and habits of the consumers changed practically overnight, many companies simply could not catch up. The increase of online shopping is one instance, where many small and medium businesses could not adapt to the new trend and were not able to survive. Those who are on the macro level without offering a deep explanation of the expected results. This created hesitation on the micro level to submit, fearing to be excluded from the market in the long term while supporting to increase the wealth of those on the macro level.

Ultimately, new forms are a natural result of the accumulation of knowledge and inventions, thus transition is a vital jump that could be effectively used if the leader is skilled enough to do so. Where the transition is more painful in its uncertainty and therefore needs coordinated collective energy and acceptance to overcome any challenges.

Despite the presence of the macro level at the top and any government policies supporting this change, this shift would be impossible without a buy in at all levels. Important to note that women and youth are the major players at the micro level, they are the new point of focus for the macro level. There is now almost a sense of urgency to include them in this transition in order to allow for it to even take place.

The same scenario applied to the internal structure with all types of organisations in both public and private sectors (and non-profit). Since the global transitions can neither be commanded nor controlled, the single organisation transition becomes more complex to manage.

Let's try to categorise transition management as a model through analysing its principles and activities that help the sustain of systems as well as organisations (Silvestri et al. 2018). Figure 6.7 shows the transition management principles where strategic activities are related to the 'culture' of a society. Among these activities, processes of the vision development, strategic discussions, and long-term goal formulation are crucial for transition management. Tactical activities are leading activities that are benefit driven and connected to controlled structures and its institutional network. This includes policies, as well as regulations and rules. The framework of transition management can be viewed as a model of sustainable development which ultimately aims to redirect development (Kemp et al. 2007).

Operational activities are short-term actions and administration of practices that manage the daily activities (Silvestri et al. 2018). Reflexive activities is performance management, assessment, and a comprehensive evaluation for the internal and external dynamics. Reflexive activities are performance measurement as a comprehensive assessment of internal and external dynamics. This is necessary to measure system efficiency to align operational activity with strategic objectives as well as alert in case of disruptions.

Over a century, societies in the MENA have been going through long-term processes that shake the existing structures. Stability was never the real status of daily life. The private sector had consequently experienced many transitions that impacted social dynamics which caused demographic transition in several cases like in Palestine, Iraq, and Syria.

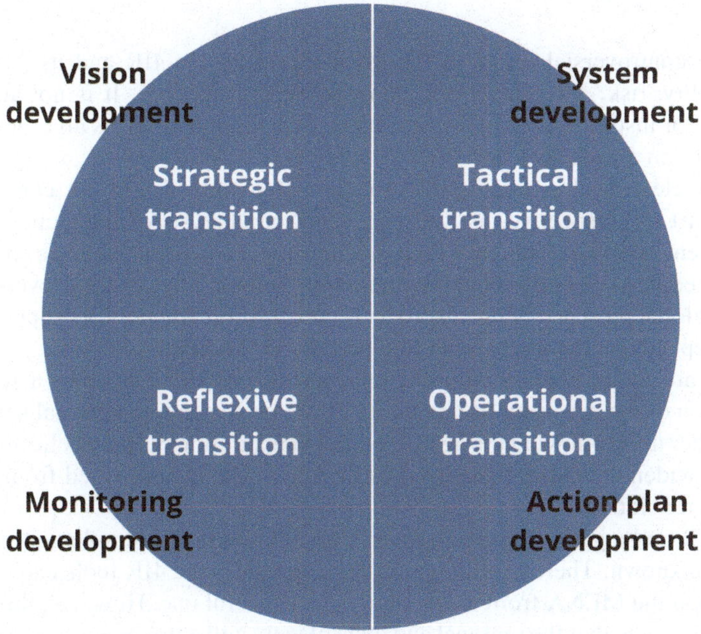

Fig. 6.7 Transition management elements (*Source* Author's own resource)

The transition in some MENA countries might be seen as less complex, from an institutional point of view than the one in more advanced countries. This is due to several reasons. First, people are less equipped to protest against government interference. Second, the transition proposed to be in line with advocating political and economic reforms that the people have been waiting for (but it is not). Third, the high flexibility of institutions to reform in regard to its connection to the centre of the financial system. However, it is astonishing how important the link is between economic transition and individuals beliefs. The transition in the MENA also requires its own time, as the role of AI continues to draw more controversy as a man waves further into its potential. Potentially leading us to try to "play god". The region which is still heavily influenced by Abrahamic religions must find a way to reconcile technological developments with their own faith in order to allow progress to happen without fear of compromising their values.

This *status quo* creates opportunities for people to change their perspectives about employment. In addition to this, the need to create new business models which allow new forms of sustainable and flexible employment to respond to the uncertainty of the 4IR. This calls for a specific response from academic institutions to offer learning-experienced based programmes as a main element that moves the wheels of SDG. Eventually, this contributes to the regional transition from terror status to a peaceful one which is in line with the SDG that leads to economic growth and development.

6.5 Summary

There are controversial views in the ME concerning the 4IR and its "dark side" of inequality, risk, and unexpected consequences in its core. It is not an internal transition for institutions or industries. It is a transition that affects all aspects of life and society on a wide scale.

Nevertheless, such a large transformation of society would not come without a huge shift in perspective, as well as a renewed analysis of interacting with the changing environment. This calls for a specific innovative response and a cooperation from the people as this shift would be impossible without a buy-in at all levels. Despite the huge global presence of the macro level, any government policies supporting this change depends on the micro level (the people) to succeed.

There are many players who are reluctant to cooperate without a reasonable explanation of the necessity of transition. Those prefer finding national solutions to issues rather than following the agenda of global institutions as they believe imitating will only widen the current gap even further than what had resulted from previous industrial revolutions.

The 4IR and a great transition is necessary, but on how to implement and adapt remains unknown. There is still a hope that eventually the 4IR tools can contribute to transition the MENA from terror status to a peaceful one. However, this remains dependent on whether the regional and local players will employ this in an innovative way for the benefit of the people rather than for their own job security.

Bibliography

Abd-Almenem H, Ismael M (2021) Research project on the economic implications of the Fourth Industrial Revolution

Chui M, James M, Mehdi, M (2016) Where machines could replace humans—and where they can't (yet). The technical potential for automation differs dramatically across sectors and activities

Dankbaar B (1993) Economic crisis and institutional change, the crisis of Fordism from the perspective of the automobile industry

Diakopoulos N (2019) A knowledge economy: how artificial intelligence can enhance journalism. http://www.milwaukeeindependent.com/syndicated/knowledge-economy-artificial-intelligence-can-enhance-journalism/

Feridm B, Rabah A (2019) The Middle East and North Africa cannot miss the Fourth Industrial Revolution. https://blogs.worldbank.org/arabvoices/middle-east-and-north-africa-cannot-miss-fourth-industrial-revolution

Ismael HAM (2021) Research project on the economic implications of the Fourth Industrial Revolution

Kemp R, Loorbach D, Rotmans J (2007) Transition management as a model for managing processes of co-evolution towards sustainable development. Inter J Sustain Dev World Ecol 14:78–91. https://doi.org/10.1080/13504500709469709

Kimur F, Rashesh S, Dionisius N (2019) The digital and Fourth Industrial Revolution and ASEAN economic transformation. Economic Research institute for ASEAN and East Asia

Kotuliĉ EŠRVIKVaR (2020) Knowledge economy indicators and their impact on the sustainable competitiveness of the EU countries. Sustain 12. https://doi.org/10.3390/su12104172

McGinnis D (2020) The 4th Industrial Revolution (4IR) is a fusion of advances in artificial intelligence (AI), robotics, the Internet of Things (IoT), genetic engineering, quantum computing, and more. https://www.salesforce.com/blog/what-is-the-fourth-industrial-revolution-4ir/

McGinnis J (2013) Innovation and inequality. https://www.nationalaffairs.com/publications/detail/innovation-and-inequality

Mckeon C (2018) Why the automotive industry will always need humans. https://blog.v-hr.com/blog/why-the-automotive-industry-will-always-need-humans

Nations U (2015) Transforming our world—the 2030 agenda for sustainable development

Ofori G (2003) Preparing Singapore's construction industry for the knowledge-based economy: practices, procedures and performance. Constr Manag Econ 21:113–125. https://doi.org/10.1080/0144619032000079680

Pakhomov EAKYYRNN (2018) The role and importance of knowledge economy as a platform for formation of industry 4.0. In: Industry 4.0: industrial revolution of the 21st century. Springer, pp 73–82

Samara W (2018) Performance measurement in the public sector Berlin

Schwab K (2016) The Fourth Industrial Revolution world economic forum

Shearer E, Stirling R, Pasquarelli W (2020) Government AI readiness index

Silvestri G, Wittmayer JM, Schipper K, Kulabako R, Oduro-Kwarteng S, Nyenje P, Komakech H, Van Raak R (2018) Transition management for improving the sustainability of WASH services in informal settlements in Sub-Saharan Africa—an exploration. Sustain 10(11):4052. https://www.mdpi.com/2071-1050/10/11/4052

Soni oaN (2019) Impact of artificial intelligence on businesses: from research, innovation, market deployment to future shifts in business models. https://www.researchgate.net/publication/332898261_Impact_of_Artificial_Intelligence_on_Businesses_from_Research_Innovation_Market_Deployment_to_Future_Shifts_in_Business_Models

UN (2015) Concepts of inequality, development issues no. 1

UNICEF (2020) Annual Report. UNICIF

Chapter 7
Perspectives on Education in the ME

Malaka Samara

7.1 The Educational System's Perception

The education system gets more difficult considering the complications and conditions that the ME has been experiencing for a century. The education system in areas where there is political strife necessitates methodical formulation of policies to ensure access to education. This comprises teaching methods and curriculum, as well as regulations that balance the environment's receptiveness to global and regional changes and requirements.

Hence, it is critical to progress toward an alternate paradigm that can generate people who can collaborate to address barriers in various domains. According to various studies, organisations and corporations are increasingly realising the benefits of education in achieving specific SDGs. However, innovation in industry and technology that comes from up to bottom alone will not be sufficient. It requires a paradigm shift from individual innovation to a collective adoption of new education methods, as a fundamental element, is required for sustainable change. In short, education is a serious means of instilling new perspectives for society and the economy (Ludwig 2020). More specifically, a transitional education is a conclusive asset to set a transitional economy.

The manifestations and activities of the 4IR are increasing so is education, which means re-identifying the current educational model as corresponding to the new needs brought from a transitional environment. AI is expected to replace around 30% of the jobs which means 30% of the people must be engaged in a new form of learning in order to be able to compete within the new economic social order. Analysing the current education output is necessary to understand the reasons for its decline in the ME and to provide a realistic framework to transit education system. In order to do that there are three aspects of perceptions to consider: The educational system's perception, the educational providers' perspectives, and the engaged individuals' perception.

W. Samara and M. Samara, *The Power of Perceptions in the Middle East*,
Perspectives on Development in the Middle East and North Africa (MENA) Region,
https://doi.org/10.1007/978-3-030-99150-0_7

In the last three decades, several industries started recruiting higher qualified employees and in response multiple policies promoting education as a tool for higher income and well-being. Societies have witnessed a significant increase of new providers for education even in marginalised communities. Despite this trend, it has become more obvious these days, that most jobs no longer require the common degree-level academic qualifications. Not only in the ME but also in the developed societies as well. For example, in the US in 2010, only 20% of jobs required a Bachelor of Arts (B.A.) degree, 43% required a high-school education, and 26% did not even require any educational degree. Yet, 40% of the population continues to pursue higher education (Spicer 2016) perhaps for other reasons, such as seeking social status. In the ME, this social status can even pertain to personal aspects such as marriage.

This environment has led to a large discrepancy between the output of education and market demand. The quality of education and the skills of graduates are incompatible with the needs of the market rapid change.

Research conducted in the field of education has concluded that the MENA is facing great difficulties in this area, especially countries that experience heavy political conflict. Furthermore, the adoption of traditional approaches in policy formulation has less connection with the new era requirements of the workforce. The absence of strategic planning in the region hinders the interaction with the requirements of the knowledge-based economy. Hence, the output of education, in most of cases, cannot compete on either the regional or the global level. Figure 7.1 shows the process through the educational input and the impact. Where Table 7.1 explains the gap of each level.

Through several reports, the World Bank indicated that the main causes of educational delay:

- The relationship between education and economic progress, as well as a lack of the knowledge, skills, and values required to participate meaningfully in economic activity.
- The gap between educational outputs with the needs of the economic development process, has tiger the unemployment issue.
- The gap between the domains of communication and information technology, as well as the knowledge-based economy in comparison to industrialised countries.
- The disparity between the levels of competencies required for development activities and the competencies of graduates of the regional educational systems.

Political, social, and economic development policies in the MENA follow a conceptual and applied pattern dictated by a globalised perception. This is then adopted by local authorities that employ a wide range of pressure methods to promote its concepts without investing in the quality of the education and its output (Khasawneh et al. 2014) see Fig. 7.1. The purpose of the educational system has changed and now there is a loss in the balance in all levels that education was created for from the beginning.

The result is an ever widening gap between the output of education and the demands of the labour market. The output of education continues to suffer from

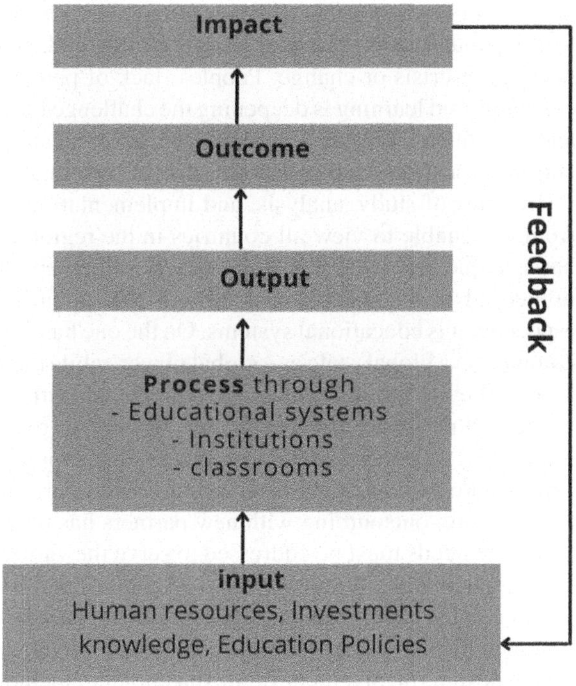

Fig. 7.1 Education input and impact (*Source* Author's own design)

Table 7.1 Education Index

index	The gap	Level
Local economy and market needs	Output does not fill the need	Outcome
Regional needs	Quality, curriculum, and critical thinking not in the focus	Process
Knowledge- based economy/4IR needs	Innovation, knowledge production and technology development are absent	Process and education culture
Development needs	Monopoly and absence of competency	Impact
Policies needs	Ill advised public and private leadership All stakeholders involvement	Purpose and input

an outdated and unadaptable curriculum, with little to no inclusion from technological or competency-based approaches to close this gap. Moreover, a lack of competent authority to implement and supervise educational policies has only exacerbated this issue.

For instance, the curriculum is no longer designed for teaching and learning certain personal and professional skills such as leadership, communication, innovation and other meta-competencies (Samara 2018). More importantly, there is no self-reliant learning that is work-based learning that allows adaptation to any transition occurring in times of crisis or change. Peoples' lack of perception of the difference between education and learning is deepening the challenge to achieve quality education output and outcomes. However, as expected in the meantime, the increasing quantity of current education continues to devalue its own quality (Kamel 2014).

In terms of study, analysis, and implementation of educational policies, it is far from reasonable to view all countries in the region in the same light. Each country has a unique set of internal challenges, development indicators and policies that have influenced the overall course of events in that country that can affect many aspects but especially it is educational systems. On the one hand, there are regimes like Qatar that compete on a global scale as a global player, while there are regimes like Yemen at the bottom. Figure 7.2 shows the quality of the educational system in fourteen countries in the region. Qatar has realised the urgency to radically change their educational system and its policies so they emphasised on employing technology, increasing the expenditure on education, by creating various curricula in different school systems. Furthermore, outsourcing with new partners has played a main role.

Future needs must be addressed to serve the various goals of education and make them applicable to all economic sectors (Schröder 2019). In general, education should respond to the rapid changes occurring in the surrounding regional and global environment. This response is usually reformed which consist in a framework of smart policy design, involvement of all stakeholders including society, a favourable institutional, policy and social context and a successful policy implementation process (Viennet and Pont 2017).

Preparing frameworks in the ME, at first sight, does not even seem unfeasible. The documentation for certain policies, they are well written and even well-strategised.

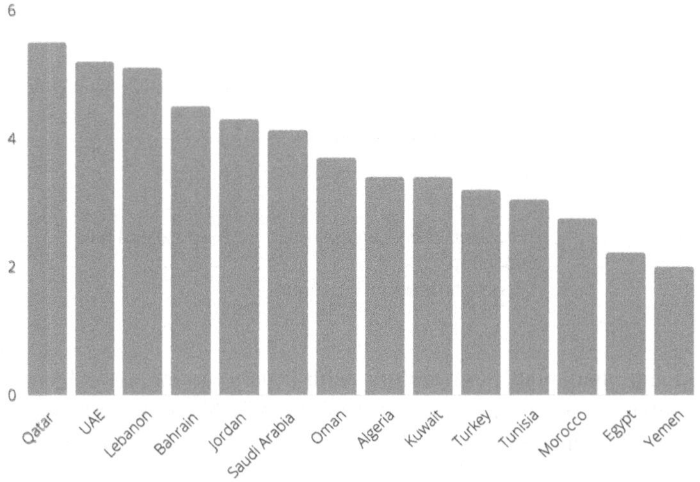

Fig. 7.2 Quality of MENA's educational systems (*Source* Author's own resource)

However, while written with some strategy of implementation, the intention to implement is still lacking. Such policies require competent leaders to bring them to the people, but the current state of incompetency in leadership has continued to affect this.

There are several reasons, obviously, those who prepare these strategies are either foreigners or local experts who no longer live in the country and therefore their role is limited only to a written strategy and do not take a role in executing their strategies. In most cases, these experts do not have enough understanding of the intersection between education and the economic and development aspects as well as the political conflicts impact on education in many regions in the ME. Therefore the strategy is often to simulate plans of the developed countries which does not consider the culture of education in the ME.

Another reason is the lack of local infrastructure in education meaning that there is a constant external influence in the system. One more parlous reason is, to put bluntly, budgeting. The more vulnerable countries in the region are currently in debt from vast loans they originally received as 'assets'. This has naturally affected government funding in certain institutions and education and healthcare have unfortunately suffered in order to repay these loans. Moreover, the expansion of security and warfare have further drained the budgets of the main sectors. While many eco-political leaders have good understanding of these implications, they prioritise their own interests at risk of keeping their countries in crippling debt, even if maintaining their own interests comes with its own set of difficulties.

7.2 Educational Providers' Perspectives and Collective Perspectives

There is a proverb that states: "Egyptians writes, Lebanese print and Iraqis read". This was considered almost fact up until Western colonisation. Children were often sent to Cairo, Damascus or Bagdad for education and then come back to benefit the community with their acquired knowledge. Thus we see the initial purpose of education as an exchange to build and maintain societies where everyone must be educated to A certain level. Obviously, in the last seven decades, this purpose has changed over time and THE general narrative about education has changed.

In the last two decades, there has been an increasing number of private schools and private universities that all are commercial and profit-driven prompting the changing role of public universities (Robertson 2010).

Private universities have evolved in adapting to market needs, with local authorities assisting in closing the gap by avoiding the bureaucracy of public university education and providing development in areas not covered by public university curricula. Private universities, on the other hand, use profit and loss criteria to choose which degree programmes to teach. Just as any other company in the private sector, the tendency is to opt for the lowest investment cost and the highest profit margin (Sahab et al.).

It is by now well known that the huge illusionary "demand" on education is created by private providers in the field to generate high profit as an industry. Yet this revenue, rather than going towards education and quality outcomes, goes directly to investors' personal profit and to expand administrative duties. The management of the process itself became more important than learning. To briefly summarise, the core for people is learning and living while the providers for such services became a profit generating private sector under a decade without any government intervention on their policies and fees (Heyneman 1997).

Consequently, a graduate gains some reputation as a holder of a degree despite its holder is not being qualified to meet the needs of the market. While on the one hand, we have an increasing number of graduates who have attended higher education, on the other higher education lacks the foundations of scientific research and does not focus on producing knowledge and enhancing learning and creativity (Mahmud 2013).

The majority of people perceive educational degrees as the highest form of learning that one can achieve. However, as previously stated, many of these degrees are now devoid of their content and are mere certificates. The result is that its holders can compete for neither at the domestic nor the international market. For example, a lack of foreign language ability such as English is a big challenge to promote higher education and research for knowledge production, especially in science and technology majors. This renders non-English speaking students unable to study in competitive universities, so their own hard-earned certificate holds little value for the major studied, thereby further reducing chances of employment for their holder. University is less of an educational institution and more of a lifestyle. It is a kind of prestige and aspirational goal but lacking in any practical use. The reality is that degrees have now become not adequate and an obstacle to their holder from progressing and seeking real competencies that are required for the 4IR.

With the 4IR fast approaching, it is imperative to promote a culture of lifelong learning and not simply learning to obtain a degree and then stop. This life-long learning requires experimentation as we approach new challenges. For certain SDG indicators focussing on skill development within education, there remains the focus of life-long learning as crucial to attain these.

The 4IR and out-coming challenges need people who are self-motivated, accept and adapt to change through various forms of lifelong learning (Schröder 2019). Learning is a necessity as life-long learning, it should be combined with experiential learning and depends on individuals to seek further and advanced skills, competencies and knowledge (Aggarwal 2005). For SDGs, there are efforts to strengthen skill development in education within a framework of lifelong learning (Comyn 2018).

The illusion of obtaining a certified degree has created a group of incompetent workforces including those employed in the educational institutions themselves. For example, lecturers may be experts in their field of study, but they possess little to no expertise in teaching or mentoring. As of now they only deliver defined information to a class without teaching critical thinking, reflection and searching. Students study only for requirements—the grade and for the exam, not for gaining real knowledge for personal development. There is a level of awareness that students must have about knowledge obtainment. Allowing as a result to neglect the pupil as an independent entity who has their own characteristics that ought to be addressed at an early age in school. At the same time, the responsibility of the instructors remains limited and unable to teach at diverse levels. This is again because of the lack of self-reliant learning for most teachers. This educational model is designed in a way led to hindering the students' ability to form their own perceptions about life, societies and the way they interact with themselves and others. Besides that, during the past five decades, instructors have been gradually developing a negative view of the teaching profession and the regressive nature of the educational process in the region. They intend to be employed with the respective national Ministry of Education for social security and to earn a steady salary. Concluding that most of the education systems in the MENA region do aim to direct the students' perception and life style that affected the education quality output.

It is somewhat commonplace now that education systems tend to be "employee factories", where the curricula should be designed in order to provide the economic system with the workforce it needs. However, these institutions do not obligate people to pursue their programmes and hence self-learning was always an option that very few people in the region chose. Some independent local centres or non-profit organisations have played a crucial role here, offering various educational programs outside the scope of mainstream educational institutions. This allowed the self-learners to explore new areas. Yet, self-learners find themselves over qualified for their respective industries so either they compromise to find employment there under the supervision of less qualified but result-driven leaders or they leave to another country where their expertise is more appreciated. To be blunt, these local institutions are not designed to include and empower competent people.

Without understanding the requirements of the 4IR, people in the MENA would not be able to realise the urgent need for having a competent workforce. However, people's intentions behind pursuing higher education are not always to gain skills and competencies. We can define three categories of undergraduates: the ones who are aware of their limited abilities and therefore deliberately opt for degrees in order to climb to the top of the system quickly. The second is the group of people who unconsciously undergo a weak learning process yet find themselves satisfied with the limited end result from their education. The third group concerns the few scholars and researchers who are keen to seek genuine knowledge and learn, but simply do not have the means without support or scholarships. The first two groups become convinced by the benefit of social recognition and actively engage in perpetuating this illusion. Even though, neither are really satisfied, admitting to the reality of the situation is simply not an option. These people lose hope and motivation as their energy is hindered and misdirected culminating in a less productive and competitive workforce. The first two groups are likely to be the ones who lose their jobs as a result of digitalisation.

The money accumulation has hugely influenced the region and its economic perception, most notably with the illusion of the demand. The educational institution represents the popular belief that one thinks their newfound knowledge will allow them to open up the sky and change the world. These institutions clearly analyse the psychology of the people as clients as they must guarantee the demand from people to keep up their huge profits. The by-product is to keep the positive popular perception about these institutes. This perception allows people to simply accept what these universities offer without question; if you can pay, you join the class. No other criteria are required. Well except school results, but it is rather used against the student under what they called "equivalent study", which is a new trend in the educational system that allows unqualified students to join the course only if they are willing to pay three or four times the ordinary qualified students. Competition and aspiration are sorely lacking in such cases and is becoming limited only to those who can afford it.

Despite all the facts, there are several varying perceptions about private education in the region (Wilkens 2011). Those who view the private educational institutes as an important tool for development and enhancing students where public schools fail to do so, while others perceive this as a corrupted system that will lead to a bigger gap between the education system and the market. Business-driven institutions have left many people borrowing loans from the banks to obtain a degree which has become now part and parcel of getting educated. The original idea is that people learn a skill or a job in order to make living out of it, not to borrow money to get a certificate without any practical skills. This hinders any development in society and wastes the energy of the young people who are not yet aware of the reality ahead. A third perception views both public and private institutions as similarly designed to some extent, where the curricula, for example, are not carefully developed and updated based on external intervention.

The only distinction, in this case, is each individual and the way the man interacts with the educational environment. Here, the student as a product was influenced by several factors like the awareness of the family, the way this person identifies life goals, adding to that the extra training, workshops and other programmes this person was investing in. As a result, the graduate can become more skilled than their peers even if they have attended exactly the same programme for several years. Thus, the national economy counts on those who are willing to be innovative and competent not only to implement a successful transition but also to assure sustainability (Širá et al. 2020). Research must be conducted in order to understand how education should respond for the 4IR and the impact of digital transformation on 'creating or deleting' new jobs in all economic sectors.

7.3 Education Transition

As mentioned in Chap. 2, most of the educational systems in the region were influenced or even designed by the West colonising countries to maintain their interests in the region. Even though many policies and strategies have undergone reform, there has been a significant shift in several countries, especially in the Gulf region as they are highly aware of the requirements of competing in the current era. For example, the UAE is competing on the global level to be ahead in AI and IoT. But the case is a lot worse for the less fortunate countries in the region. Learning from other systems and exchanging external knowledge through cooperation with specialists, scholars, and scientist is essential for each nation to grow. But the national goals must be clear to everyone engaged in the process.

The 4IR requires a new order for educational systems, especially due to the increasing trend of distance learning. This opens an opportunity for the countries in the region to re-evaluate their own faulty systems and align the national goals of education with global ones. In particular, all stakeholders (the education system leaders, the participants, and the providers) have to find a common strategic interest which is in line with strategic national goals.

A transition to a knowledge-based economy requires a comprehensive response as reforming current models is no longer sufficient. This transition also means a shift in collective understanding, in which a new model is introduced together with identifying the long term goals of education. Figure 7.3 shows four necessary principles to develop an education system where serious decisions and actions must be taken

Fig. 7.3 Developing education system (*Resource* Author's own resource)

in the strategic, tactical and operational levels. This includes monitoring and performance management that assure improving the learning process and the benefits of education as a sector. Otherwise, a growing unemployment rate is waiting just around the corner. If education continues to be perceived as an industry producing human resources only for the economy, it reduces the quality of knowledge production in society. It should be viewed in a more holistic way that is linked to development, prosperity and well being.

Eliminating the learning process by educating the required technical skills is maybe, sufficient for the capitalist market. Both the market and the economy are crucial for the sustainability of a country. But the economic system is not the nation, it is only one element which was at the first hand formed from the need of societies. A state or nation is not solely a market. People should be more qualified to deal reasonably with their communities that need their own "*raison d'etre*" beyond generating profit. Plato stated that the fundamental task of education is to value reason and encourage the student to be reasonable—essentially foster good judgement (Siegel 2020). This includes valuing wisdom above pleasure, honour, and other "less-worthy" pursuits. This is exactly the opposite of the current education systems in the region. People are pursuing an information gaining system that teaches techniques and information produced by the forces influencing the market. People educate themselves into in a way following instructions and burdening themselves with life responsibilities of a high standard living, even approaching banks for more loans to cope with the promoted idealistic lifestyle. The result is no space to find purpose, to find wisdom, no ability to participate in good judgment. Communities then lose their balance, and sooner or later the economy as well.

We can all agree that the economy is essential for the existence and continuity of a nation. The current AI era needs more than ever both learning directions in parallel. The learning direction provided by those developing the software for AI, and the more traditional intellectuals in order to maintain its social responsibility. The combination between both was, to a certain extent, effectively implemented in the past, when the family was the core of production in the ME societies.

A comprehensive experience was a package to be taken from one generation to another. A profession was not only limited to professional skills but also personal skills and competencies. This includes language learning, creativity, systems understanding, the wisdom of natural intelligence and thus winding the perceptions. This is what was called in the past the traditional vocational education.

For decades, many factors have been affecting the educational system in the ME and thus hindering the quality and relevance of education, that in its turn hinders social and economic development. The 4IR is based and depends on highly competent people. Education systems in the ME have no capability to respond to future needs if they refuse to adopt certain strategies in teaching and learning.

The educational system in the ME has been and remains dependent on external policies, international funds and implementing agencies rooted in colonialism. British, German, French and Ottoman schools were built with the aim of creating vocational schools for students from poor families and orphans to teach them a certain profession to achieve self-sufficiency. However, education never addressed the national interest or identity of any country. Educational systems in the ME have been working on devoting a culture of indoctrination and memorisation instead of understanding and freedom of thought and creativity. This culture has failed to provide the necessary skills to succeed in the labour market at both levels; the individual and the professional levels. This has created a very high level of unemployment and has laid the foundations for the culture of ignorance, unawareness, and unwavering acceptance of any given information.

There is a difference between unemployment and unemployability. Unemployability is not a catch-all statement for those not working, rather it concerns people who cannot meet the needs of the market and thus creating less productivity and effective output at the workplace. In other words, there is no quality for the work because of a lack of quality in education. As a result, the issue is not the level of unemployment, but the high level of unemployability (Usulor 2018). Due to ineffective tracking strategies, this is unfortunately, the case in many ME countries.

Separating learners from experiential and self-regulated learning hinders social and economic development in communities and will contribute to the level of unemployment among academic graduates (Comyn 2018).

In times of crisis, the first areas of employment and education to affected are the vocational areas, or "Worked-Based Learning (WBL)". Someone who is training to be a carpenter for instance, must be present in the workshop to receive the required practical training. Nevertheless, as remote learning becomes the trend (especially due to the ongoing COVID-19 pandemic), past professional skills such as these are at risk due to the lack of available and adaptable teaching methods (Samara 2021). Thus, experiential learning, as well as the self-regulation processes of the learner are crucial to meet the current demands in terms of skilled employees for today as well as the future of work in general. Current economic crises are a call to awaken governments and individuals to the importance of the rapidly changing nature of work to address the challenges and be able to prepare education programmes focusing on immediate youth employment.

In general, the educational system in the region has not been modernised in what was supposed to be compatible with the second and third industrial revolutions. Therefore, it has not been viewed as a pillar of development. Rather, it was significantly neglected. If we look at the experience of other countries in Southeast Asia that placed great importance on education, such as Singapore. Singapore is a remarkable example of a third-world country that transformed into one most competitive economies in the world. Some may point to its strategic foreign diplomacy and its ability to attract investors as an explanation for this development. However, many forget the importance of its collaboration among the population and their trust in the Singaporean government. One could argue this trust was built through the transparency and lack of corruption provided by the authorities. However, to really understand this trust and this collaboration is to understand its education system. An effective education system will always lead to high productivity, not simply because of the benefits for the market but for the whole of society (Tan 1997, pp. 303–312). This education system experienced changing curricula and new methods to allow Singapore to make its mark as one of the modern success stories.

While other previously mentioned countries have played with the idea of adapting educational curricula, Singapore had intensified their investment into education and training programmes that match market needs. For example, as the Information Technology sector continues to take a central tole, Singapore established MySkillsFuture portal to provide all citizens a space for learning necessary IT skills. This not only is providing teaching, but also empowering the population to teach themselves and engage in life-long learning and address their own knowledge gaps.

There are four official languages in Singapore; Mandarin Chinese, Tamil, Malay and English. Although, the country is primarily unified by English, there remains a bilingual policy in education where all students are required to learn another language. This enabled researchers to not be limited by language, as well as enabling cultural interchanges inside and outside of Singapore. This is also bolstered by the training provided for teachers which adhere to a WBL strategy to develop their ability to teach.

Akin to the ME, and really is applicable everywhere, is the importance of family encouragement and support. In Singapore, the success of education has led to families understanding its importance and even becoming stakeholders in its success.

As conclusion, a holistic framework engaging all stakeholders and factors is needed in order to adapt to the I4R. The ME can learn on several levels, diplomacy and long term partnership, the engagement with the external expertise and research, transparency and the people trust, as well as innovation and workforce importance.

7.4 Summary

We have established the need of shifting the common perspective, and one of the biggest controllers of that is the education system. Currently the education system in the ME is facing various challenges simply to meet the changes in the labor market due to AI. However, these challenges vary from one country to another depending on the economic and political situation.

Education is typically viewed as a crucial asset for social and economic development. However, the region finds that education has become even a hindrance to this development as there is a clear gap between education output and the market demand in the region. Therefore, it becomes inevitable necessity to invest in education and change its paradigm that can provide the market and the people with the knowledge to manage the 4IR.

This analysis of education in the ME consist of understanding what the intentions and perceptions are of education. Namely, the perception of those running the educational system, the perception of those providing education, as well as its students and the perception on digital transformation.

4IR and digitalisation have created a new demand for new competencies in response to the changing nature of work itself. This requires teachers and students now to engage in self-reliant learning, experiential learning, and life-long learning and training programs to address their own knowledge and skills gaps that will arise more frequently in the wake of new technological breakthroughs.

Education systems in most countries in the ME have no capability to respond to future needs if they refuse to develop and implement certain strategies in teaching and learning especially in light of the absent of strategic planning and effective implementation for education policies and strategies. This will hinder development and prevents the economic growth in many countries.

References

Aggarwal A (2005) ILO recommendation 195 concerning human resources development: education, training and lifelong learning

Comyn P (2018). Skills, employability and lifelong learning in the Sustainable Development Goals and the 2030 labour market. Int J Training Res 16. https://doi.org/10.1080/14480220.2018.1576311

Heyneman S (1997) The quality of education in the Middle East and North Africa (MENA). Int J Educ Develop 17(4):449–466

Kamel S (2014) Education in the Middle East: challenges and opportunities international conference ICTO, Paris

Khasawneh S, Jaradat I, Muna Ho (2014) The reality of education in the Arab world and ways to develop it. http://www.alecso.org/publications/wp-content/uploads/2020/11/العربي-الوطن-في-العام-التعليم-واقع

Ludwig V (2020) Transition to circular economy: the role of education from youth to higher education. https://epale.ec.europa.eu/en/blog/transition-circular-economy-role-education-youth-higher-education

Mahmud S (2013) The higher education in Iraq. Challenges and recommendations. J Adv Soc Res 2(9):255–264

Robertson S (2010) Challenges facing universities in a globalizing world. International seminar on quality in higher education: indicators and challenges, Bristol.

Sahab E (2019) Al-Shakhori I, Hassa, A-Z, Khairy A. Private universities in the Arab World.

Samara M (2018) Curricula approaches and competence development for secondary vocational education schools in Palestine. In: TVET@Asia 11, 1–12. Retrieved 15 July 2018, http://www.tvet-online.asia/issue11/samara_tvet11.pdf

Samara M (2021) Towards E-learning in TVET: setting and developing E-competence framework for TVET teachers in Palestine. TVET@Asia 16.

Schröder T (2019) A regional approach for the development of TVET systems in the light of the 4th industrial revolution: the regional association of vocational and technical education in Asia. Int J Training Res. https://doi.org/10.1080/14480220.2019.1629728

Siegel H (2020) Philosophy of education. Encyclopedia Britannica. https://www.britannica.com/topic/psychologism

Širá E, Vavrek R, Vozárová IK, Kotulicˇ R (2020. Knowledge economy indicators and their impact on the sustainable competitiveness of the EU countries. Sustainability 12. https://doi.org/10.3390/su12104172

Spicer A (2016) The knowledge economy is a myth. We don't need more universities to feed it. https://www.theguardian.com/commentisfree/2016/may/18/knowledge-economy-myth-more-universities-degree

Tan J (1997) Education and colonial transition in Singapore and Hong Kong: comparisons and contrasts. Comp Educ 33:303–312

Usulor N (2018) Unemployment versus unemployability (The case of Nigerian graduates)

Viennet R, Pont B (2017) Education policy implementation: a literature review and proposed framework. OECD.ORG
Wilkens K (2011) Higher education reform in the Arab World. Islamic World Forum

Chapter 8
Development Opportunities

Warda Samara and Malaka Samara

8.1 Nations Branding and Development

Warda Semara

The region has moved from geographic division, economic division and currently 'digital division' this perhaps emphasises the current division between the developed and underdeveloped countries in the region. These divisions are based on the criteria of the contemporary global economic system that blooms in some countries and actively hinder others. A region like the MENA—which contains more than 6% of the world's population—is classified from the globalisation perspective, there is an unfairness in the right of many countries. There may be a convergence in the lifestyle, history, culture, and economic development between the populations, but several remarkable differences still exist, such as the global and regional roles. The extent of the differences between Lebanon, for example, and Sudan, represented in the way of social life, culture, customs and traditions and the consequences of not adhering to them. The political structure and the basis of its dynamics interaction, in addition to the climate, environment, tourism and economy are distinct from each other. Adding to that, the separated history and colonialism that affected each country. Despite all these fundamental differences, the two countries are classified under the same name 'developing'. This comparison is not to preference any of them, but it had led to an undeniable impact on both countries. This is an emphasis on the importance of the peculiarity of individual states. What makes the cooperation between individuals or between nations possible and necessary is indeed the differentiations that feature. Therefore, the identity and the image of each individual state must be defined and distinguished which requires collective cooperation on a national level.

Divisions in countries are created by global forces as these forces have a lot to invest in these countries' resources. Therefore, 'branding' them under terms like 'developing' directly serves external best interests. It is important to perceive the regional interaction between functional and symbolic theories of borders. It is

W. Samara and M. Samara, *The Power of Perceptions in the Middle East*,
Perspectives on Development in the Middle East and North Africa (MENA) Region,
https://doi.org/10.1007/978-3-030-99150-0_8

possible to differentiate both sides. Therefore, a consideration of both distinction and cooperation through these borders is essential (Sendhardt 2013). There is no doubt that manifestations of globalisation have invaded all aspects of life in countries that neither possess the brakes nor tools that enable them to interact in a balanced manner. Globalisation advances systematically in these areas, where diplomacy is employed at first, and then escalated to attractive economic prospects, humanitarian aid, urbanisation, and in many cases, even armies were used. This has created an acceptance in both the population and their leaders of the solutions of globalisation, and completely ruling out the validity of any solutions presented on the ground.

Consequently, the way MENA region is perceived by the rest of the world is shrouded in misrepresentation. The region is poorly represented through main narratives that are dominated by different kinds of institutions, not limited to the media. It is true that the region is politically unstable with uncertainty and high risk. However, the region is rich in the diversity of its resources, oil, gas, history and connection to ancient civilisations, and its people as human resources, specifically youth. Therefore, a new narrative should be adopted locally and reflected internationally in order to change the way that the world is interacting with the region on a popular and political level. This narrative should brand each nation as a separate entity within a bigger rebranding of the region. For example, the 'Fertile Crescent' was a successful label representing Iraq and Greater Syria at that time which was basically based on the archaeological studies and the direct connection of this region with ancient civilisations. This is an example of a nation branding without affecting the identity of the people. It rather opens opportunities and cooperation on different levels. Branding is not only limited to the whole nation, it includes branding individual cities like Jerusalem, Damascus, Bagdad, Berlin, London and Hong Kong which is necessary to enhance the local economy and diversity and exchange among other nations. These cities soon began to create fixed brands of notoriety which also became representations of their countries over generations.

Moreover, there are coastal cities that were destroyed in modern warfare, such as Haifa and Tripoli. These cities were marked by their development in culture, arts and architecture, and were mentioned extensively, explicitly, in Arabic poetry and literature as centres of civilisations.

Understanding the mechanisms and the reasons of the destruction of these cities is essential. It not only concerns physical destruction and its associated consequences, it affects the image of the nation that includes the spiritual and cultural standing of these cities and their nations. Besides, the current struggle that is trying to erase them from the '*machine experience mind*' and the collective global memory. Some of these capitals were the centres of learning and education. Egypt, for example, is one of the countries in the region that has recently increased its attention to its national branding through culture, art, history, and education. Cairo, throughout human history, has been a centre for learning and knowledge exchange knowledge through research. Despite any ongoing challenges, it remains the capital of learning in the region. Enhancing the role of *Al-Azhar* university as a learning centre, pre-university education system, was essential as it is a metaphor for both Arabs and Muslims as one of the oldest higher educational institutions in the world that was established in AD 972 (Saat 2018). To this day, it is still a very important institution for learning in the region. There is a fundamental argument concerning the relationship between national GDP and development. Nevertheless, from a purely economic point of view, GDP growth is still to be considered economic progress according to global standards.

Egypt is transferring its main three challenges into motivations, the use of energy, human resources, and governance. These expectations could shift the political and economic power in the region that restores the historical position of Egypt as a major player. Figures 8.1 and 8.2 show the remarkable expected economic growth in Egypt by 2030. This would be a significant indicator of the construction in the ME. On the other hand, the Egyptian Central Bank has announced that the external debit in Egypt have dramatically increased from 33.694 billion in 2010 to 123.49 billion in 2021 which is a high national risk. Despite all arguments, Egypt started recently to focus on aligning the national branding within a national strategy in harmony with new global changes. By implementing AI programmes and software, Egypt was demonstrating a serious attempt of re-branding itself.

In fact, the methods used for infiltration bears a lot of similarity to national branding. Infiltration is most successful, when a group is divided and vulnerable to instability. Branding thrives on similar divisions, however to be more optimistic, they may refer to these as 'categories.' These categories can refer to the education sector, nonprofit sector, etc., it is not divisibility of culture, it is rather categorising it in a way facilitates development in each category, where each category is still

Rank	Country	GDP 2017 Trillion	Proj. GDP 2030 Trillion
#1	China	$ 23.2	$ 64.2
#2	India	$ 9.5	$ 46.3
#3	US	$ 19.4	$ 31.0
#4	Indonesia	$ 3.2	$ 10.1
#5	Turkey	$ 2.2	$ 9.1
#6	Brazil	$ 3.2	$ 8.6
#7	Egypt	$ 1.2	$ 8.2
#8	Russia	$ 4.0	$ 7.9
#9	Japan	$ 5.4	$ 7.2
#10	Germany	$ 4.2	$ 6.9

Fig. 8.1 The biggest economies in 2030 (*Source* Author's own design based on IMF data)

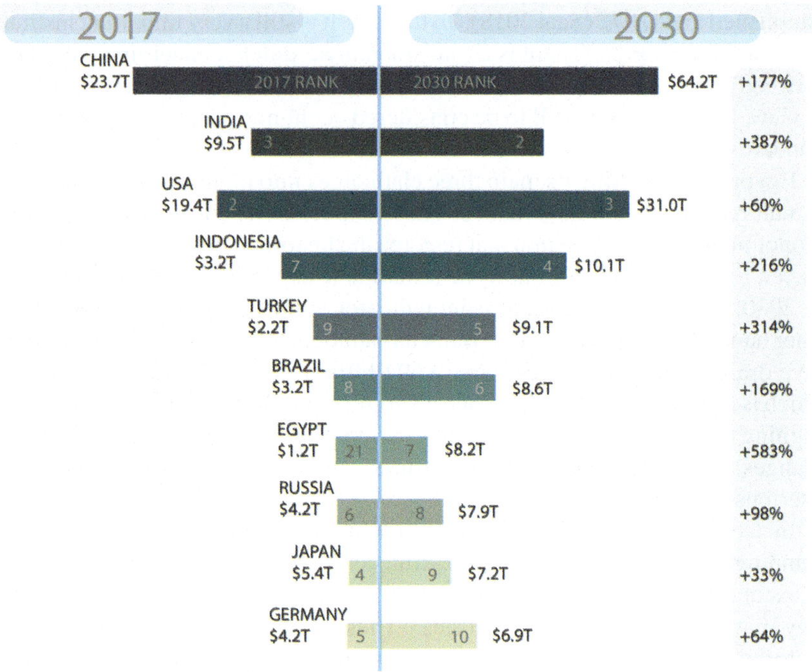

Fig. 8.2 The percentage of GDP growth between 2017 and 2030 (*Source* Author's own design)

connected with the rest as part of one vision. This applies in the case of national branding.

In other cases, there was the creation of new cultures within the culture in the form of the '*development culture*' essentially focussing on the culture of security and technology. This then gradually assimilates and eventually overtakes the wider local culture. Youth were fascinated by globalisation and its manifestations. However, Fig. 8.3 indicates that the meeting point of globalisation culture with the local culture brought arguably economic change and growth in many aspects, but remains overshadowed the side effects of destruction and damage from external intervention.

What does this have to do with local and regional development and national branding? This model of cultural transition in favour of globalisation blurs national branding and eliminates its existence in the future, potentially devastating the collective awareness of the '*machine experience mind*'. It might aim to even delete the local culture if this continues to progress in the same direction.

Yet upon review of this categorisation of cultures as part of national branding, China poses an interesting alternative. Within its own culture, China was able to interact positively to globalisation. Globalisation could not swallow China as a civilisation. China has always been moving with deliberate plans to take advantage of global progress without harming the culture of the local community. Regardless of

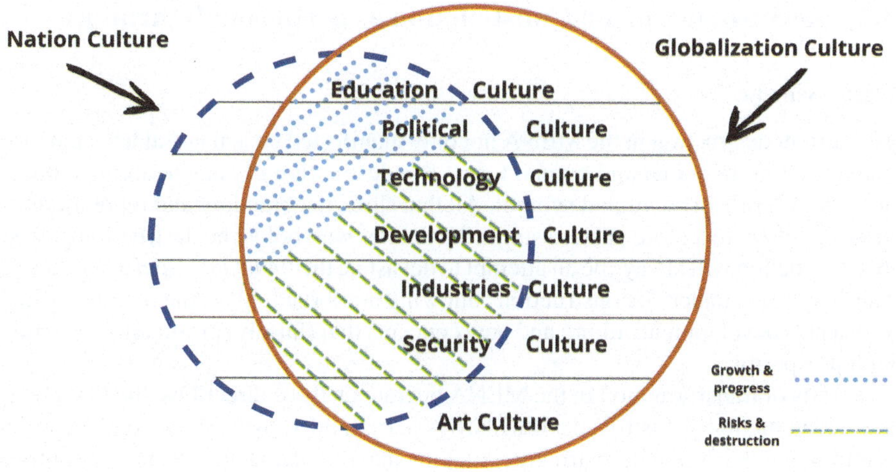

Fig. 8.3 Example of categorising the whole culture (*Source* Author's own resource)

whether local cultures are reasonable or strange for others, it is the belief of China to protect its whole originality and other aspects originality in the country. A continued absence of an internal strategy will hinder development. In order to solve the emerging issues in the wider local culture, there must be a long term vision for each sector to develop towards. A long-term goal will allow for realistic objectives on the ground. This requires a collective awareness. Otherwise, the systems of the national culture become an extension to globalisation culture, which allows the "profiting" of every thing or being.

National branding necessitates, what I call, '*centring*'. This means prioritising the problems facing a nation internally and enhancing the structure to allow rational interactions on a domestic and international level. To simulate this image, MENA countries have to be committed to changing the existing geopolitical environment. Including but not limited to replacing ill-advised leadership, rebuilding the state and defining its social role and function, and introducing necessary reforms (Ghaliun 2005). Reforms in this case would be to enhance and identify the regional identity and collective culture that eliminates partisanship and sectarianism. This then creates a more fertile ground for democracy, where people return to the field of political decisions and develop independent economic systems. All this could happen once the public is educated to do so and understands cooperation for nation-building. Rather than branding the region under 'terror' or 'developing countries'.

8.2 Reconstruction or Construction as a Thorough Strategy

Warda Samara

The current destruction in the MENA not only manifested on a material level but also manifested in the social and human form. The destruction of ancient architecture is not simply a ruin of a national symbol. All that shifts the branding and reputations of these countries to a more passive status. No matter who holds the destruction power, this destruction will always be an attempt to devastate the '*machine experience mind*'. Then to place it under "reconstruction" allowing new branding for the region covered with a new development culture and new concepts that (falsely) promising the region with prosperity.

Efforts of transformation in the MENA operate on three directions, the first one is the reconstruction of destroyed areas like Syria, Iraq and Yemen. The second direction is improving the digital infrastructure, looking in particular at the advanced countries in the region. The third direction is the reforming of the whole geopolitical case in favour of economic progress in regions like Palestine and Kurdistan. All directions are in line with a new world order, AI and increased technological advancement.

Reconstruction in the region, especially in Syria, Yemen, Libya and Iraq is supported by international aid which makes sense from the perspective of the global institutions who also support a new world order according to their perspective. Thus the building of the new structure, especially in the aforementioned countries, is part of the new world planning. Therefore, the World Bank is calling to construct a new system entirely rather than reconstructing the old system. Construction as an industry complies with complex regulations that need time, effort and money to be introduced (MEED 2021). Therefore, I conclude that any construction in the region is not going to take on a traditional form. Its unique interaction of IoT and AI with communities is not similar to any previous construction that humans have ever witnessed. Construction is operating on several dimensions that all must work and interact together, the infrastructure as the main material part of the construction, technology and people.

People in the region view the starting point of any construction or transformation as nothing more than a national holistic effort. Comprehensive understanding of self-sufficiency along with the ability to cooperate must be promoted on the grassroots level. For example, agriculture which is a significant part of the construction, as the rehabilitation of its would increase productivity and reduce the unemployment rate. The supporters of this perception emphasise on the importance of developing a common understanding for all the stakeholders in this construction. Acknowledging the fact that the political dynamics on the ground have changed since the 'Arab Spring' revolutions and the main parties in these countries are no longer the sole influences.

People are highly aware that any reconstruction is always an inherently "political" process in which gains are distributed to the stakeholders, which also means that some parties are deprived of it. The parties being another term for the people. One would therefore think imposing external solutions should be avoided to prevent any attempt that imposes external visions for the region. This perception opens a question: Who will be responsible for the construction and transformation of these ares and what is at the core of their ambition?

These approaches are reminiscent of the consequences from WWI on the region and fundamentally ignore the expanded awareness of the ME. People of the region will no longer accept being treated without dignity. Therefore, there is an appeal for a regional effort for the construction for the benefit of the people. This should include a comprehensive understanding of the local conflict in each country and finding strategies to get out this cycle (Barakat 2016). Those with a capitalist leaning do not like this approach, they prefer not to cooperate and allow the indigenous people to decide their fate and the way they deal with their own resources and take ownership. The region is more than capable to achieve the desired construction for its own people but will the global forces allow them do so?

We can see many instances of external forces competing to reconstruct the region. For example, Russia is assuming a lead role in rebuilding Syria. They have approached several governments around the world, such as China and the EU. As a consequence Chinese business through the BRI, may become one of the important forces in the reconstruction of the Syrian economy. Wang Linzong, the Deputy Director of the Institute of West Asian and African Studies of the Chinese Academy of Social Sciences, describes this as an experience that deserves investment that comes with vigilance and caution (Blue Book of Syria; Annual Report on Development of Syria 2020). China presenting her role in Syria as participating in the process of reconstruction as channelling through the direct investments that guarantee joint returns in its interest and the interest of the country concerned. In Iraq, the capacity of chain companies in the oil field competes heavily with Western companies. This is an indication that China will increase its investments in the country, especially with its participation in the BRI in neighbouring countries (Arabi 2020).

The debate of whether to accept the digital construction or not seems sterile. A digital ME offers a promising economic prosperity and political benefits. This case allows some groups who are highly skilled and able to learn new technological tasks are rewarded with prospects while the majority lose their traditional livelihoods. This road is welcomed by the regional and international financial forces and therefore they provide the maximum facilities to implement this vision. Thus, most countries have already announced their initiatives as ‘digital Egypt’, ‘digital Morocco’, ‘digital Turkey’, and others. All with the aim of transforming states into an information society interacting through AI programs that changes the public lifestyle. Notwithstanding the many issues that these initiatives would bring (see Chap. 5).

Among all these risks, there is hope that reconstruction will not create further divisions between the ME countries through technology. However, defining risk as ‘an unwanted’ event which may or may not occur. Thus recognising risks determines how to deal with the constraints and views around complex systems, such as the global economic system. In a capitalist system, the risk is an essential feature that impacts the role of the entrepreneur. Decisions and activities in the markets are understood from the perception of the risks involved. Therefore, it has a central role in economic dynamics. People, nations, entrepreneurs differ in their attitudes to risk. Some perceive it as opportunities to be taken which others deem much to go

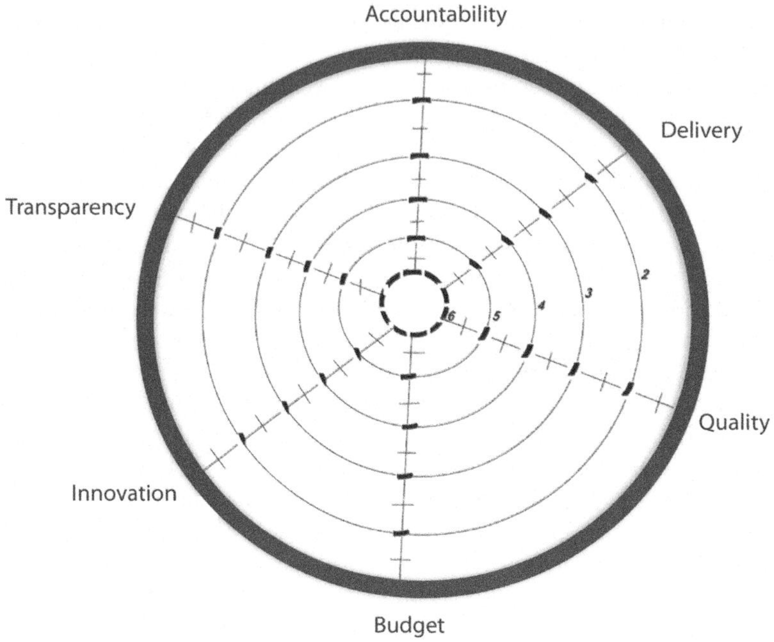

Fig. 8.4 Institutions performance indicators (*Resource* Author's own resource)

through (Hasson 2018). Thus, risks these days are influenced by the current economic and political understanding where capturing hearts and minds is crucial. Planning and applying the necessary mechanisms on the ground are essential to help reduce consequences.

Yet development opportunities differ across Middle Eastern countries depending on the quality of governance indicates. Figure 8.4 shows the main indicators of institutional performance in the public sector. These indicators are quality, delivery, cost, innovation, transparency, and accountability. This quality is defined by the following indicators: accountability, transparency, innovation, budgeting priorities and the ability to deliver their results. I have developed Fig. 8.4 as a model that enhances the quality of governance based on: models of international excellence plus the analysis of the external and enteral environment of a public institution (Samara 2018). An institution in this case being defined by a collection of man-made limitations that influence how individuals interact internally and externally. This model was applied to measure the performance of one public institution in Germany in Freiburg as part of a thesis I did focusing on Performance Measurement Systems in the public sector. Hence, such models should be applied in all institutions in a comprehensive matter before starting the construction to assure that the institutional environment from the beginning is subject to governance principles. This fosters both economic growth along with development in the long term. The country that

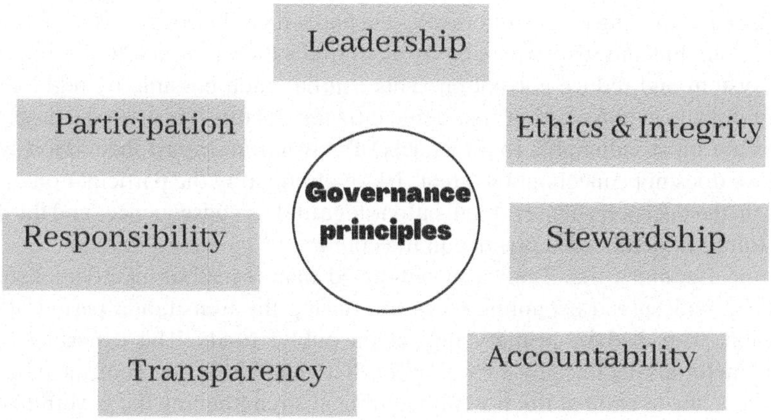

Fig. 8.5 Governance principles (*Source* Author's own design)

can achieve economic progress is the one that enjoys high standards of governance and institutional performance that includes accountability and transparency.

Adopting governance can be identified as a tool to apply it in all fields at all levels. It can play a thorough process in this through the political level including political parties; the economic level including private sector; the administrative level including citizens, the Public Private Partnership level including public relations, media just to name a few. The indicators of both the performance measurement system and the governance are very much alike, see Fig. 8.5.

High institutional performance is an indicator on less corruption that creates trust among the public which enhances the rule of law thereby leading to political and social stability and an absence of violence (Bruinshoofd 2016). The groundwork has now been laid for economic growth to follow. This economic growth as a product of this system indicates good governance.

Institutional capacities vary in the countries of the ME, and as a result, corrupt practices vary (mentioned in Chap. 2). Hence, the economic, political and social response to transitions varies, especially when dealing with new data. In countries of ongoing conflict, like Libya, Yemen and Syria, the level of governance scores very low. Whereas in Egypt and Tunisia, there is a hard attempt to shift the functionality of institutions as well as the structure to adjust laws.

In Egypt, institutions were characterised by neglect at the administrative level especially in regard to the public funds' corruption that occurs in the ministries, municipalities, and parliament. Many changes and efforts have been done to make development in eco-political institutions such as activating increased supervisory responsibility, progress towards digitalisation, encourage the investment sector and promoting entrepreneurship. Meanwhile, in the background they started increasing penalties for corrupt practices, finally marking illicit wealth as a fundamental issue. Obviously, the bureaucratic interests are resistant to this change. Within the framework of Egypt 2030 or 'Digital Egypt', a unified databased has been developed to make decision making process more efficient and with reduced risk. The 2030 agenda assures to include all institutions by using digitalisation as a tool to develop governance system and reduce corruption. This can be made possible by regulating the interaction between institutions' staff and citizens. As this it is often the case, where citizens are most vulnerable to direct acts of corruption against them. However, all the above does not cancel out the great risk of eliminating the participation of wider society in the decisions of the digitalisation stage and its consequences and the danger to the future of democratic practice in the country.

As for a country like Tunisia, it witnessed manifestations like demonstrations caused by widespread economic recession during the transitional period after the revolution. This had its primary impact on public funds. The export of oil and mineral materials declined by 83% between 2010 and 2011. The Tunisian parliament approved a law to combat illicit wealth aiming at strengthening the government on a large scale, ensuring transparency and preserving the national public funds. However, Tunisia's economic prospects are unstable in light of its high debts, causing a growing concern for the country. Combined with the unstable political situation, there is a lot standing in the face of economic development as the economy is simply not yet open for investment. There still needs to be greater efforts towards any economic progress and social solutions.

As for its democratic participation, Tunisia had seen a greater number of people involved in new political parties who actively try to prevent any corrupt authority from the rule. However, no noticeable eco-political progress has taken place. Meanwhile, in Egypt, the participation of the public has declined justified by the current regime as knowing what is best better than the people. All while the public expresses its concern of no democratic future in the country.

These two examples show the difference in response to similar political events in the last decade. The internal characteristic of each country's environment led to different outcomes and consequences that affected the required methodologies in order to eliminate the resulting uncertainty.

It is obvious that political institutions must be of high quality because they lead the national economic institutions as well as its market. It is therefore imperative that authoritarian leaders are not centred on political institutions (Samarasinghe 2019). This is one of the public primary demands in Tunisia as its economic progress is heavily reliant on the decision-making of the political elites. In Egypt, the political system will determine many, if not most of its economic interventions.

8.3 International and Regional Aid

Warda Samara
Malaka Samara

The origin of foreign aid is based on the adoption of economic and financial policies and reforms aimed at achieving stronger economic performance and higher standards of living and governance in the name of democracy. Some perceive it as altruism from richer countries, with foreign aid really serving as an instrument of foreign policy rather than genuine humanitarianism (Challand 2014). Thus, there are many complications surrounding foreign aid and there is a great debate about it. While indeed it is an aid to countries, there are many who view it as risking the real independence and prosperity of countries especially under impossible conditions but the leader they still unable to deal with it.

The foreign aid that flows to the MENA has different faces as it stems from different sources. There is regional aid that comes mainly from the Arab Fund like the Arab Fund for Economic and Social Development based in Kuwait. They offer loans and grants to Arab countries aiming to achieving Arab integration and consolidate interstate cooperation. Loans are concessional; by providing easy financing conditions to assist these countries to implement their development plans. This Arab Fund continues to provide non-refundable grants as a contribution to various fields of studies, particularly to the least developed countries in the region. This has also included institutional support and training including for emergencies and country specific circumstances. There is particular emphasis on contributing to projects involving the interconnection of electrical power, transportation and communications. The Arab Fund also pays close attention to social development and reducing poverty by financing projects covering health care, education, drinking water, rural development, and social welfare (AF 2008). Statistics showed that the total value of the various cumulative operations of the Arab Fund for Economic and Social Development, from 1974 until mid-August 2020, exceeded $37.7 billion, for the benefit of millions of citizens in 22 Arab countries.

This is one of the examples of the active regional funds that aims to directly support the people of the region. On the other hand, up to 2021, the war in Yemen has claimed 112,000 lives and about 14 million face mass starvation. This was caused by the contribution of other regional and international funds that support the opposite parties in the country.

International financial aid is a formation of the structure of the network of relations between the centre of the world capitalist system and backward societies. This happened in a way that the less powerful societies are put in front of two options; to be forced to rely on the centre of the system in order to survive or to face chaos and sanctions when necessary by global forces. This is not only for the MENA region, it applies to many countries under constant subjugation.

In some cases, some even consider aid as an outright form of neo-colonialism or imperialism while endless power can use, and has been used (Issaev 2021). Chomsky has argued that the "neoliberal onslaught" of globalisation was brought about by the IMF and World Bank through the resultant shift of power away from governments and towards markets. Where the current economic order is designed for accumulating capital that is not serving the people. Rather, it widens the gap between the rich and the poor because the agreements themselves are made strictly for and between the rich whereby the rich control policy with their capital (Uzamere 2000).

The global financial institutions reform th**eir narrative all the time to fit with their new** strategic and global aims without considering the destruction that is left because of their policies in the first place. The major IMF strategic documents and loan agreements continue to be underpinned by a prioritisation of private sector-driven growth, fiscal austerity focusing particularly on subsidy reform, and the liberalisation of markets, industries and trade.

The IMF seemed to ignore the obvious signals of regression and persisted on the same policy despite their negative impacts on the social and economic indicators in many countries like Egypt. Hence, the recent loans from IMF have been met with a divided public opinion and even protest over their economic consequences. Despite this, governments are still continue to accept these loans (Mossallam 2015).

For example, Cairo is one of the most prominent Arab capitals that has resorted to the IMF, obtaining 20 billion dollars in the last five years. In Mauritania, the IMF has agreed to grant the country $167 million, covering the period between 2017 and 2021, with increases in 2020 of $29 million, to meet financing needs due to COVID19. In 2020, Morocco borrowed $3.2 billion. Jordan received a 2020 loan of $1.3 billion, and in May 2020, $413 million. In 2016, Tunisia received $1.7 billion. Iraq received a loan in May 2016 worth $5.34 billion. Yemen received a 2014 loan of $553 million. Lebanon is seeking to borrow from the IMF in order to fill the financing gap that the country suffers from (Al-Shal 2021).

From here, many view this as obvious financial domination of the MENA through the imposed ambiguous terms using the influence of global financial institutions or major monopolistic companies (multiple nationalities). Hence, if any emerged government is committed to making the desired local development, it would always collide with the payment terms of these loans. This renders repayment of any loans almost impossible, what was initially supposed to help the people has simply become a curse on them.

Policies of obtaining loans or foreign financial aid have extended into different dimensions where local associations and even individuals are relying more and more on banks and lending institutions. With the rising standard of living, loans have become a primary part of social culture, which increase the burden of debt at all levels and leading to increasing asset ownership by the banks. This we can call '*the loans culture*'.

Looking to Lebanon as a current example of demonstrating the huge power that global financial institutions have in isolating countries and leave people to face social and economic difficulties. At the time that mainstream economists in Lebanon perceived global aid as the only solution to get Lebanon out of disaster and negotiate for a new loan from the IMF. I see this as a great opportunity and a call to the Lebanese to find other ways to fix the economic and social difficulties internally to avoid sinking the country into further debts with unfair conditions which will cause more damage in the long term.

Economist, Elie Yachoui, states that the loans to Lebanon from the Global Fund will not help, rather it will worsen the situation and lead to increased poverty. Domestic solutions can serve the vision better which requires trust between the people and the government. The government though did not show serious actions in regard to the main issues: how to get back the looted funds, how to run the administration of new service sectors, and how to suggest a solution to the state's reliance on oil extraction. There are internal solutions but no one resorts to them (Baydoun 2020).

Foreign aids are not always financial support, it takes different shapes. Some of these shapes for example when a country get a loan of some billions to build a dam and the term is the implementation company must be from a certain country. This means a high percentage of the offered aid does not even flow to the recipient country. It stays outside. In other cases, Russia, for example, offers support in security and military industries and direct engaging in wars like in Syria. While China uses its aid to other countries as a tool for securing the political support of developing countries in times of conflict with the West. China is clearly offering a lot of support in logistics, trades, economic strategies, and recently support in the medical field during the COVID-19 pandemic. This has been seen as an attempt to make it visible that humanitarian motives are behind foreign aid especially with dispatching medical teams around the world (Fuchs and Rudyak 2017). Moreover, China established the Asian Infrastructure Investment Bank to develop the historic BRI, which links China with Europe through Central and Western Asia, to which about 50 countries have joined, including 19 Arab countries. Nevertheless, some consider international aid as always associated with the eco-political agenda in some way (Issaev and Zakharov 2021).

What we learn from all these examples is that social justice and development can only be done through the internal holistic effort with smart interaction with other forces. Growth and development do not occur when money is the main tool that moves the whole system.

This method of loaning has yet to prove any benefit in countries where no well-developed social protection systems exist. This means that the current promoted economic agendas are leading to further impoverishment and widening inequality gaps which became even more obvious after the ‘Arab Spring’.

In a world of transition world where China grows and where the US declines, the leaders of the MENA region must remember and be aware of not repeating the same mistakes when collaborating with China and its allies. A proverb describes similar situations; “Stick with your current sinister, or you will get a worse sinister”. It is important not to see external forces as the saviour because, no matter how good their intentions, they will not care about improving the lives of other peoples in the long term. Any true saviour for trouble can only happen from within.

8.4 Small and Medium-Sized Enterprises (SME) and Entrepreneurship

Warda Samara
Malaka Samara

The 4IR is defined by new business models and innovative solutions which presents a chance for prosperity for less fortunate countries. Fulfilling any vision from the

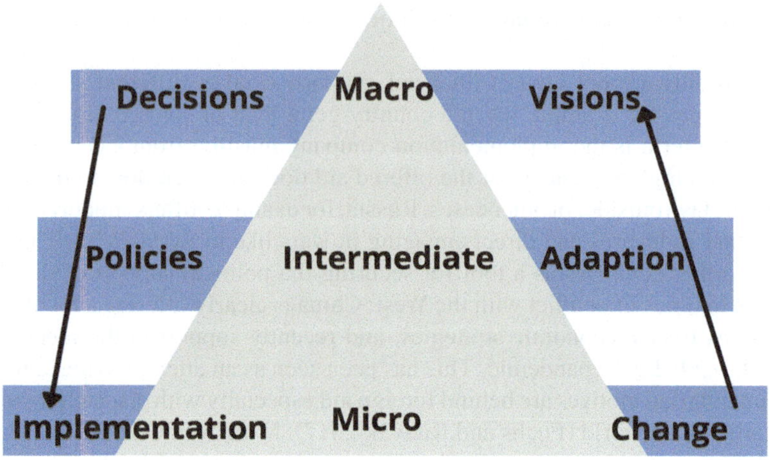

Fig. 8.6 Transition levels (*Resource* Author's own resource)

previous industrial revolutions required collective adaptation and acceptance at the micro level. This made the role of the MSEs more vital where women and youth who run these businesses at the micro level play a fundamental role in consolidating the changes desired from the macro level (see Fig. 8.6).

For local individuals, it becomes inevitable to take the risk to start a business in order to survive and improve their social and economic situation. The micro level initiatives and solutions were forced into existence after having to wait endlessly for solutions from the macro-level. Even though these people are exposed not only to loss but also to danger. People are taking the responsibility to continue moving on through these risks believing that it will pass by one day and they will be able to overcome the current challenges. Therefore, many social and economic initiatives and small business ideas are rapidly increasing in the MENA. These people perceive the regional current risk as a hungry illusion manufactured in order to eat the national resources for the benefit of the macro level. This encourages them to invest in more projects that help individuals to gain income and help the society to grow the SMEs at the national space.

SMEs have the great advantage of resilience and the ability to adapt to economic circumstances. It is also seen as one of the most contributors to poverty reduction, job creation and participation in the national GDP (Stan 2014). Therefore, this sector is in an advantageous position to face challenges and changes. Resilience, in general, is a key to understanding coping during and following crises. In the AI era, SMEs need to take measures to increase their resilience and response to crises in a way that assures sustainability for these projects. Since the announcement of these digital initiatives in the ME, female and young entrepreneurs received by far the most attention. They recognised the progressive image such representation brought and saw it as crucial for exposure to a larger audience. This has actually been very beneficial, as it required pioneering new roles for these new entrepreneurs and thus diversifying the economy further.

Some economists saw additional reasons why small businesses would become a more crucial part of the economic landscape. In the highly competitive and rapidly changing global economy, they argued, less hierarchical management systems could innovate, customise products, and adapt quickly to changing circumstances. For instance in the face of declining transportation costs and the emergence of the internet made it easier to innovate and be real competitors on the global stage (Stan 2014).

The growth of the digital economy in the MENA could become one of the key aspects of this progress. In the ME, SMEs represent more than 94% of companies operating in the region, providing jobs for more than 86% of the workforce in the private sector. Such companies comprise of nearly 95% of all companies in Dubai alone – contributing around 40% to Dubai's GDP (Sommer 2021). Learning from the European experience where the 20 million European SMEs play an important role in the European economy. In 2012 these have secured jobs for 86.8 million people. This is accounting for 66.5% of all European jobs for that year (Stan 2014).

Any chance of future prosperity depends on the creativity of entrepreneurs and the highly trained workforce. Most SMEs address the lack of trained workforce as the main challenge (Soni 2019). This calls the educations systems, consulting and coaching firms as well as highly skilled experts to respond to these gaps through developing and updating their training methods. By training their staff in a way that deepens their knowledge and competencies, they can provide the necessary innovation and creativity. This training expanded to self-reliant learning in order to be adaptable to the ever rapidly changing work environment. This also opens exchanging and cooperation channels between local and international entrepreneurs (Harden 2021). Nevertheless, digital literacy is in rather short supply in the ME, as a result of a brain drain, even if the higher-income countries in the Gulf.

SMEs are a vital tool for local economic recovery when transiting the communities to peace. In any post-conflict situations, employment is a major role in enhancing stability, socio-economic progress and sustainable development. It is an important alternative to social unrest (ILO 2010). The remarkable phenomena in the MENA that almost everyone in the society is looking for an opportunity to reintegrate and participate in the healing process, as this is part of their culture. They realise the features to run SMEs has changed, but many of them still do not have access to gain further training.

For SMEs, the biggest challenge, operationally, in the 4IR is the increasing cost of required technologies to function. This can only be mitigated through regional support and policy adaptation, both of which are required in order to provide better structures for SMEs. While large corporations are expected to lose more jobs, MSEs can play a fundamental efficient role in term of, cost, delivery, quality, and innovation in line with social responsibility.

8.5 Women Perceptions and Role Through Entrepreneurs—Case Study

Warda Samara

The importance of women's entrepreneurship for economic growth and development has seen increased recognition in the MENA. Thus far this has been significant in creating new jobs and reducing unemployment and poverty. Besides, it is empowerment for social and economic development in the community that in the long term will affect the national social and economic level of development.

Promoting the concept of security only by having a regular job with the government or main corporations is hindering creativity, independence and accessing new possibilities. Being capable of breaking away from an unsuccessful yet persistent social norm and adopting a new one is important about women role in the 4IR. The following case study, is a simple example with huge lessons to learn from. Besides the ongoing threat of political conflict, women in the ME have also fought a persistent battle against the male-dominated societies they live under.

Many statistics indicate that the percentage of unemployed women in the MENA is very high, demonstrating the lowest female labour force participation rate in the world. It is important to be aware that unemployment does not only mean that someone is without work. Alternatively, it indicates a lack of certain professional skills and competencies to obtain employment. Between 2015 and 2021, I designed a project to enhance women entrepreneurs in Palestine. During the implementation process I conducted a study in collaboration with Logica Center for Consulting and Rural Women Cooperative Association in Tulkarem, and supported by The Arab Fund for Social and Economic Development. Despite the low income and the rise of poverty among women in marginalised areas, the study questioned the reason that women are not interested in entrepreneurship and do not invest in available resources such as neglected agricultural spaces.

One of the findings was that 77% of the participated women do earn income via home industries rather than visiting a physical work space (before remote work became as commonplace as it was today!). These home industries included agricultural production, film production, and beauty cosmetics, etc. (Coaching 2020). Yet, most of these women are still registered and considered unemployed, even though these projects enhance the economic growth in the communities and in the national GDP. They still perceive themselves as unemployed as long as they don not have a regular job and a salary. Another finding was that the way women perceive themselves leaves a remarkable impact on their personal and professional life.

The study included 400 women from Palestine who come from mixed income areas. People in these villages suffer from several difficulties mainly lacking water and accessing to facilities and brain drain. It was implemented to enhance women creativity and innovation that improve their financial and social circumstances. With the programmes focusing on various methods on interacting with and making use of all available resources at their disposal.

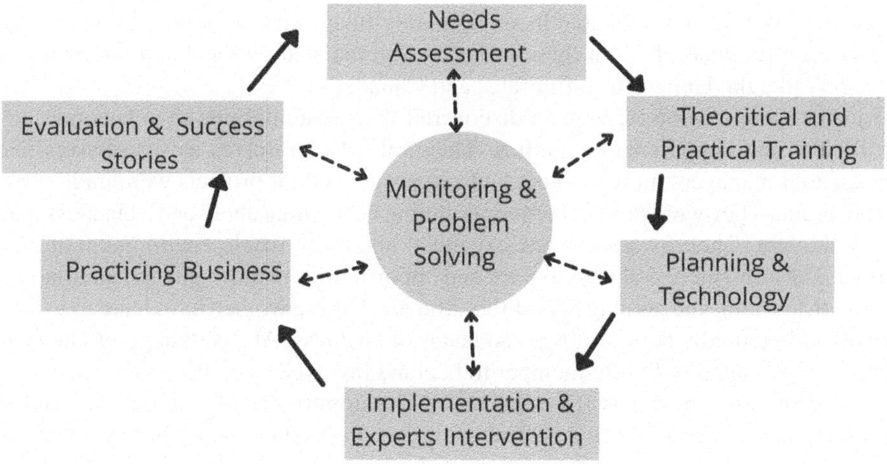

Fig. 8.7 Implementation process of socio-economic development projects (*Source* Author's own design)

Prior to this programme, the attendees perceived themselves as unable to have a role in society and unable to run any kind of projects often mentioning difficulties they would not overcome. 88% of them had no prior experience an therefore obtain no weak skills. They showed fear of not being able to balance between raising their kids and running a small business. A comprehensive needs assessment was conducted in order to analyse the environment and the needs. Based on that intensive training sessions, both theoretical and practical, were held. Experts from different fields were facilitating these sessions and supported women to have better understand to the importance of their role in the social and economic development of the society. Figure 8.7 shows a successful implementation process of the socio-economic projects. By providing these women with the required materials to launch their business initiatives and experts to consult, they had full rein to enhance any necessary skills, manage their project and take full advantage of the exposure. In the end, they were ready to compete in the market.

This was an intensive intervention-style programme over a period of 18 months. At the start, the participants were taught in entrepreneurial and technological skills—with a great focus on how to use their smart phones to their advantage. After three months, the process begins of planning and eventually establishing their small enterprises. This project was repeated 24 months later, and the third 24 months after that.

The third group had achieved after eight months to set up "smart greenhouses" as part of their agricultural production. These greenhouses had automated computer irrigation systems, sensors and ventilations. All were run from their smart phones, where they could track and export all data. The participants now had the opportunity to track and control their resources on a remote basis, a previous unthinkable task in agricultural production. 73% of the women are running their own projects successfully with a remarkable income, mainly in agriculture, food production and handmade products. 12% of these projects even reached regional and international markets like the United Arab Emirates and Canada.

After the intervention, women discovered their potential power to become self-sufficient and support their families. They valued themselves as housewives and household managers more than ever, unsurprising as their projects were mainly run from home. They were more effective at running both a household and a business than they thought. Their awareness has expanded about the whole environment around them. They find there is always a space and opportunities to grow and find alternatives through learning and gaining new skills. Above all, these women have learned to start small and gradually build to advanced levels of business. At a certain point, they can even include another family member to become involved as well.

We learn several things from this case. The importance of mindset and understanding in order to allow change. Enhancing the understanding of these women has a huge impact on the domestic economy and self-sufficiency. Gaining new skills and competencies have led to changing behaviours and has changed their interaction with the environment around them. Therefore, this program has opened their awareness to wider possibilities at the personal and professional levels.

A medium scale program has influenced the way that people interact with the same resources around them. The program did not need to change anything in reality rather than changing the way they see themselves by providing access to new kinds of knowledge. Only this has changed their role in the family and increased their home financial income as well.

This case study now raises a fundamental question. Why did women perceive themselves as unable to take the risk to run their own projects before the intervention?

8.6 Sufficiency Economy

Malaka Samara

Capitalism has its own philosophy, where capitalists produce goods for the consumers. This gradually became the dependable and acted model and no longer saw the use for self-sufficiency. This is intended to encourage people to identify more as a consumer, rather than a citizen. Therefore, there are many local and regional calls for self-sufficiency, its importance and its role in developing individuals and communities. Additionally, it is important to be aware and realise how other countries and communities depend on the Sufficiency Economy for development at several levels.

It is an important point to mention that the Sufficiency Economy is not only limited to agricultural activities and food production. It also goes beyond that to include any kind of activities or hobbies that we practice to produce any kind of product that we use in our daily life at the individual level such as sewing, making clothes, etc. (Brewer 2008).

This applies at many levels to individuals, societies, and countries. Self-sufficiency does not necessarily mean that the person or the state would completely refrain from buying consumer goods. That never was the case, it was always concerned with cooperation in order to produce at least the minimum of the need in order to keep the social and the economic balance. The need behind it is not material, rather more personal needs of empowerment through dignity, freedom, and decision making (Brewer 2008).

The real unemployment rate increases when countries go through national crises that eliminate SMEs because of the lack of access to resources and raw materials. For example, the economic collapse in Lebanon starting from August 2020 was accompanied by economic destruction because of COVID-19 regulations that have caused catastrophic wealth destruction, especially for the middle class. Poverty rates may reach more than 40% of the Lebanese population in 2021, leaving 1.6 million Lebanese unable to secure their basic needs (Nasif et al. 2020).

Self-sufficiency will not change things overnight, even if it did, it would require first a change in the mindset of the people as well as a proper process of implementation. Above all creativity and thinking outside of the box is key. Returning from the global stage to independence and finding solutions of domestic level, would allow societies and nations to be able to interact with each other in a way that is more beneficial to the Global environment.

Put simply, people have always been able to have great thoughts and ideas. What has been difficult, however, is their practical implementation. This is mostly attributed to a fast-paced lifestyle which has made its way in nearly all facets of life, including our attitudes. We have simply become accustomed to wanting these fast and effortlessly as everything around us changes fast and effortlessly. The result is that people started to depend largely imported goods from the supermarket distancing themselves further from the roots of agriculture. With the new generation, the focus will soon become only on the city centres. In reality, agriculture has been the largest contributor to the GDP and foreign exchange in the ME, and it is still the second-largest employer.

This is not common knowledge among the new generation, who has been showing a greater leaning towards the cities. Hardly unsurprising as they are sold as centres of technology, industry, modern life and economic development. This further leading to a depletion of young educated people in the villages and a massive surge in large commercial units. These are not always ME native businesses.

Moreover, the increase on demand for goods, including technology has obligated pushed locals to increase their productivity by using technology, whether willingly or not. Meanwhile, other people have developed dependency on their devices and technology relationship with their devices and technology. That dominant perception may not necessarily be for the benefit of the people.

In conclusion, we cannot treat technological dependency (at least on a widespread scale) as an inevitable cost of development. We can use technology to our advantage on an individual level, and even on the national level. All it takes is the required understanding of the real power of our devices and technology.

8.7 Summary

Any age of post-chaos will usually consist of reconstruction and construction of nations and societies and in the MENA, there are several aspects of consideration. In Syria, we see the aspect of physical destruction and who will support this. In various regional digital initiatives, where no domestic digital products exists on a wide scale, who is then securing and protecting their data? This forms the bedrock of discussion concerning the contemporary role of external aid and support in the region. How would one provide the major support required for nations post-chaos while also leaving them empowered to implement their strategies themselves.

This chapter discussed the opportunities of economic growth, the risks that stand in the face of sustainable development and the importance of governance and national branding to face internal and external risks. Where creating the integrative relationship between national GDP and development depends on the educated population and the competent workforce is the main challenge to cope with the 4IR. In this context, The Small and Medium-sized Enterprises (SME) and entrepreneurship have been viewed as a catalyst for this era of change, where women and youth are at the forefront in these groups to promote change.

Although the progress of technology is fraught with danger, especially for less fortunate countries, it above all displays a huge advantage of all levels. All it takes is realising the way the people perceive themselves while interacting with the resources around them, and the moving dynamics of the current era. This allows them to understand the real power of devices, technology and find their own way to cope with the 4IR.

References

AF, A. F. f. E. a. S. d. (2008) Arab fund embodiment of joint Arab action. Arab Fund for Economic and Social development

Al-Shal T (2021) A 10-year journey between Arab countries and the "International Monetary"... Exorbitant costs. A. Agency. https://www.aa.com.tr/ar/ تقرير-باهظة-تكاليف-الدولي-والنقد-العربية-الدول-بين-سنوات-10-رحلة/اقتصاد

Arabi MA (2020) A Chinese marshall plan? What are the determinants of the Chinese role in the reconstruction of the Middle East? https://ewc-center.com/2020/09/28/ الدور-محددات-هي-ما-الصينية-مارشال-خطة

Barakat S (2016) The case for a regional reconstruction strategy for the Middle East. https://www.brookings.edu/blog/markaz/2016/03/04/the-case-for-a-regional-reconstruction-strategy-for-the-middle-east/

Baydoun H (2020) Lebanon in crisis is at the mercy of the International Monetary Fund. Al- Arabi Al-Jadded. https://www.alaraby.co.uk الدولي-النقد-صندوق-رحمة-تحت-المأزوم-لبنان

Blue Book of Syria; Annual Report on Development of Syria. (2020). (3rd edn.). The Center for Syrian Studies at Northwestern University of China and the Publishing House of Social Sciences Literature

Brewer P (2008) Self-sufficiency, self-reliance, and freedom. https://www.wisebread.com/self-sufficiency-self-reliance-and-freedom

Bruinshoofd A (2016) Institutional quality and economic performance. RaboResearch—Economic Research
Challand B (2014) Revisiting aid in the Arab Middle East. 281–298. https://doi.org/10.1080/13629395.2014.966983
Coaching LCfCa (2020) Rural women initiatives
Fuchs A, Rudyak M (2017) The motives of China's foreign aid. The International Political Economy of China. Edward Elgar Publishing Limited
Ghaliun B (2005) Globalization and its impact on Arab societies ESCWA Expert Meeting, Beirut
Harden CTA (2021) Doing business in post-conflict zones: why SMEs are key
Hasson S (2018) Risk. In Stanford encyclopedia of philosophy. Metaphysics Research Lab, Stanford University. https://plato.stanford.edu/archives/fall2018/entries/risk/
ILO (2010) Local economic recovery in post-conflict
Issaev L (2021) Russia's "Return" to the Middle East and the Arab Uprisings. Al-Sharq Strategic Research
Issaev L, Zakharov A (2021) Federalism in the Middle East—state reconstruction projects and the Arab Spring. Springer
MEED (2021) Digital awakening—the digitalisation of construction in the Middle East
Mossallam M (2015) The IMF in the Arab world: lessons unlearnt. SSRN Electron J. https://doi.org/10.2139/ssrn.2705927
Nasif F, Asaeleh E, Bzi B, Bejani H, Basat A, Shaol H, Diwan I, Al-Sayyed H, Yousef A, Al-Zain S, Jaber NFF, Nader S, Nasrallah M, Rafeal, P, Salti JRN, Al-Saeedi N, Shahadeh K, Yahya M, Yameen B, Zween J (2020) The economic crisis in Lebanon: a ten-point action plan to avoid a lost decade. https://carnegie-mec.org/2020/01/14/ar-pub-80785
Saat N (2018) IThe Al-Azhar University: A historical sketch. In: Tradition and Islamic learning. ISEAS–Yusof Ishak Institute, p 15–33
Samara W (2018) Performance measurement in the public sector. Berlin
Samarasinghe T (2019) The relationship between institutions and economic development. Munich Personal RePEc Archive, MPRA. https://mpra.ub.uni-muenchen.de/97755/
Sendhardt B (2013) Theoretical perspectives on borders. in borders and border regions in Europe: Changes, challenges and chances, p 21–44. https://www.jstor.org/stable/j.ctv1fxhcq.4
Sommer A (2021) Middle East construction sector eyes innovative technology to improve operations. Oracle Construction and Engineering Blog. blogs.oracle.com
Soni oaN (2019) Impact of artificial intelligence on businesses: from research, innovation, market deployment to future shifts in business models. https://www.researchgate.net/publication/332898261_Impact_of_Artificial_Intelligence_on_Businesses_from_Research_Innovation_Market_Deployment_to_Future_Shifts_in_Business_Models
Stan StA (2014) The role of small business in economic development of European economy. http://sceco.ub.ro
Uzamere, ELaPA (2000) Chomsky offers insight into IMF. World Bank. o. e. The Tech

Chapter 9
Future Perspectives and Outlooks

Warda Samara

9.1 Future Perspectives

It is generally agreed upon that the current immense structures and dynamics emerged from a multitude of historical processes. These processes, above all, was influenced by the West colonialism and its extension as in its more subtle forms in society as the main tool of shaping that history (Robinson 2017).

This is significant as some of the most devastating historical events were allowed to happen by manipulating the common narrative. However, as we are experiencing the forward momentum of the 4IR, many countries in the MENA may be subject to *'digital classifications'*. In order to respond to the 4IR, we cannot focus on the historical common narrative but rather focus on the strategies on the domestic and international levels. After all, some of these strategies can form the basis of the current common narrative depending on public perception. These strategies should include drawing several scenarios for any potential risks and how to act accordingly. Another layer of preparation for this is required which I will explore further in this chapter.

Although this chapter (and the entire book) refers to the ME, any of these future perspectives could be applicable for most nations. It is intended for any communities who wish to understand and develop comprehensive prosperity through the following recommendations. However, as we have learned, there is no one size fits all for development models. Therefore this should be read more as a guideline that provokes the mind and not an instruction manual.

People are experiencing a distinct era on data management and taking decisions to adapt for 4IR, it should be an era of thinking beyond borders, beyond geography, beyond maps, and beyond political solutions. Youth should find creative alternative solutions that work for everyone's win–win-win situation. The advanced technology is there, all the information to operate it is there and its results are more than promising. It stands to reason that we should refrain from imposing limits due to

W. Samara and M. Samara, *The Power of Perceptions in the Middle East*,
Perspectives on Development in the Middle East and North Africa (MENA) Region,
https://doi.org/10.1007/978-3-030-99150-0_9

potential undiscovered risks. However, also not neglecting to handle, understand and learn from any risks and malfunctions which may occur.

Conceptually, questioning and redefining concepts and terms to have a common understanding is essential for creating a common understanding towards future improvements and development. This becomes more urgent in light of the radical change that comes along with the 4IR. Acknowledging that the shape of familiar terms is changing. This includes the role and the shape of the government, and citizenship. As well as the identification of a state and its borders.

Historical events are happening in the MENA region which is an appeal to the urgency of change and effective decision making. The whole world seems to be planning for the ME except for the ME itself—at a time of new possibilities that were previously unthinkable. Like technology and the internet both allowing swift access to information. At the same time, there remains ever present demand for MENA natural resources. Here I highlight the main perspectives that are important to be investigated in the regional centres of studies while planning for the future of the region:

9.1.1 Con-federalism and the Digital ME

The geopolitical and economic rules have changed, and it is now clear that governmental institutions are acting independently of the people it should serve. The shift to digitalisation is increasing the gap between the people and their governments, as well as creating new classifications among countries that might become 'digital classifications'. This is possible for main two reasons: First, those countries that have already started the smart cities initiatives import most of the AI programs from external forces. Second, the countries lack of the essential elements to cope with the 4IR procession. I view both as subject to *'digital colonising'* on different levels. What we have to do with this is taking the advantage of 4IR and technology advancement to innovate tools that assure countries independence while getting involved in the new era.

These new indicators show that the traditional classifications 'geographic division' and 'economic classification' are no longer the case. Which has to change people's understanding of the most popular aspects like Con-federalism and its symbolic role, the shape of government and its fundamental role, and 4IR and its advantages. Even if the 'digital classification' is taking hold where people and organisations interact digitally, crisis consequences will be more harmful on the ground. To avoid that we need:

- Regional effort: to collaborate as a region and not on an individual basis by finding mutual benefits and a common vision. This must include a clear agenda of digital independence that prevents the region from becoming 'digital colonies'.
- Innovative workforce, to enhance technological innovations and prepare skilled people to develop domestic products in the field of technology and AI.

- Alternative solutions: to agree on alternatives due to the expected crisis scenarios associated with technological development, particularly with cyber attacks and technology dependency.

9.1.2 The Power of Perceptions and Awareness

There are two strong conflicting forces in perception, '*the machine experience mind*', the perception of people and "the machine of globalisation". The main difference is the first one hold the truth with in and the second one holds the power. The contemporary structure of capitalism together with advanced technology is heading in a direction that is perceived negatively by the people, especially those who live in poverty and underdeveloped areas. But they are still unable to deal with it and stop its negative consequences. Or at least find a mutual point of interest.

The selective access to data is designed to build an incomplete picture and draw attention to unnecessary material elements or events without real discourse. Therefore, 'the machine history mind' loses its ability to deal with the modern leaders who are unable to lead nations for the benefit of the people. In essence, the result should be that people believe that there is no alternative to the 'holy guidance' of their ruling authorities. Not only this, but also people perceive and analyse others according to the limit of their knowledge, experience and data. This not only limits one's horizons in general, but they begin to have a distorted and limited view of understanding the environment around them. Their understanding is depending on facts, analysis and an intention to understand. Rather these mindsets become unsettled and even violent in the face of novel solutions.

Furthermore, the flow of mass data and changing indicators urge the need of having a new pattern of leadership that is able to clarify the roots of the events and develop a domestic understanding of events and actions to make strict decisions accordingly. Includes educating their population about the importance of their role in the process.

This is not only applicable to the mass population, governing authorities are actually more likely to fall prey to this trap. Especially that authorities seem more interested in passionate debates with each other rather than providing accurate information on ongoing events. It is a drama, and does not even bear much resemblance to a political drama, rather an overly dramatic soap opera. This, is then what is broadcast on TV for the population. This has no doubt led to a huge impact on accumulative awareness in an attempt to exploit 'the machine history mind'. Which facilitates promoting the false narratives that assure the continued exploitation of certain people and certain areas.

9.1.3 The Impact of Historical Events

In the details presented, it was concluded that the dire multidimensional consequences in the ME case after WWI were not caused solely by the Sykes-Picot treaty. It was in fact a series of treaties, almost one after the other, starting from the Basel Conference in 1987 until the Treaty of Lausanne in 1923. Adding to the failure of internal administrations including weak and inept policy and public relations infrastructure, it has played a major role in the unfair division and instability in the region.

Additional regional efforts are needed to enable people and local leaders to reconsider their perception of the contemporary historical sequence of events. This would require an approach from multiple different perspectives including scholars, politicians, economists and experts in all fields. The indigenous knowledge forming part of the "machine experience mind" should not be neglected. It stands for the deep knowledge, experience and understanding of the sequence of events which would explore ways to bring peace and prosperity. This knowledge is 'heritage' and should be protected accordingly.

Micro and macro history are both experiences related to all aspects of life such as social, political, economic or cultural aspects. Studying history enables people how previous generations lived, evolved and developed over time. This includes opportunities and challenges these previous generations went through to teach people to adopt, sustain or avoid certain behaviours, methods, models, beliefs or thoughts that help to evolve as individuals or nations.

9.1.4 The Global Forces Influence and the ME Leadership

The world is going through a comprehensive reset of the global eco-political system, especially with the rise of China and Russia as global powers. Both challenging the US as a significant decision-making force in the region (and elsewhere). This shift in paradigm has birthed a new opportunity, one that removes the shadow of Western dominance over the region for the first time for a century.

Including highly qualified leaders who are able to draw and implement strategic visions is necessary in order to avoid repeating historical mistakes. New mechanisms, new structure, new methods and a new pattern of actors.

This Inflection Point in terms of the global system necessitates a deep understanding and response to reshaping the political, economic and social systems. This requires a fundamental change in the current leadership structure on both local and regional levels. In short, the region needs creative leaders who can lead their communities and nations through the maximum benefit of the fourth industrial revolution, IoT and technology. Meanwhile, leaders who can deal with the repeated historical events in another way must lead the divested scene of the MENA. It would not even need to be one leader, it could even be a coalition of leaders as these leaders have to work together on different levels. The focus should be here is not repeating any mistakes that were made in past critical situations and take advantage of the new era. If such a step could be achieved, it will not be ignored by the Superpowers and it will open an unexplored chapter of renegotiation. By involving academics, experts, and, professionals when necessary, there can be effective collaboration on the strategy to serve purely independent public interests and that promote rational political decision-making.

9.1.5 Enhancing Knowledge Production

Reconsidering ancient science and the responsibility of intellectuals regionally and internationally is a key that leads to real civilisation where economic prosperity, development and well being are coming together. This could happen by empowering scientific research and studies for all fields of science and education. Producing knowledge and providing accurate information to the people is not the only element to be done, ending some phenomenons is essential as well.

Reforming the patterns of the massive commercial education that produces people who are neither skilled nor competent. Which did not serve the people rather than creating groups of unemployed frustrated youth. This has been approved with the high unemployment rates in many countries in the region. Furthermore, the use of 'imported' terms and concepts has attracted the locals, however, its use has hindered the progress of learning and understanding. In the MENA region, many concepts are imported from the West while implementing the content is failing in many places. It is known only conceptually, thus its deeper meaning or applicability remains elusive to all. This is most notable in school, teachers for example are teaching these educational concepts that they do not really understand. It pertains to no part of their personal experience and they lack a suitable teaching methodology.

These are two manifestations among many, that can be solved if there is education on how to teach and how to learn by experience and critical thinking. Consequently, re-identifying education goals is a key element in any future progress in the educational sector. This includes engaging regional and international scholars, scientists and special experts to supervise the process. The model should be supervised in order to ensure the benefit to the pupils rather than to profit-driven investors. People's awareness about education as a concept to be taken into consideration. Furthermore, education systems should produce people are able to rapprochement between different cultures and exchange knowledge.

9.1.6 4IR as an Opportunity

The result is always depending on the way that people interact and respond to changes. If we look to the 4IR as an opportunity, individuals, societies, groups, institutions and countries are examined to re-set priorities, goals and behaviours. For example, rather than rejecting AI People should take advantage of using and developing AI programs in a way that not to harm societies.

The nature of AI requires skilled people in new professions that need new knowledge and new competencies. For example, the tremendous expansion of Fiber-optic communication network offers a great opportunity for many states in the region (see Chap. 5). This requires training millions of people to deal with the new emerging jobs.

States should know where they stand and what are their capabilities in regard to technology, knowledge and possibilities in the region that mostly serves and is dominated by external and international investment. When the MENA region leaders and local players open their eyes to new perceptions, they will find advanced possibilities like higher solutions to the current chaos.

The MENA region is the least competitive region in the world in the field of internet and technology. This makes it a fertile ground for huge demand. This includes digital banking. This also creates more demand where regional and international companies are investing in. This must result in new negotiations and new political formula. The MENA can exploit the potential of lines to become a centre for connectivity and communication between all parts of the world and develop the foundations of the digital economy in the first place because the region has broadband markets the most concentrated and least competitive in the world so far, but it is a fertile market for competition.

9.1.7 Reconstruction and Governance

Corruption is cancer to the region. Without any medication, the only solution with any cancer is to remove the tumour altogether. Likewise, the most corrupt institutions should be completely replaced with new patterns: One major issue of previous revolutions in the region, especially notable with the 'Arab Spring', is the lack of a proposed alternative to the system they were fighting against. Successfully toppling a regime did not always lead to any improvements, and instead, often lead to more chaos.

Once construction starts it will be affecting the division of the region for the next century or even more. Civil society across the region has raised concerns about the actors involved, the proposed plans and the potential exploitation during any reconstruction efforts. This brings to the fore the negative experiences and consequences of post-conflict reconstruction in the MENA region, specifically in Iraq. Now the global reset is finally taking hold, even in the ME.

Despite this, expectations in the region remain low, hence a serious effort must be taken in order to be able to formulate their own reforms. Without the support of the people, local authorities will look to external support once again to implement policies mostly to ensure their own security in an era of change. Undoubtedly, this does not revoke the value of international and regional cooperation as part of the process. But with that may come to the risk of digital colonising where the relationship with the MENA and the rest of the world will remain unchanged and even worse. Which is the main concern for the locals.

Without proposing organised solutions coming from the people, the relationship with the MENA and the rest of the world will remain unchanged. With dialogue and finding a common interest chaos stops start where all regional actors should be involved in the planning process and the final decisions. While no one should be excluded, external interests and influence should be reconsidered in another way. Most importantly, people who are the source of the corruption of the political and economic system must not be left without legal actions.

9.2 Frameworks and Strategies

While the understanding of events and dealing with the main narrative are changing, new frameworks and models should be developed to adapt to the technology as well. Here I suggest some models and considerations:

9.2.1 Public Private Partnership + Society = PPSP

In its most simple form, the purpose of the public sector is to manage and organise the needs and interaction of societies domestically and internationally. Whereas the private sector provides products and services to both the public sector and society. Under the 4IR, societies across the board have become more demanding, especially on the technological front. Traditional processes are now rendered ineffective for meeting the needs of society. Governments began to struggle as a gap emerged between their capacities and what they were expected to deliver. As a result, governments decided to re-organise the public sector, which turned out to be at the expense of investing in its population.

The most long lasting model public/private sector in the ME is the Public Private Partnership (PPP). In brief, PPP is defined by arrangement between two or more long-term public and private sectors. This as a development model does not meet the development needs in the eyes of the people anymore. Despite the presence of a public sector, which by its very name should represent the public, the wider population feels excluded as a stakeholder in its own economic processes, see Fig. 9.1.

Since both the public and private sector exist to serve society, it would make sense to reconsider who the real stakeholders are for growth and development. Therefore, a new form of entity or institution that represents purely the needs of society and not for profit or ruling authorities. It would exist outside either sector and would spark reorganisation of the established model. Represented by S, these institutions form part of the new suggested model of PPSP (borne out of PPP + S), represented by Fig. 9.2.

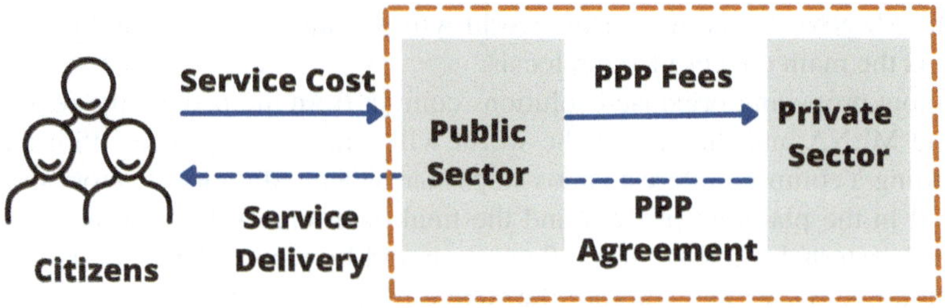

Fig. 9.1 Public private partnership model (PPP) (*Source* Author's own resource)

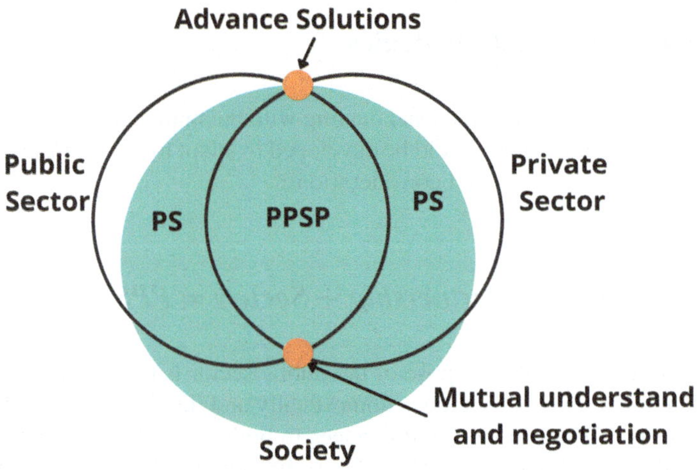

Fig. 9.2 Private Public Society Partnership Model (PPSP) (*Source* Author's own resource)

The inclusion of society or people as stakeholders, ultimately holds the institutions accountable and would increase transparency. To create such transparency, an open dialogue would be required among all parties leading to advanced solutions or at least more clear and understood solutions to all involved. This would also require an educated and well informed population in order to allow the success of this model. Otherwise, ignorance would leave any attempts of reasonable dialogue fruitless. In times of uncertainty, governments become insecure about their capabilities to meet the challenges ahead. Ultimately, a genuine success would require support and buy in from their people. Without the opportunity for an open dialogue, the other alternative would be brutal suppression which would benefit no one in the long term.

9.2.2 *Model Two: The Countries* 'Centring' *Strategy*

Balancing the short term and the long term in countries necessitates the adoption of holistic culture and practical initiatives where all the domestic stakeholders recognise the mutual benefit to move the country towards prosperity. However, it would be insufficient to simply agree on general national goals (National Vision Matter: Lessons of Scucess 2005). Achieving prosperity would require a "reposition" of societies, which I will refer to as *"centring"*.

The nature of states position is 'urgency' or undeclared wars where countries are all the time either ready to defend itself or to declare war. *'Centring'* is the opposite that enables the domestic environment to achieve certain goals that booster their prosperity which counts on the Global level. This strategy is based on collective efforts on several levels: The relationships and partnerships with regional and international forces, as well as a holistic inclusion of all the domestic stakeholders including the population. Basically, it is to give more attention to two dimensions of socio-ecological framework, the individual dimension, and the relational dimension represented in Fig. 9.3. Once these dimensions are strong enough, the state can be more effective in establishing sustainable change on the other two dimensions. In all levels, technology advancement and 4IR are key factors to be considered.

'Centring' as a strategy should be proportional to all of its social and political players' participation and commitment (National Vision Matter: Lessons of Scucess 2005) as long as its vision is clear to all. For example, to establish coordinated

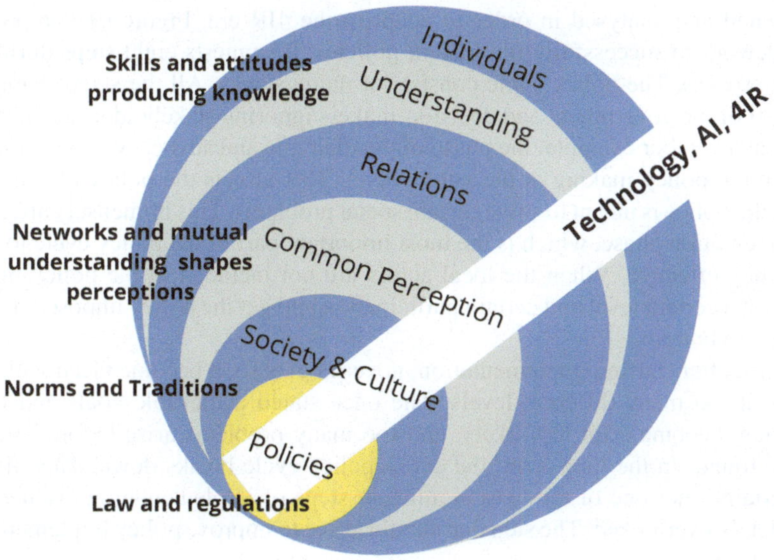

Fig. 9.3 Socio-ecological framework (*Source* Author own design)

regional or international councils and various programmes with ambitious goals of prosperity.

In other words, it presents an opportunity of self-reflection for nations. Self reflection of all domestic aspects and analysing all data currently available to create the appropriate projects and initiatives. This creates an atmosphere of stability amidst negotiations with external forces before potentially locking themselves into any commitments. Some may argue that this position is impossible under the 4IR, as its dynamic and fast-changing nature creates a constant sense of urgency to not fall behind. However, we should not neglect the timing that this creates to renegotiate. Such a model is impossible without trusted leadership and a clear vision, particularly in the case of post-war where reconstruction with long-term consequences are at the forefront of discussion.

The approach of '*centring*' is needed now more than ever in the 4IR as it allows the processing of all information and internal data before proceeding. This is a notable change from the climate of pressure as since 1916 the region was subject to being prey to external forces.

9.3 Policies Framework

Implementing policies face many challenges and even fall in many times, however, the same policy frameworks are continued to be used. In many cases institutions attempt to impose these policies. The failure of implementing policies must be researched and analysed in order to adapt to the 4IR era. Figure (9.4) represents a framework to successfully implement policies. It suggests eight steps during the whole process. The policy cycle consists of many stages. All the stages happen at the level of the government and decision-makers ignoring stakeholders and actors at the local level. For example, the phase of the dialogue and advocacy almost does not exist in the policy-making at the public level. This affects the policy effectiveness where the policy is meant to solve certain social problems. This immensely affects the implementation phase, which is the most important part of the policy cycle to make the policy effective. When the local actors are not included in the policy-making phases at a certain level and certain participation and get the policy imposed on them from up to bottom.

Hence after starting implementation, governments soon become faced with challenges at too many different levels. The once stated achievable goals and objectives now become a lot less likely, and too many problems arise before solutions can be found. In the long term, the entire policy cycle breaks down. Then the last but certainly not one of the least significant steps of implementation evaluation is completely overlooked. The step that should strive to improve policy implementation for the future.

Fig. 9.4 Reform policies (*Source* Author's own design)

9.3.1 Final Statement

The historical paradox between what happened in the ME after the Sykes-Picot treaty and what is happening today is not more than a political scrambling from the same perspective with different tools. The local players are still limited in their ability to gather and analyse information that will enable them to employ and implement efforts in an organised manner in the short and long term. This prevents most of the ME states from reaching the required political maturity at a stage such as the Fourth Industrial Revolution (4IR), and thus puts the whole region to the test.

Therefore, countries must commit to understanding the essence of this progress in depth and analysing all its aspects in order to prepare to deal and respond to this exceptional transformation and to adopt reforming policies in all sectors. Hence, this book is an invitation to individuals and societies to take advantage of the current era as an opportunity. In addition to calling on local leaders to rationally use public resources and renegotiate with global powers for the benefit of the people.

9.3.2 Book Summary (Warda Samara)

Science and technology are advancing in an unprecedented way, despite the ongoing wars and conflicts on the ground, people are distracted by their tragedies while the driving forces of the technological race are preoccupied with how to transform reality into a digital model.

The interaction of topics and events in the ME is an extension of global complexities at all levels and fields. The relationship between the region and the West appears simple like a co-dependent relationship, however its complexities make it difficult to imagine any solution to escape. The prevailing historical narrative of this relationship does not put it in the right place, and therefore it is difficult for people and local leaders to analyse, especially young unexperienced leaders. Adding to this is the changing face of this relationship from one form to another according to the repercussions of each period and the will of the global forces.

The world paid a heavy price for the two world wars. Mass destruction was everywhere, but perhaps the most devastating repercussions were reflected in the ME with continued ongoing destruction until now. Most of the major decisions taken on a global scale, especially in Europe, are directly or indirectly reflected on the countries of the ME. For instance, the geographical division of the ME between 1916 and 1923 came within a series of several international agreements in which the countries of the region were viewed unfit to rule themselves. These national divisions marked the ME as well as many other countries around the world as we know them today. This was the compromise of the region's inclusion in the global eco-political system.

The turn that took place in World War II on the global level forced the players to change the methods used in dealing with the colonies, especially once the MENA countries declared their independence. The regional dynamics changed and the Gulf states rose as promising economic powers for individuals and societies, however, only as models of capitalism in the region. This was a new compromise of reshaping the global economic system that allowed the economic divisions that increased poverty in marginalised areas at the expense of GDP.

The core of science, knowledge, research and exploration disappeared from the mentality of individuals in the ME, while capitalism was progressing relentlessly until pure materialism became the master in the region. Between the absence of the former and the progress of the latter, it becomes difficult for the younger generations to be able to distinguish between reality and illusions. In fact, the dominant narrative and the truth are both present in the same field, but each of them operates on different frequency. Illusions form part of reality for many people, for so many even that it can become accepted truth, thereby making the search for truth difficult or even impossible.

The ME journey is marked by a series of divisions, first appearing in the geographical form, the economic and now evolving into the digital. While the region has proved its limited capability to strategically respond to the first two, it will be a real test to handle the complexity of the digital age. Only at the start, its chaotic tendencies have become clear especially in conjunction with the COIVD-19 circumstances. Many people are ignorant that there is a Fourth Industrial Revolution (4IR) as one of the few turning point during one century, the opinions differ globally and regionally about how to deal with this event, as some consider it as a renewed cold war, where the knowledge race between the great powers is the determination of who rules the world. The confusion at the regional and local levels will make many areas in the ME vulnerable to digital divisions, a new form of colonialism of the region since the beginning of the century.

This scenario confuses local players who still believe in traditional solutions to issues such as those of the Kurds and the Palestinians. These people may be surprised that they are under certain digital classifications and have to redefine their identity in order to be part of the new world order, or that an unknown fate awaits them, especially in the absence of alternative solutions by organised regional efforts.

In fact, the dominant narrative and the truth are both present in the same field, but each of them operates on different frequencies. Illusions form part of reality for many people, for so many even that it can become accepted truth, thereby making the search for truth difficult or even impossible. However, there is no doubt that there is already a significant shift in the population's understanding of events and the moving dynamics. Organising the regional efforts remains a big challenge.

The 4IR and a great transition is necessary, but on how to efficiently implement remains unknown. In particular, there are several aspects of consideration in regard to reconstruction and construction in the ME. In Syria, we see the aspect of physical destruction and who will support this. In various regional digital initiatives, where no domestic digital products exists securing and protecting the data remains a critical issue. This forms the bedrock of discussion concerning the contemporary role of external aid and support in the region. How would one provide the major support required for nations post-chaos while protecting the main national issues at the same time.

Bibliography

National Vision Matter: Lessons of Scucess (2005) Proceedings of a public-private sector development forum, issue

Robinson DAJ (2017) The economic impact of colonialism https://voxeu.org/article/economic-impact-colonialism

The manufacturer's authorised representative in the EU is Springer Nature Customer Service Centre GmbH, Europaplatz 3, 69115 Heidelberg, Germany. If you have any concerns regarding our products, please contact ProductSafety@springernature.com

Printed and bound by CPI Group (UK) Ltd, Croydon, CR0 4YY
30/09/2026
02225465-0018